Robin Greenwood is Vicar of St M; the Diocese of Newcastle, UK. Ove combined practice with strategic re opment. He has held diocesan, cat........ ments in England and Wales, resourced conferences in the United States, Australia, New Zealand and Britain, and was a Director of the Edward King Institute for Ministerial Development. His previous writings include *Transforming Priesthood: A New Theology of Mission and Ministry* and *Practising Community: the Task of the Local Church*. He is married to Claire, also a priest in Newcastle Diocese. They have three adult children.

PARISH PRIESTS

For the sake of the Kingdom

ROBIN GREENWOOD

First published in Great Britain in 2009

Society for Promoting Christian Knowledge
36 Causton Street
London SW1P 4ST

British Library Cataloguing-in-Publication Data
A catalogue record for this book is available from the British Library

ISBN 978–0–281–05538–8

1 3 5 7 9 10 8 6 4 2

Typeset by Graphicraft Limited, Hong Kong
Printed in Great Britain by Ashford Colour Press

Produced on paper from sustainable forests

For Claire

Contents

Acknowledgements		ix
Introduction		xi
1	Church for the world's true life	1
2	What's in your diary?	28
3	Church: communal practice of Good News	52
4	The navigator: *episkope* of the local church	90
5	Practising *episkope*	121
Appendix: Projected numbers of employed clergy in the Church of England, 2008–17		157
Notes		162
Bibliography		188
Index		201

Acknowledgements

This book began life four years ago, when *Transforming Priesthood* had been in print for ten years. I am grateful to the dioceses, parishes and colleges in those Anglican, Episcopalian and Lutheran churches that have continued to encourage me to explore the role of the presiding priest. Although the churches now talk about mission, ministry, priesthood and discipleship in relational terms, there is still an urgent need to draw together many strands of thought and experience, asking: Precisely what is now the role of the priest who, with the bishop and other ministers locally, exercises *episkope* for the sake of the Kingdom? This study is a mixture of theory and practice, relating to real examples of contemporary Church experience.

Many relationships, conferences and conversations have contributed to this book. One man who has had a deep influence is the late Daniel W. Hardy, who brought his considerable wisdom to these issues over several years. I offer thanks too for the stimulus of the support of those in the Newcastle Diocese who have reflected with me in the completion of this book: Bob Burston, Tony Chesterman, Frances Dower, Colin Gough, Margaret Hobrough and Allan Marks. An especially vital thread came through those who interviewed bishops and parish priests and those who agreed to be interviewed, in Australia, New Zealand, the USA, Wales, Scotland and England.

I am glad to express my gratitude to the Diocese of Canberra in New South Wales, mentioning especially the hospitality of Bishop George Browning, Frank Hetherington, John Stead and Stephen (now Bishop) Pickard. I was grateful also for the hospitality of Ross Fishburn, Rachel McDougall and Charles Sherlock at Trinity College, Melbourne. My thanks go also to the Dioceses of Brechin and Glasgow and Galloway, and Bishops Idris Jones and John Mantle for their invitations to lead discussions of ministry and mission today. I am also grateful to the Evangelical Lutheran Synod and the Episcopal Diocese of New York for their 2007 invitation to contribute to conferences: Bishops Stephen Bouman and Mark Sisk, together with David Anglada, Barrie Lawless, Richard Hill and Gayle Ruege. I want to mention also the stimulus of the 2007 conference of the Church of England Ministry Development Officers and also clergy study groups and retreats in Fareham, Durham and Newcastle.

Acknowledgements

I acknowledge warmly the parishioners of St Mary the Virgin, Monkseaton, in the Diocese of Newcastle, for entering into the possibility of creating together a church that values and draws out the vocation of all its people, to make Christ known in the parish and beyond. Especially I acknowledge the staff team for their courage and love: Eileen Noble, Eric Lewis, Sue Hart, Mary Cooper and Val Cowan; and the mission co-ordinators: Katy Bell, Tony Garland, David Lax, Vicky Scurfield, Mike Stoker and Alison Stroud. I wish also to appreciate those who have held office as wardens in this period and all who contributed to the 2008 review of the parish's mission.

Others who have personally made a contribution include: Ken Bennett, Ken Booth, Stephen Brown, Richard Bryant, Stephen Cherry, Philip Davies, Jenny Dawson, Bill Day, Stan Dye, Dave Elkington, James Francis, Richard Giles, Martin Groves, Malcolm Grundy, Roger Hindley, Judy Hirst, Peter Kenney, Bob Langley, Alastair MacNaughton, Geoff Miller, Alison Moore, John Osgood, Manon Parry, Caroline Pascoe, Alan Payne, Peter Robinson, Trevor Smith, Malcolm Squires, John Thompson, John Tiller, Anne Tomlinson, Rosemary Tucker, Carol Wolstenholme, Max Wood and Mark Worthington.

In terms of funding, I have been grateful for a grant from the Lord Crewe's Charity towards the costs of books, conference fees and travelling. I record my warm thanks to Ruth McCurry, commissioning editor at SPCK, for her constant encouragement and alert awareness of the needs of readers. Also, among those who have creatively critiqued the text in its final stages, Charles Sherlock has made an immense contribution.

Bishop Martin Wharton, through inviting me to be Vicar of St Mary's, Monkseaton, Diocese of Newcastle, gave me both the security and opportunity for developing and reflecting further on the theology and practice of parish mission and ministry. I dedicate this book to my wife, Claire, who having moved from her work in psychotherapy through selection and training for ordination, currently serves as curate in a Newcastle parish. Our constant conversations on leadership, evangelization, Scripture, God's character and purpose, prayer and the Church's future are implicitly woven into this text. I thank her for her love and challenging support.

Introduction

> Let the pain of this world seize us by the throat. Listen for Jesus
> calling us all out of our tombs of despair and apathy. May the shock
> of baptismal dying once more set us on fire. This place we call
> home is meant to be a new heaven, a new earth, a holy city, a new
> Jerusalem. It is the sparks in the stubble that will make it so.[1]

This study is a frank invitation to Churches to be bold in their
expectations of those now called to be parish priests. Precisely what
is required from those in this role is a question for Churches as
institutions and for those who are now parish priests. The signs are
that in the future the number of full-time, stipendiary parish priests
will continue to reduce (see Appendix). As new patterns of ministry
continue to develop it will be essential that Churches know what in
particular is being called for and made available through the parish
priest, differentiated from other clergy and ministry team members.
Clarity about the critical role of parish priest will sharpen the selection process, initial and continuing clergy education and the preparing of job descriptions. A greater incisiveness about the vocation,
role and skills of the parish priest (working collaboratively with
other ordained and non-ordained colleagues) will stimulate vocations, increase parish confidence and promote the local church's
mission. There will be resonances here for many ministries, ordained
and lay, readers and Local Shared Ministry teams. However, the
sharp focus of this study will be on the role and tasks of the priest
or presbyter who, as 'incumbent', shares with the bishop the 'cure
of souls'.[2]

   The manner of working and relating of this particular member
of the 'presbyterion' (team of elders and ministers[3]) deeply affects
the culture and operating style of the entire local church. What
forms of connectivity, locally and in the diocese, are desirable? It is
not the preserve of parish priests alone to decide what they are for
and how they should function, but rather of the entire church and
those within its wider neighbourhood. The *Virginia Report* suggests
that 'the bishop and parish priest will maintain the highest level of
communication possible, so that encouragement, advice, and, where
necessary, correction, can be given, together with new tasks as occasion arises.'[4] What constitutes the 'local' church will vary ecumenically and within particular contexts and theology. In simple terms,

it is always the most authentic and vibrant particular situation in which the entire church becomes engaged in the mission of God.[5]

Ordinals, role models, events, personal skills and compassion will all compete for space in an incumbent's diary. This book suggests that, whether paid a stipend or not, parish priests (within teams of many kinds) should not regard as their primary role the provision of ministry to others. Rather, precisely through the celebration of the sacraments, preaching and pastoral care they are to stimulate, interweave and support God's calling of all. So it is the entire church that enacts the *episkope* that releases God's love within the whole church, for the fulfilment of creation.

The very identity of the Church lies at the heart of this debate. How does the Church best serve God's mission in the world? Do we begin from the internal dynamics of the Church as a society itself or from the sense of God already at work in the world, of which the Church is a graced agent of salvation? In a society cast adrift from many previously held certainties, there are crucial issues of how people individually and in communities find their true personhood and freedom. Society needs agencies that connect diverse people and groups in the interactive space between the national and international and the deeply personal. Many would doubt today that Christianity is a potential ally of social change and alternative forms of citizenship, suspecting that religions spell war, terror and outworn authority patterns. It is a vibrant theme of this exploration that churches, serving the triune God's mission, and less concerned for their own growth or survival, do indeed have unique opportunities to contribute to public discourse concerning every part of living: economic, political, medical, educational, civic and legal.[6]

In an era when there are justifiable fears about the sustainability of the institutional life of many Churches, this book is offered as an aspirational stimulus rather than a response driven by anxiety. This vision of priesthood for today's Church enters into no direct conflict with others whose analyses are very different. However, in an era when many are modelling an ecclesiology that is rigidly authoritarian, obsessive about sexual issues and regards tradition as a static norm, I believe there is a pressing need for Churches to rework the practice of local churches as a passionate affirmation of the trinitarian God.

The idea of the 'navigator' offers a deep insight into how the local church can be stimulated by the *episkope* exercised by the parish priest. This idea came to me when travelling in New Zealand and on reading Anne Salmond's remarkable account of the journeys both of the crews of Cook's various eighteenth-century Pacific expeditions and those of the Polynesian islanders who first inhabited Aotearoa. The latter, especially, learnt to navigate intuitively towards a destination, as yet unknown but attractive to them. Both sets of voyagers were courageous companions in highly dangerous enterprises. In both cases, achieving their aims was in strong competition with their chances of physical survival; in both cases, though differently, they relied on the particular crew member who was the navigator. His accumulated experience, intuition and acute powers of observation made a critical contribution to the corporate achievement of the ship's company.

Internalizing a reading of the stars, the waves, the birds' flights, the wind and colours of the spray, the navigator informed the crew of their likely position and offered guidance for the next stage of their journey. Among the Polynesian voyagers, the navigator had to watch the stars changing as they travelled south and then re-play the picture returning home. Also in Polynesian culture the navigator is the high priest and captain, a sacred role.[7] There are resonances too with the *gubernator*, the helmsman, who governs the direction of the boat from the stern with a rudder. The *Shorter Oxford English Dictionary* connects the skills of piloting, guiding or governing a ship on a journey in unknown territory with shaping one's life, administering and conducting business safely among many influences.

The notion of navigator, in combination with a reappraisal of *episkope*, gives new impetus to the Church's call and effectiveness through a reappraisal of the work of parish priests, and colleagues, called to exercise authority in the churches. As I shall explore in Chapter 4, navigators in many disciplines provide inspiration for understanding the connection between the unique and interrelated work of each person and the synchronicity of the whole community.

Throughout my adult life, the call to ordained ministry has brought immense opportunities, rewards and challenges, professionally and personally. A pivotal time for me was as a parish priest in Leeds in the 1980s. My aim was to be instrumental in stimulating a congregation to grow in faith, celebratory and inclusive worship, prayer and confidence as a missionary community within the various estates that comprised its setting. There were clear signs that the lives of people, whose everyday circumstances and self-expectation often diminished rather than lifted them up, were given fresh hope. A liberation occurred, partly due to a renewal in the way of speaking about and practising community as a church and also to the encouragement of many to find and take support for developing a personal spiritual pathway. My encouragement came from the pastoral, liturgical and theological tide flowing at that time from the documents and subsequent practices of Vatican II. They expected an *aggiornamento*, through a revived engagement of the Church with the modern world. The Document *Lumen Gentium*, the dogmatic constitution on the Church, sets out in Chapter 1 ('The Mystery of the Church') a thoroughly trinitarian understanding of the Church, as agent of the coming Kingdom. An ecumenical endeavour to create authentic speech and practice of the Church, which has deeply influenced Anglicanism, was released through this Roman Catholic initiative.

The influence of the reforming impetus of formative voices surrounding the *nouvelle theologie* of Vatican II, such as Congar, de Lubac, Danielou, Philips, Rahner, Schillebeeckx and Suenens, critical of the received Thomist tradition, opened up the possibility of interpreting my role as parish priest as an agent of transformation.[8] Energized by a re-engagement with Scripture and the early fathers, Congar, presenting the Church's role as central to the reconciliation of creation to God, shows how the ordained, while having particular sacramental responsibilities, share profoundly in all other aspects of the priesthood of the *laos*. Edward Schillebeeckx, combining scholarly patience with an eagerness for the Church's renewal, revisited the history of the development of ministries in the early centuries, showing how no authentic ministry stands apart from a particular church community. There were strenuous contrary factors, such as inherited attitudes and habits of clergy, the assumption that only articulate congregations can be directional in mission, and that laity are reluctant to be lifted fully into their overlapping vocations.[9]

Reflecting on that experience in *Reclaiming the Church* (1988), it became clear to me that the widespread passivity of the laity, influenced by normative cultural patterns of self-deprecation, was a characteristic formed by the projection that ordination puts priests into a separate or higher spiritual plane. I became convinced that attitudes of benign patronizing that characterized long-term patterns of Church (and society), could in part be reshaped through the subversive expectation that the laity, in all aspects of life, have a full part in the Church. In 1994 I published *Transforming Priesthood: A New Theology of Mission and Ministry*, as an academic contribution to the reimagining of the role and tasks of the parish priest within the local church. The time had arrived, I believed, theologically to reconsider the work of the parish priest (incumbent) within, rather than separated from, the vibrant flux of the baptized and baptizing community of Christian people. My subsequent book, *Practising Community: The Task of the Local Church*, published in 1996, popularized the theories of *Transforming Priesthood* in connection with the search for good practice in Local Shared Ministry.

In dialogue with Leonardo Boff, David Ford, Colin Gunton, Daniel Hardy, John Milbank, Jürgen Moltmann and John Zizioulas, I proposed that it is only possible to speak of ordained ministry in dialogue with:

1 the contemplation of the relational triune God;
2 an articulation of the passionate desire of this God;
3 an understanding of the nature of the eschatological *communion*[10] that, amid the contingencies of life, takes as its intention the furthering of this desire.[11]

Adopting the language of the newly published *Alternative Service Book* (1980), I contended that the work of the parish priest is essentially one of 'presiding' among the other ministries in mission. I explored this presiding role in terms of transforming and building up the entire church in the interactive ministries of discerning, blessing and witnessing. This discourse on the priest as stimulus for the body of the church, I suggested, had the potential to bypass former polarities between clergy and laity.

In this new study, I work from the basis that, as God's triune life invites all creation into mutual play, the practice of church and theology has always to be reconstructed within the particularities of neighbourhood, society and world. An essential part of the task of theology is to be aware of situations where unexamined concepts of God breed attitudes of domination rather than of liberation for people and the natural world. Scriptural texts testify to the long history of God's people, constantly being re-formed through God's sovereignty acting within successive crises and alliances, with a distinctive character and purpose. *Transforming Priesthood* was published as the first women were being ordained priest in the Church of England, and *Parish Priests* is appearing as the Church of England negotiates the code of practice within which women will be ordained bishop.

Jesus reinterpreted the Jewish people's past experience and language in forming a messianic Spirit-led community.[12] After centuries of experiment among many races and nations, the amazing possibility of a *communion* of people, dedicated to showing the world

God's final purposes, continues to linger and generate hope. The practice of church has a unique capacity for transforming concepts of belonging, power-sharing, citizenship, freedom, the roles of women and men, the inclusion of difference and the choices we make in our common speech. This ecclesial journey is now enriched by feminist theologians, such as Marion Grau, Elizabeth Johnson and Catherine Keller, through their search for the affirmation of relationships characterized by difference, particularity and multiplicity.[13] Churches that choose to embody the politics of difference stand in a unique position, both to contribute to these urgent human agendas, as well as to receive from them.

I have been grateful that SPCK has continued to make copies of *Transforming Priesthood* available throughout the last 14 years. In this renewed conversation to clarify the life, work and experience of priests within churches, I shall examine how far Christian theology and churches are consciously working towards mutually co-creative relations in speech and action.[14] It seems vital that parish priests and associate ministers of the twenty-first century be given the support needed for the difficult and rewarding task of finding how churches can most truly be an echo and instrument of God's own passion for the world's good end. To what extent is the reinterpretation of the role supported by continued theological thinking, by developing role models, by the wider institution of the Church or by the expectations of the laity? How far do the complex immunities to change produce competing and mutually debilitating agendas?

1

Church for the world's true life

[T]he church by being the church serves the world. My oft-made claim that the first task of the church is not to make the world more just but to make the world the world, has never been a call for the church to retreat from the world. The church can and should only exist in the world. Indeed the church needs the world as much as the world needs the church. What the church owes the world is what the church has been given, that is the privilege to be a community capable of confessing our sins before God and before one another.[1]

Aspects of contemporary church contexts

At a time when people are choosing from a variety of spiritualities and making syncretistic amalgams of religious experience, can Churches still be a sign of salvation and an inspiring and effective witness for the rejuvenation of the world? I believe the world crucially needs Christian communities, open to the world and at the same time fired with inexhaustible, transformative resurrection life (Rom. 10.12). Churches are those groups of people who know, and intentionally practise, the stupendous truth that all are God's beloved and that all life is 'charged with the grandeur of God'.[2] A Church truly responsive to God's mission in the world will choose to embody ways of relating that reflect that mission most fully. But in reality, routine experience of churches, institutionally and locally, examined in this light, raises a strong element of doubt.[3] My intention in this book is to map elements of the contemporary ecclesiological discussion to help clarify the role of the parish priest for today. It is just not appropriate to discuss ordained priesthood separately from the work of the priesthood of God's Church for the world.

I shall set the present and future role of the parish priest, therefore, as navigator for the whole Church's emerging identity, within the contemporary challenge to:

- face up to the disintegration of ecclesial institutions and the unravelling of past securities;

1

- rediscover how to be church here and now;
- respond in expectancy as God calls us to new responsibilities and ways of faithfulness in a changing world.

When we engage boldly with the mystery of God through Scripture, Eucharist, prayer, preaching, celebration, lament, thought and conversation within many contexts, we recognize the inadequacy of inherited conceptions, power structures, language, identity and limitations, and move on.

The public practices of the local church are built from the fine detail of situations, personalities, buildings, money, memories, aspirations and very particular and shifting circumstances. But also the practice of local churches is interconnected with faith embodied in the wider structure or network of the whole Church in every age and in every place. Each local church is an expression of the world Church, not least through the guardianship of the bishop in a relationship of mutual accountability and through *communion* ecumenically with sister churches.[4]

No single take on the 'state of the Church now' can be held in isolation. In a single week we may read about the relationships between human and religious life in villages, about immigrant workers boosting church attendance, about 'our vicar' identified and expected in a family crisis, public lack of interest in denominational loyalty, statistics of falling attendance, the move towards ordaining women as bishops in the Church of England, media opinion that the Church is drifting into oblivion, and anxiety that new emphases on disciplined commitment has disenfranchised the general public from 'their' church.[5] Positively, there is rich evidence of many vibrant ecumenical moves by those who are discovering transformative possibilities in and through the Church.

A growing body of literature, from varying perspectives, testifies to the scriptural basis for and everyday practice of 'total' or 'mutual' ministry. Paul defines church in terms of *koinonia* (*communion, community, communication*) based on and expanding the original meaning of a partnership of interest. We must avoid the false binary position that a church rooted in *koinonia* has no interest in the neighbourhood or world.[6] In Paul's theology it is a real, functioning community of interest and trust for the whole world (Philemon 2.1; Gal. 6.6; Rom. 12.3–6). Just as the outpouring love at the heart of God who is Trinity cannot be contained, so the wellsprings of a *koinonia*-shaped church are unbounded and overflow unpredictably.[7] However, we shall need to be constantly on the lookout for the mistake of suggesting a literal, rather than an analogical, connection between the life of the Trinity and that of the church.[8]

But a focus on church as reciprocal *communion* is not at the expense of excluding the individual's journey, a sense of the numinous or intimacy with God in silence. In enthusiasm for generating community spirit and involvement, we do not want to humiliate and exclude those who prefer the back row for reasons known to themselves, and probably not even held in consciousness. Holding together competing values requires a growing maturity. For example, it makes perfect sense, in so many ways, to enable the embodiment of mutual community by arranging seating so that everyone sits close and can see and be seen. Yet the sense of threat and self-disclosure that this entails for some is unbearable. This is not to say that churches should collude with a pervasive sense of unworthiness. We have, as yet, little experience in addressing such unhealthy shame, communally or personally, partly because some of our inherited organizational patterns induce shame rather than build self-esteem.[9] It is a demanding project for churches to learn that they are not merely collections of individuals who 'come' to worship. The fears of some have to be balanced with the needs of the whole, as together we discern God's will. In Chapter 3, I shall explore how difference and otherness are not to be resisted, but are indeed precisely what constitute *communion*.[10]

Parish priests in a 'missionary' and 'collaborative' church

Synodical documents and much of the growing literature on ministry take for granted a 'collaborative' and 'mission-focused' methodology of church. The ARCIC report *Gift of Authority* affirms that: 'The church cannot properly be described as an aggregate of individual believers, nor can its faith be considered the sum of beliefs held by individuals.'[11] Yet the perpetuation of a culture of dependence on clergy for faith and ministry in local churches, without clarifying their role, dilutes the capacity of the Church to practise *koinonia* for the world's healing. To offer consolation and encouragement to hard-pressed and conscientious parish priests and their colleagues is a vital task. But this must not collapse the proper tension that looks to expecting and empowering all to become a collaborative, mission-shaped church, sign of God's welcome of and respect for 'the least'.

In this study I recognize and appreciate the resilience and skill required in the exposed and often lonely ministry of the parish priest. It requires changing focus from moment to moment, it invites engagement with a huge range of human, spiritual and communal issues through the day. Increasingly, parish priests hold responsibility within clusters of churches and are encouraged to work in partnerships with other clergy, readers, local ministry teams and laity, as well as, ecumenically, with those in sister churches. Overall, the picture is one of many-layered subtlety, requiring with practice the learning of a high degree of negotiating skill. Building community clearly involves real contact and friendship, but also for the priest and close colleagues sufficient detachment to be able to minister to anyone in need and to exercise *episkope* in relation to the discipleship and ministry of everyone in the community.

But inherited expectation of priestly detachment and independence is part of the problem. There continues a wide freedom for incumbents and priests in charge to arrive from elsewhere and begin to adopt their own preferred ways of working. In the local church, as in all human endeavour, the task is always that of juggling the possibilities for the group, the task and the individual.[12] Depending on role models, personal views and ability, and the inherited situation in churches, parish priests live and function often according to competing and unfocused agendas. Important matters of policy and community-building often lose out to people and situations presenting themselves as urgent cases.

At the same time many clergy face dwindling, ageing congregations and a sense that decades of hard work show little return. In such a public ministry, parish priests without the commitment to taking self-support (cell groups, work consultancy, retreats, spiritual directors, sabbaticals) can have nowhere to take their fears, doubts and natural shifts in the journey of faith. Means of measuring levels of burnout, stress, strain, depression, anxiety and frustration have been developed, revealing a complex relationship within clergy between satisfaction and dissatisfaction.[13] The situation is exacerbated by the resistance to change that can occur within the dynamics of diocesan leaders and bishops.[14] Also, parish officers are increasingly asking when it will be recognized that the scale of the diocesan operation must be reviewed against the situation in which there will not be infinite increases in finance to keep the present system going. There are hard choices that dioceses need to make about ministerial patterns for mission for the next 20 years, including how many stipendiary parish priests would be desirable, for what task, and on which criteria. How would such choices combine with strategies for learning, local ministry, deanery development or completely different expressions of church?

The General Synod of the Church of England is currently introducing legislation on clergy terms of service that will see Human Resource provision for these issues viewed more corporately, rather than left to the discretion and limited skills of the individual.[15] Radical changes are being debated in the 'contract' between parish priest, people, neighbourhood and bishop and the general culture of the Church.[16] However, accounts of the past, such as Robin Gibbons' *House of God, House of the People of God* (2006) and Roy Strong's *A Little History of the English Country Church* (2007), serve as a reminder of the long expectation of elusiveness and freedom of parish priests and parishes. Within the complexities of the institution, centrally planned strategies, for example on review or work consultancy, take a surprisingly long time to mature and take root. One of the chief factors in the current situation lies within the succession of pivotal office holders, clerical and lay, within any given local church and the power they possess to mould situations to their understanding of faith and personal strengths and capacities.

While no single concrete expression of church could be regarded as definitive, some forms of church organization lack the capacity to bear a relational trinitarian insight. The 2007 conference of Ministry Development Officers from Anglican dioceses in the UK reached the consensus that Churches distributing authority and responsibilities, essentially as a stepped-down linear hierarchy, cannot fulfil the criteria for 'church'. The *Virginia Report* suggests that it may be possible to use the word 'levels' in a non-pejorative way to indicate the diversity of spheres of activity. But I believe it would be preferable to abandon language that gives an impression of some people fixed permanently over or below others.[17]

The method of 'preferment' of clergy to institutional posts of increased seniority combined with a routinely low expectation of the participation of the entire *laos* illustrates a degraded and inadequate expression of the Body of Christ.[18] Consider, despite recent revisions, the still opaque culture and processes of making appointments of clergy to 'senior' posts within the Church of England. As a result, we continue preferring and promoting those who have served effectively and imaginatively within the inherited structures against the odds. So in their new post, on a wider scale, working extremely long hours, the role model offered specifically denies the value of trinitarian approaches to how to be church now. Experience shows the cost to persons, families, parish priests and laity, and dioceses. No one, however dedicated, can do the ministry that God intends for another. Bishops who overwork in hierarchical systems inevitably create guilt-inducing role models. No single part of the field or system can be changed without the co-operation of the others.

It is time for established Churches to get real about the way we misrepresent God. The Church's normative behaviour maintains a wounding split between the priestly and prophetic ministries, encouraging the dominance of the 'Royal Consciousness'.[19] In *The Prophetic Imagination*, Walter Brueggemann challenges forms of power that are a false witness to God's character revealed in Scripture, bringing despair not hope. His treatment of the Old Testament traces the movement from the radical vision of Moses for a people governed by God, to the solidification of royal power in Solomon, to the prophetic critique of that power, with a new vision of liberation for all, in the prophets. From Exodus, through Kings and to Jesus, the prophetic vision not only emphasizes the pain of God's people but reveals an energy that comes from amazement at the new thing that God is performing.[20]

Taking into account the history of the Church of England and the cultural baggage attached to it, I have a serious doubt that there is a critical mass of energy for the development of a Church rooted in *koinonia*. Urgently, our society now requires a Church committed less to its own institutional survival and more to becoming a navigator of hope throughout the whole of society. This requires a Church that deliberately raises the voices of the powerless and that in its inner relating symbolizes and articulates a Kingdom approach to human living.

A significant part of the Church's deficit lies in continuing to present the local church as a service in many forms offered by parish priests with occasional lay help. Despite alternative scenarios in the literature of the past half century, the general public, most of our congregations and many newly trained priests, not to mention bishops in institution sermons and appointment-making, continue to equate the church with the parish priest. One bishop recently described the stipendiary clergy as 'our greatest mission resource'. Although in one sense the contribution and quality of the clergy matters a great deal, I believe his remark requires a great deal of clarification.

Educators and parish priests in the Church know that learning how to be an interactive agent for the birth of a 'mutual' or 'reciprocal' Church that serves God's mission in the world requires alert and persistent attention. In honesty we also know how, through ambivalence and immunity to change, we are ourselves a major blockage. Even as I write this I am aware of the paradox of myself as one person advocating a collaborative approach to understanding the dynamics of church. It has been very important to have consulted with colleagues and parishioners in the evolution of this book; the supreme irony would be to hear myself saying, 'I've concluded that God wants us to be a community of mutual disciples working for the Kingdom and we're doing it this way and starting tomorrow.'

A common way of disqualifying mutual or collaborative ministry is to label it as a passing fashion, possibly now even over, merely mirroring secular movements of thought and probably a distortion of Anglicanism. Another is that it inevitably turns the Church into a sect by encouraging an introverted community. It would certainly be inconsistent with Christian tradition for our patterns of authority to bear no relation to those of our environment; equally, it would be inconsistent if our practice were not a contribution to the revisioning of all power dynamics.[21] Churches will recognize how their work of reshaping relationships and power dynamics is both part of the cultural development of their locality in every aspect, and also properly a critique of it and so an invitation to new ways of being in society. What I want to highlight is how the very nature of *koinonia* itself bypasses bipolar habits of thought that insist on there being only one 'correct' and adversarial response to any question. Deeper constructs, distilled from the long Christian tradition, arise through an interweaving of reflecting on faith (theology), with many human experiences in particular contexts and among a variety of personalities.

The need for theological criteria in finding how to be church

As, certainly in the UK, theology cuts very little ice in considering the future of the Church, I sense that a case for bringing to bear theological criteria certainly needs to be made. Part of the problem stems from inherited habits of theological education. Parish priests hold a collective memory of theological education presented in an indigestible, didactic form likely to discourage further study.[22] Fortunately times have changed from when those who had banked up an objective knowledge of Scripture and theological concepts merely then re-presented them to others for consumption and memorizing. Courses and colleges today set out to become reciprocal communities of learning, even though bound by systems of accreditation and the requirements of synods and reports. Theological education for ordinands, readers and laity, individually and corporately, is a principal key to developing the Church in imagination and hope. I have often witnessed how, in an appropriate environment and with encouragement, those who previously were afraid of books and thinking discover their latent intelligence and hidden creativity. When experience, context, narrative and emotions are included in dialogue with theological ideas and with the fields of human knowledge, the potential is huge for encouraging a culture of life-long learning. I shall discuss these here under three headings in relation to my own experience.

Nurturing imagination for another world

Imaginative scriptural and theological reflection has been for me a primary source of inspiration, firing my own commitment and capacity to reconsidering the Church's character and task. In recent years, students of Scripture have shown how texts are not only informative but also performative, critiquing power abuse and nerving Israel subversively to sing and enact alternative practice.[23] The Church's task, in each new situation, is to retell the story of Jesus Christ, not only to elicit faith, but to embody and proclaim what happens when people deliberately *do* the gospel together. We *become* what we say or sing or how we sit and stand with one another. So, for example, in the Introduction I alluded to how the texts of Vatican II and the evolving ecclesiological discourse, led by Council experts, prompted my lay-focused alternative parish practice in the 1980s. I attempted to 'preside' in the parish's mission and liturgy on the assumption that the role of the one 'in charge' is not to make decisions, even after consultation, but to enable the whole community to decide God's purposes for them and then support them in following it through.[24] Spiritual direction for laity taking up leadership roles then became a high priority.[25] The insights of Vatican II were complemented by the ecumenical theology of the Lima texts on *Baptism, Eucharist and Ministry* (WCC, 1982). The continuing debate about the future of the Church has been influenced by the renaissance of a trinitarian understanding of God and through feminist reworkings of the nature of the Church (ecclesiology)[26] in terms of relationality and friendship.

Unconscious choices behind forms of church practice

We should openly recognize how much our chosen ways of seeing the Church are formed by our personal circumstances and faith journeys. So we pursue vocations to a large extent because of our own personal needs, and fortunately many others benefit as a result. When we look honestly, we see that the character of church to which we aspire is to a great extent bound up with our perception of our needs and the way we choose to tell the story of our lives, and is therefore always in flux. Recognizing this openly is a vital starting point for each of us to respect the needs of those who are different. Such openness can save us from, unconsciously, projecting our fear of change onto others.

Local churches, when detached from developments in the wider Church, can become especially nervous of deconstructing inherited habits. This may be connected with fear of losing touch with a God who is familiar or with loyalty to ancestors. Liturgical experiments, perhaps interrupting habits of facing East or standing to 'share' communion, rather than kneeling to 'receive', can generate high octane anxiety.

The Church of England is socially aspirational in a way that other Churches are not. In 1965, the *Paul Report* on the future of the Church of England brought into awareness the assumptions that senior leadership would naturally be derived from the upper middle classes. I can illustrate this from my own experience, as you the reader might uniquely for yourself. In the 1970s, as a curate in two successive parishes, I identified with the language generated within Liberation Theology and Industrial Mission to clarify how the Church of England's life and leadership could combat social misery and in practice embrace a wider demographic range. This had been sharply accentuated for me through the collection of experiences of being an only child, the product of a broken family and a council estate childhood, combined with the potency of a lively grammar school, university and theological college education and, over decades, many nurturing relationships, especially in marriage and family living. I recall vividly how becoming an ordinand suddenly raised my social standing in a Yorkshire village. It is not my intention here to dwell on a sense of personal deficit. I am using my particular experience to suggest that we all explore and recognize how our life's journey has formed our notion of church. I know from conversations over many years how my own experience resonates with others who are urgent in expecting the practice of church to be inclusive of the dignity of all, rather than being patronizing or humiliating.

Theological criteria for identifying church

Decisions are often made based on what works, is popular or familiar. Though often attractive these are seriously limited.[27] 'Try it and see' or 'What will attract most people?' approaches need to be counterbalanced by an array of tough questions. These arise from placing the long wisdom of the past in conversation with a discernment of the agenda of the Church, in any particular place now. Adult Christians only let go of tried and tested shared meanings when they become convinced, to their core, that they are now unproductive and that a new proposal will serve better.[28] Management gurus Senge and Covey remind us that strategies and ideas for improved performance have to be interwoven with the revising of outdated attitudes and concepts.[29] Uncritiqued long-established habit is so often confused with unchanging and reliable certainty.

An example of this is the Church of England's response to the *Tiller Report*. A quarter of a century ago, John Tiller exposed the default Church of England myth that every parish, historically and ideally, requires its own resident stipendiary priest and the dualist opposite, that dioceses fail when this proves impossible to deliver.[30] Reneging on this unachievable vision continues to generate institutional anxiety. As a member of Bishop's Council and Deanery Chapter, I believe the ministry agenda now urgently requires a diversified approach, according to different principles. Freedom to act creatively could come from finally detaching from the assumptions in the quip, 'While we have just sufficient money and just sufficient clergy to continue in the old way, we'll keep the ship afloat.'

The Trinity in a reconsideration of ecclesiology

Some leading theologians with varying emphases, beginning notably with Karl Barth, have offered overlapping concepts and terminology in attempting to find speech for a concept of the triune God. To take seriously the mutuality of interpersonal *communion* experienced in the life of the Church is to open up the most fundamental issues concerning the *communion* that characterizes the mystery of the Holy Trinity. An ecclesiology that is a sign and foretaste of

God's final ordering of all relations in Christ will be informed and nurtured, however cautiously, by a social trinitarianism.[31] The Christian West continues, even after decades of a renewed contemplation of the triune mystery, to be impoverished in its vision and practice through a lack of trinitarian intuition or imagination.[32] Most contemporary enactments of church and ministry continue to demonstrate the limiting consequences of developing an ecclesiology predominantly on a Christological basis, with regard both to the historical shape and direction of Jesus' life and also its doctrinal significance. The lack of a concern for the work of the Spirit (pneumatology) leads to a rigid, oversolid and controlling ecclesiology.[33]

By contrast, the Church called into existence by the triune God, however analogously, may be said to have the potential through the coinherence of Christ and the Holy Spirit to portray that *communion* that is the being of God and the shape of God's desire for the ultimate ordering of the entire creation.[34] In the light of the Trinity, everything looks different:

- First, God's being is most deeply understood by Christians as Trinity: *communion* of Father, Son and Holy Spirit.
- Second, it is essential to God's purpose for the universe that all relationships should be conceived as yearning to follow the trinitarian pattern.
- Third, the Church, having a particular part to play in preparing the way for God-shaped relationality in society and creation, must allow its ministerial and institutional arrangements to echo the trinitarian *communion* of overflowing love.

John Zizioulas has been in the forefront of propounding the significance of the faith expressed by the early Fathers of the Church, rooted in a deep bond between the being of humanity, of the world and of God. Like Moltmann, he invites us to recognize the Church as part of creation, called to reflect God's being in humility and contingency, and to reject patterns of systematic domination. Zizioulas' starting point is the divine givenness of a *communion* relationship between the natural world, its people and God. This must dictate to the Church, analogously, its ways of distributing its responsibilities and its way of relating with people and groups. Indispensable to unlocking the concepts of Zizioulas are two themes:

1 There is no true being that is not an expression of *communion*. Nothing exists as an individual conceivable in itself alone. *Communion* is an ontological category.

2 *Communion* that does not come from a concrete and free person (*hypostasis*) and does not lead to concrete and free persons
   (*hypostases*) is not an authentic image of the being of God.

Every form of so-called *communion*, therefore, that denies or sup-
presses the unique freedom of the person is not an expression of
authentic Christianity.[35] The triune God, whose life is revealed in
Jesus Christ through the Spirit and has been expressed in terms
of *perichoretic*[36] being, evokes a church in which there are no permanent structures of subordination, rather overlapping patterns of
mutual relationship. The same person or group of persons will be
sometimes subordinate and at other times superordinate, according
to the gifts and graces exercised, appropriately, on different occasions.

Elizabeth Johnson finds metaphors for the profound Christian
experience of God in egalitarian, mutual and reciprocal terms. She
believes that God is 'constitutively relational' and lives in the movement between persons we call love. Suffering is a sign of the essence
of God's being 'insofar as it is an act freely engaged as a consequence of care for others'.[37] Vitally for the argument of this book, she
cites the kind of power voiced by women as 'power-with' rather than
power-over or powerlessness, and as 'a deep joy of connectedness
with others'.[38] Johnson commends Moltmann's exploration of how
Scripture makes it possible to conceive of the trinitarian persons
in patterns of relation rather than as a set of linear progressions.
Moltmann rightly argues that 'The unity of God is to be found in
the triunity of the Father, the Son and the Holy Spirit. It neither
precedes nor follows it.'[39] The three persons of God interweave
with one another in varying patterns of saving activity and can be
spoken of in concepts such as giving over, receiving back, being
obedient, witnessing, filling and being filled, and actively glorifying. This stands in contrast with inherited pictures of God and
church that assume that unless a single ruler is in control, chaos will
ensue, and personal identity will be lost and harmony destroyed.

Johnson urges the Church to abandon literalness in using metaphor, remembering that this dense triune symbol of God's mystery
arises from historical experiences of Jews and, later, Gentiles
coming to salvation through Jesus in the Spirit's power.[40] Trinitarian
language can only ever serve analogously, reflecting on experience
of relating with God, as mere 'speculation can degenerate into wild
and empty conceptual acrobatics'.[41] She suggests that rather than
being an attempt at a literal description, the trinitarian symbol has
the capacity to reveal the dynamic movement of *shalom* drawing

near. The word 'Trinity' is a condensed way of speaking of the availability of God's wisdom, *sophia*, as compassionate love for each person and every unique situation. So Johnson invites the Church now to rediscover possibilities of trinitarian concepts by lifting up the threefold experience of the mystery of God as the centre for understanding:

- First, the symbol of the Trinity expresses the very essence of the God at the heart of all reality and shown to us in the dynamic of Christian community and the Eucharist as relatedness.
- Second, this symbol indicates that the particular quality of relatedness, more than anything we could conceive, is not one of hierarchy implying permanent structures of sub- or superordination, but rather one of genuine mutuality in which there is both a radical equality and respect for distinctions.
- Third, the trinitarian God cannot be spoken of except as a divine outpouring of compassionate, liberating love in the historical world of beauty, sin and suffering, so leading to the expectation of God empowering human living along the same patterns.

The continuing ecumenical debate on trinitarian *communion* at the heart of God and of all creation invites us to take an interactive dynamic of participation as the clue to the proper nature of human personhood, baptism, church community, Eucharist, priesthood and ministry.[42] All of these are provisional signs of the new creation, the Kingdom that the triune God will ultimately bring into being. To take part in making such a form of church happen means that, by growing in *communion* with the mystery we call Trinity, we accept a shared responsibility for the regeneration of all relations: between humanity and our global environment, between faiths and nations and within society generally. The still-persistent remnants of a deist theology make little of the Trinity. The prevailing ministerial patterns of the contemporary Church reveal few connections with the interrelatedness of God, of people and the entire cosmos.[43]

In a world increasingly alarmed by other persons, nations and faiths, who are perceived as frighteningly different, a Church rooted in a social trinitarian theology potentially has a vital role. This Church is possessed by a vision of God and of the created order as generous, open and engaged in a life-process. Unity is not a static entity, equated with the denial of difference or a desire for reductionist homogeneity. Rather it points to the mutual interaction and interpenetration of elements of radical difference. Thus the Church can imagine and attempt to model a society formed positively and hopefully in mutually constitutive relations. Individualism denies the need for human relating, except in so far as our needs are served. Collectivism falsely reduces all members of society to the status of disposable cogs in the machinery of corporate enterprise. Both lack a profound sense of reciprocity, so that power groups may arise and dispossess or make redundant relatively powerless persons in the name of efficiency or in the pursuit of effective economics. A social trinitarianism, by contrast, refuses to treat any person or group either as totally isolated or as a mere unit in a collective game.

Zizioulas shows how the true understanding of personhood, based on an accurate vision of God as difference in *communion*, is the Church's unique contribution to the human quest for fulfilment and meaning for all. 'If God does not exist, the person does not exist'.[44] As the Father, Son and Holy Spirit are mutually constituted in their unique difference, precisely through otherness-in-relation, so the Church has the mission to show society how, in a healthy culture, each particular person is both unique and yet mutually related to the being of the whole, uniqueness-in-relation.

The vital contribution of Christoph Schwöbel, in dialogue with Zizioulas' claim that to be in God's image is to be persons in *communion*, is to further the trinitarian basis of Christian belief for the contemporary Church. Rather than describing Christ as *possessing* the divine nature, Schwöbel suggests that Christ becomes agent of salvation for the world, as an *event* of *communion*, of sharing relations with the Father, the Son and Holy Spirit. Jesus shows the salvation of every human being as similarly related to the triune God.[45] So humanity, in Jesus Christ the second Adam, is restored to its destiny.[46]

People of God and the 'Church of the Poor'

A key question for ecclesiology in our present era is the relationship between the Church and the world. The World Council of Churches and the Roman Catholic Church's Second Vatican Council led to a rebalancing in thinking about the Church, towards a more open engagement with the world. However, more recently the balance has in many ways swung in the opposite direction, towards a Church as more world-*renouncing* than world-*affirming* community.

A fundamental assumption throughout this study is that faith is ecclesial, lived in and from interactive community that embodies the gospel.[47] A community with a distinct identity and shaped by a particular story, the *ecclesia* lives in the world distinctively. Although I find inspiration in some of the insights of Milbank and the 'Radical Orthodoxy' movement, I have reservations about working totally with a contrast model of church, shaped wholly by revelation, with a radically different worldview of the pagan.[48] Milbank writes of Paul seeking natural justice not just in relation to life but specifically in relation to resurrection, as a gift of 'sonship', coterminous with life itself.[49] There is not space here to give an account of this debate, which is well summarized by Gerard Mannion.[50]

I believe the Church has to avoid exclusivism by performing more of a balancing act in which we are constantly pushed in two directions. The dangerous lure of the world has to be held in tension with staying connected and becoming better equipped to serve there. This study advocates an ecclesiology that espouses a Christian community of distinctive character that is also in deep and respectful contact with – including a relationship of critique – the whole of its surrounding context and in dialogue with other faiths and philosophies.

The concept of dignity is one of great complexity as the inherited demarcations of class in British society are overtaken in significance by degrees of measurable prosperity. For followers of the Jewish–Christian story of God there is an unambiguous and countercultural demand that all human persons are due an inalienable value. Churches have a unique place and opportunity in weaving together the spectrum of agencies that dedicate themselves to forming networks of trust for building up the store of goodness and care within localities. This relates to two critical dimensions implied in the scriptural metaphor of humans being created in God's image. First, human beings are not alone because we are 'transparent to another reality', resembling God our Creator. Second, human beings are designed as not wholly to ourselves, in that in regarding ourselves, we see also one another.[51]

In the 1980s, working with parishioners on East Leeds estates, I grew in my determination that the Church of England should redefine itself to honour each human person and embrace their gifts. A *koinonia* Church will avoid posing false alternatives to describing reality.[52] It will be both strong enough for those who are on the edge of coping with life, and also vulnerable enough to reflect the life of Jesus who died outside the city gates.[53] This is vitally true of those who as priests personify the healing work of God in society. Selection procedures must finely balance the Church's needs of adequate leadership and perfection of character with a genuine knowledge of forgiveness and the power of Christ's healing of broken lives.

The expression 'People of God' has been a popular code for a re-discovery of a Church with more traits from the first than from the second millennium. There has been a temptation to reduce this expression to a bourgeois Church, adopting the best practices of secular democracy with insufficient reflection on their limitations.[54] Liberation theologies, spawned by the innovative work of Gustavo Gutiérrez, Leonardo Boff and Juan Luis Segundo, are committed to liberating the world's poorest from material deprivation. These writers and others who have been victims of attack and murder developed their positions out of the view that Marxist theory offered concentrated expertise in handling the data of social science. Fre-quently opposed and more recently critiqued for simplistic moral-izing and self-referencing conversation,[55] this theological movement relentlessly links the hope of salvation with a radical critique of a Church embedded within institutions and the global economic framework that fail to demonstrate God's preferential option for the poor.

The impetus of Argentinian Marcella Althaus-Reid, using post-colonial discourse, is to write not *for* but *from* the poor. From the experience and speech of poor urban women she challenges narrowly focused mainstream Christian theology and practice to a permanent process of 'serious doubting'.[56] Sobrino notably proposes five key scriptural themes that outdistance contemporary demo-cratic practice:

1 The centrality of the cross in situations of poverty and slavery, of God who hears the cries of those who suffer (Exod. 3.7). Tak-ing those who are crucified down from the cross conflicts with the agendas of prosperous democracies.

2 Recognizing solidarity with the humanity of those suffering in-justice as a test of a humane society (cf. Deut. 15.4 and Jer. 22.15). The hope of justice is the ultimate scriptural demand in the face of despair and cynicism (Mark 1.14).

3 Placing the poor at the centre, going beyond merely seeing them as equal in opportunity for development and abundance (Ps. 72; 1 Kings 10.9; Jer. 1–3).

4 Challenging the ways that rulers and democracies lord it over their subjects and encourage the strong to increase their wealth (which is a universal sinful condition), so that the poor become an underclass, despised, unseen.

5 Avoiding the arrogance by which people in democracies have aspirations to superior wealth, freedom of expression, power and standard of living. In such a world the oppressed are invisible and 'minds are darkened' to God's purposes (cf. Rom. 1.18–25).[57]

These developments, together with the insights of Black Theology (for example, James Meredith, Martin Luther King and James Cone) and reflections on world-changing events such as the Holocaust, provoke us to need a Church whose priority is critical engagement with its environment, locally and globally, and that is intentionally formed through intense contact with the living God. The 'collaborative ministry' culture of the People of God has a tendency to slide into a nostalgic reconstruction of a homogenous and strident 'early Church',[58] well-managed, egalitarian and disentangled from its exploitative environment. The study of language, community styles and the history of Christianity in the first century shows local churches with a sense of belonging to something greater than themselves, but a long way from a monochrome sense of identity.[59]

As a corrective, the notion of *communion*, when applied to the Church's household, invites connection with the scriptural tradition of the self-emptying God, choosing to stand alongside the poorest, demanding for them food, dignity and fairness.[60] The assumption is that the fundamental principle of church is the coming near of the Kingdom. All theology, like the mission of Jesus itself, is grounded in opposition to all that limits and opposes God's promise of life. Such an ecclesial group will be untameable, messy and alive with unresolved competing passions:

> Say you and I both embrace the liberationalist claim that the body is the locus of salvation and that food, water, shelter are part of God's plan for all. We would still need, however, to work out what these ideas mean in practice; we need to develop the implications of that understanding for the way we relate to ourselves, to others and to the way society is organized. For some this could mean a higher minimum wage and greater welfare benefits . . . For others it might mean radical structural change such as the replacement of capitalism for a system not based on profit and competition.[61]

Positively, living within the biblical concept of People of God has contributed to raised expectations of practices of compassion, humility and partiality towards the poor. However, rather than just being *for* or even *towards* others, *koinonia* (*communion*) radically suggests church walking *with* others as central to gospel practice.[62] The Beatitudes of Matthew 5 make clear that it is not sufficient for the poorest to be treated with equality; they need to be placed at the centre to mould the Church of Jesus' gospel. To secular democratic principle, the Church adds the compassion that God reveals in Scripture even for Israel's worst enemies (Amos 9.7). A better future for the Church arises from learning to be the unique *communion* that rediscovers the joy of placing at the centre the poor and every kind of poverty, material, intellectual and spiritual.

The vibrant 1968 Latin American Bishops' Conference in Medellin, Colombia, linking the biblical Exodus of God's people with the plight of the peoples of Latin America, invested in the concept of the 'Church of the Poor' as most profoundly gospel-inspired. Fired by a determination that the Church should be able to evangelize those facing the greatest degrees of deprivation, it counter-balanced the neoplatonic and often oppressive understanding of reality as naturally a graded hierarchy.[63] The impetus behind the expression 'Church of the Poor', arising from African and South American experience, controversially coupled with a Marxist/capitalist dichotomy, offered a shocking counterbalance to the practice of church as the rich and well-organized generously ministering *to* the poor.[64]

The invitation of Liberation Theology is to take as a new perspective in rethinking the internal structures and organization of the Church, the varied forms of brokenness and structural sinfulness afflicting the personal, social and cultural environment of the world. Only in the power of God's resurrection newness is it possible for churches to give up on the attempt to proclaim the good news hampered by too much history, money, real estate and sadness for lost glory.

More recent pastoral reflections on the capacity of churches being enriched for mission through the deliberate inclusion of those who are 'differently abled' – whether obviously physically or more subtly emotionally – is a further reminder that every worshipping group both carries and inflicts wounds.[65] The eschatological metaphor of Church as God's household invites us to consider Church offering hope to the world. Such a Church acts as an agent called to identify and urgently find alternatives to those ingrained behaviours and language that routinely treat others as mere commodities. The ecclesial task of reimagining and practising alternative and redemptive relations requires parish priest and people together, willing to live in the murky and unpredictable moment between what is and what is not yet, living in what Grau labels 'constructive ambivalence'.[66]

Eschatological company

What if a theology and embodied practice of *communion* really is the only way a 'church' can exist if it is to be a sign and foretaste of God's final desire for the world? What if the hope the world most needs from our practice of faith is evidence of a believable counter to the dominant myths? Ecclesial *communion* reveals the poverty of a culture built on the elevation of the individual, through uncovering authentic personhood as free, relational and designed for *communion* with the triune God.[67] What if we have to suffer a demanding transformation, personally, communally and institutionally, to meet the complex and often conflicting demands of the embodied corporate practice of Christian faith? There's a danger that a Church in panic about the preservation of past forms, or even its very existence, will fall into the consumerist trap of promoting itself as a commodity with market value.[68] But what if its present vital calling is the summons to renounce past glories and to accept instead that new circumstances continually require very different forms?[69]

What if a Church now needs to follow the self-emptying (*kenotic*) path of knowing that its character and task is to be a liberating and exhilarating embodiment of what we know of God's crucifying way of loving?[70]

To presume to know much of God's life must be arrogant. However, in recent decades a deepening theology of the Holy Spirit has revealed how Jesus' teaching and work can most authentically be known and made real today in terms of self-emptying *communion*.[71] Contemplation of the nature of God as a trinitarian movement of reciprocity leads the Church to demonstrate to the world unfamiliar and restorative patterns of dynamic interaction. The *Virginia Report* describes faithful Christianity as living in 'community with God the Holy Trinity', focused 'in a vision of the final and ultimate reign of God'. The Church's mission is to be 'the living and visible sign of that divine reign, when He will dwell with them as their God'.[72]

Christian hope is evoked by the Old Testament prophets' witness to the longing of God for the destabilizing of institutionalized injustice. The Church's eschatological hope focuses on the unique life-giving power of God, shown in Jesus' resurrection. The expectation of God's deliverance in situations of despair is a key dimension of church as a community and institution that is a scandalous sign of the mystery of God's regenerative love.[73] Instead of perceiving itself as a community generously including and praying for life's misfits and other people in need, the Church of the Poor comes to recognize itself as composed of those who, in one way or another, know themselves to be damaged and fragile, as well as joyfully expectant. A Church of the Poor is constituted by those called to discover their true voice in God's household (*oikonomia*) of mutuality, equality and friendship. To perform God's inclusive household rules of choosing the weak as a central way of practising church requires an urgent readjustment of attitude. Focused attention is required for the reconfiguring of inherited patterns of distributing responsibilities. Authentic church becomes aware of the need to change habits that subtly diminish others and cling to patterns of authority that fail to bring resurrection to those crushed by life's events.

Episkope: metaphor for the Church's work?

Religion in the world's press often seems frightening and a major source of violence and manipulation. Christian faith in the modern world has the urgent task of contributing strengthening bonds between world faiths. Where in humility it is accepted, the Church can perhaps become a broker in ecological matters and standing with the poorest. We have earlier noticed the possibility of Churches being agencies of cohesion and sociality for societies and the world. My belief is in the entire *laos* as an eschatological company working for the world's true life, running 'like sparks among the stubble' (Wisdom 3.7).[74] In exploring the role of the parish priest and those ordained and commissioned to serve in close association, I shall propose that for those given and those sharing by extension in 'the cure of souls' in local churches, a redevelopment of the notion and practice of *episkope* could offer an attractive and highly motivating metaphor.

The ecclesial character of the Church's unique and interanimative ministries is a key element in this study. T. F. Torrance, in his study of the Body in the New Testament, concludes:

> If the ministry of the church is primarily corporate, the ministry of the whole Body, then are there any theological reasons which insist that presbyteral or episcopal succession must devolve on individuals alone? The corporate priesthood of the church would seem to demand above all a notion of corporate episcopate, and would seem to rule out the radical individualism that lurks in so many medieval and modern views of the episcopate.[75]

As widespread studies among Anglicans and in ecumenical dialogue have recognized in recent decades, the being of the Church and of its ministries is relationally grounded in the doctrine of the Trinity.[76]

The *Virginia Report* summarizes how Anglicans since the Reformation have understood the ministry of oversight (*episkope*) by bishops in college and by bishops in council as exercising a ministry described as 'personal, collegial and communal' (3.21 and 51) for the holding together of churches in a community of discernment and reflection.[77]

Critically, the elements of episcopal ministry are not restricted to the personal ministry of a bishop. The General Synod of the Australian Anglican Church expresses it succinctly:

> dimensions of the ministry of the church as a *whole*. The whole church is called to unity, with every member conscious of his or her belonging to the whole. The whole church is meant to hand on the faith through teaching and proclamation. Within the church all are called to take some responsibility for each other's journey and well-being.[78]   (1 Cor. 12, 12–26; Matt. 28, 18–20; Gal. 6, 1–5)

The whole Church in some way shares in the episcopal element of ministry. No one is called to passive irresponsibility in this matter.

The *Virginia Report* speaks of the bishop personally exercising ministry in partnership with other bishops, clergy and laity, always 'in relation to the community and always subject to the Word of God'.[79] Collegially, the bishop represents the concerns of the local church and community to the wider Church and brings decisions and concerns from the wider Church to the local. The People of God as a whole is the bearer of the living Tradition.[80] In a parallel way, *The Gift of Authority: Authority in the Church III*, a Report of the Anglican–Roman Catholic International Commission (ARCIC), speaks of the symphony of the life of the Church in which lay people and priests express in 'synodality' their Eucharistic 'Amen', in unity with their local bishop as a 'living memorial of the Lord's great "Amen"' to the will of the Father'.[81] For my argument here I shall quote verbatim from the *Virginia Report* on the communal exercise of the bishop's office:

> The community's effective participation is necessary in the discovery of God's will, under the guidance of the Spirit. In their communal relationships, bishops meet with representatives of those who hold office, or those who exercise responsibility within the community of the local churches. This accords with the principle of subsidiarity, keeping the bishop in touch with the concerns and decisions which

belong properly to the more parochial levels of diocesan life. As representative persons, bishops have a moral duty to reflect the concerns of the whole community, especially those whom society pushes to the margins.[82]

Within each local church a mutual give-and-take between bishops, clergy and lay people characterizes the whole body.[83] Synodical government is potentially the practical expression of this account-ability of episcopal ministry to the entire Church, local and uni-versal. In terms of ecclesiastical order, Anglicans work with three 'houses' of bishops, clergy and laity. Each 'house', to varying degrees at various times, stimulates among the whole *laos* the three eccle-sial dimensions of *episkope* – communal, collegial and personal.[84]

A *koinonia* ecclesiology makes room for the separate and distinct orders of ministry to be in creative and dynamic relationship that moves beyond calculating the relative permanent significance of any one of them. Further, the ordering of particular persons as bishop, priest or deacon, always an ecclesial act, uncovers the nature of the whole Church. Although the distinctive ministry of a bishop, a priest or a deacon contributes to the effective working of the Church in the world, there is a vital sense in which these are characteristics of the Church in its entirety and remind the Church of its mission. Paul Lakeland shows from a Roman Catholic perspective how the notion of a Church characterized as diaconal is consistent with the baptismal theology of Vatican II's *Lumen Gentium*. A serving Church, before any distinction is made between those ordained and the rest of the laity, has a vital diaconal aspect in its presentation of the lov-ing presence of God to the world.[85]

John Collins has pioneered a reappraisal of the diaconal role. He combines a revaluation of accounts of early Church practice with an ecumenical awareness of the work of the Church in the world today.[86] From his research we can recognize the value of a distinct-ive ministry of those ordained deacon to context-specific and evolv-ing diaconal roles. Further, we are reminded that being a deacon is part of the work of every Christian. This is not as the bottom of a hierarchy, such as when a bishop may recall that despite his current status he is also 'a humble deacon'. But rather as a key aspect within the serving ministry of all Christians, willingness to be sent on an urgent commissioned message of love and compassion is always a key element. The same would be true for the episcopal and pres-byteral aspects of the Church's character and task. So, for example, a lay person or reader can be found exercising a care for the guarding of the Church's life, enabling learning, building Christian community or evoking ministries in others. A priest may sometimes be found concerned with the administration of the church or with a diaconal role of reaching out into contact with a local community.

A bishop's work will often be more on the edges of the Church than in watching out for the Church itself. In other words, the episcopal, priestly and diaconal aspects of the Church, held distinctively by those in 'orders' (even though the language and context that define them may continue to be debated), become at varying times the natural task of many. No one's ministry excludes that of another; rather in their uniqueness they form one another as the Church.

It must also be important for those holding office within the three orders to see a key part of their work as helping all Christians to see their role in sharing in the episcopal, priestly and diaconal aspects of mission. The content, and associated language, of the work of the three orders and aspects of ministry is strongly debated today. On the specifics of *episkope*, for example, Zizioulas argues that the Church's unity is an event formed and maintained in the episcopal gathering of the Church for Eucharist. The work of episcopacy, locally and universally, is one of searching out radical difference and gathering it and holding it in *communion*. The bishop, as representative,[87] holds together in a trinitarian unity the worldwide and every local expression of church.[88] So how can the bishop invite others to share more fully in this task of which she or he is the representative figure? If the key work of the priest is in gathering people for worship, pastoral care and teaching, how can the priest be one who also evokes these gifts and desires in many others? If the deacon is one on a commissioned errand (not a menial servant), how can the whole Church learn to be sent on urgent tasks in many situations?

There are serious problems surrounding the Church of England's deep ambivalence to the potential contribution of a continuing diaconate. The report *For Such a Time as This: A renewed Diaconate in the Church of England* (General Synod, 2001) invited the Church to move away from a merely transitional understanding of the diaconate. Biblical and theological resources were employed to suggest how a distinctive diaconate could help the whole Church in all its vocations to reach out to society in compassion, worship, sacramental life and teaching in diverse contexts. Rather than diminishing the work of lay people, the report was confident that deacons have a major role to play, with priest and bishop and all the laity, in ministering to the needs of local communities and bringing the gospel of Christ to the nation. The creation of many new deacons, notably in the context of local ministry teams, could be a trigger for the development of the laity in diaconal roles.

Stephen Croft, in *Ministry in Three Dimensions*, presented the work of the leader of the local church in terms of the everyday work (*diakonia*), sacramental tasks (*presbyteral*) and unifying, enabling and keeping watch (*episkope*). Croft fluently demonstrates an interweaving of these three elements in the vocation of the parish priest commissioned to draw out a common responsibility for mission among all ministers and within the entire congregation. Significantly for my argument, he rightly notes that parish priests often concentrate on the first and second dimensions of ministry and succeed in building up the church in pastoral and sacramental duties, but don't give much attention to the third.

Parish priests (and bishops) frequently claim to be powerless. In traditional hierarchical terms this holds true. However, there can be a very real exercise of influence and persuasion within webs of relational dynamics, when a sense of calling to a presiding ministry is combined with emotional intelligence. It is because presiding priests so often overlook this crucial element of their role that I am experimenting in this book by suggesting that, for the Church's situation today, it may be pivotal. I shall attempt to demonstrate that the exercise of *episkope* within the whole Church's corporate discernment can help to lift the entire community into mutual ministries of watching out, pastoral care, service and mission. As we have already seen, *episkope* is more than an individualistic and controlling role. Rather, it has the capacity to spark and sustain alternative church patterns reconceived in terms of participation and the re-lationality of difference. Understood along such lines, it may even be possible to regard *episkope* as a metaphor for the very nature and task for the world of the entire Church. Instead of conceiving episcopacy merely in terms of the senior figure in church structures, we could reimagine it as focusing the eschatological work of the whole Church. *Episkope* could be recognized as the watermark in the paper of a Church that watches out for the world in many dimensions. So then the particular focus of the local priest, and immediate leadership group, will be to exercise that *episkope* task and to evoke it in all others.

Could *episkope* stand as a metaphor for the very nature and work of the Church itself and therefore of those called to keep it true to its character and task? This certainly seems to be consistent with the 1999 WCC Report, *Episcope and Episcopacy and the Quest for Visible Unity*:

> Laity appointed to ecclesiastical positions may exercise personal oversight within the confines of their appointed position. Clergy exercise personal *episkope*, particularly for the ministry of word and sacraments, within the ministries to which they have been licensed under the personal oversight of a diocesan bishop. In relation to worship, preaching and teaching, spiritual life, and the administration of the sacraments, the priest has an oversight delegated directly from the diocesan bishop. In general the priest works with the parish council/vestry in this oversight but retains authority for them in his or her ministry.[89]

In Chapters 4 and 5, we shall explore in detail the *episkope* required in the work of those who lead mission and Eucharist in local churches, not merely as an extension of the work of the chief pastor of the diocese but as an expression and stimulus of the eschatological event that is the practice of church.

Learning to live without security

Finally, a key element in reconceiving church today has to do with showing the vulnerability and humility of Christ. Dietrich Bonhoeffer, in discussing the nature of the Church, points out that, rather than being a disparate collection of worshippers, the Church is 'a section of humanity in which Christ has truly taken form'.[90] A Christ-shaped Church accepts only the space the world will allow, rather than aggressively fighting its corner. It testifies to Christ's own, self-denying, way of coming into the world. In this way, rather than being an end in itself, the community of faithful Christians is adapted to God's purpose for the world, proclaiming the beginning of all that God longs for. Authentic Christian, trinitarian, *community* practice is characterized inescapably as a recapitulation on Jesus' vulnerable way of being with disciples, individuals and crowds. Jesus points to a concrete practice of irresponsible self-forgetfulness, rather than to a clinging, grasping, relentless desire to survive.

The notion of contextual intelligence, articulated by the Harvard Business School and those who train managers today, serves as a reminder that each of us has our own complex road of experience and that we should not underestimate the significance of what our lives have taught us, nor of the impact on us of authors and role

models. The impact of people we have known closely or from a distance can have more impact for change than books. However, I have
especial reason to be grateful for the incisive work of Henri Nouwen,
Richard Rohr, Jean Vanier and others who in diverse ways have connected Jesus' servant, foot-washing way with theology, spiritual formation and human maturing. Membership of the Franciscan Third
Order calls me repeatedly to live Jesus' *kenotic* way of self-giving
and descent rather than of protection and grandiosity.[91] Ignatian
spiritual exercises have also called me to follow the disenthroned
God, committed to suffering with and within creation.[92]

Resilience to find and accept healing for the most broken places
in myself has come through the growing body of wisdom relating
to the confronting of the 'False Self'.[93] A health-giving Church will
be more than busy creating superior strategies for sharing ministry
or even brilliant programmes for evangelism. Like St Peter, whose
denial was integrally woven into the story of the crucifixion and
the earliest days of the Church, our own hearts have to be broken.
We need to accept Jesus' invitation to lose life in order to find it,
personally, communally and institutionally.[94] The concept of the
False Self, formulated in the 1960s by the theorist on child psychology Donald Winnicott, has, I believe, taught us to be suspicious
about inherited hierarchical ways of church governance. The theory
suggests that most people to varying degrees are caught within a
defensive structure, arising from real or imagined deprivation in
early years.[95] It leads to our wishing to appear to be accepted as
part of the dominant paradigm to gain acceptance from those we
respect, including God. Those operating to a great extent within
the polite and mannered position of the False Self often experience
greater than usual problems in making connection with others and
in forming deep relationships. They experience a sense of empti-
ness as though sleepwalking rather than living.

Exponents of the theory of the False Self suggest that incipient
immature dependency and lack of genuine contact feed the desire
to succeed within hierarchical institutions and at the same time limit
the capacity of the Church to serve God's project, and are overdue
for reshaping.[96] The true freedom Jesus embodies and invites his
followers to accept means avoiding the shortcut of the False Self and
choosing through spiritual exercises to know the esteem in which
we are held by God's love.[97] Real Christian community, treating ten-
derly and also loving us fiercely, will contain our fears and draw out
love from us as together we show one another, in our loving, the
radiance of the one who alone loves us without qualification.

In the local church there is no consolation in fixed, predetermined certainties. A frequent assumption is that 'collaborative ministry' is an objective form of ministry that can be rolled out everywhere the same through some meetings and programmes.[98] The authentic character of church will always be a negotiated settlement between a given predeterminedness and a radical openness to any moment and situation. 'Tradition' is the vulnerable rediscovery, time and time again, of how to be church in ever new places. One of the key roles of parish priests and colleagues is to have sufficient knowledge of the tradition, as it has developed so far, and of change-processes to animate this. How do we find the will, courage, energy and skill to persevere, especially when we receive so many contrary signals in the institution and from hardworking colleagues? I know from experience that collaborative practice can become viable and normative in a wide variety of human contexts. It is possible. Over several decades, often against prevailing attitudes, I have witnessed and encouraged participative forms of church through a mixture of determination, kindness, expectation and pragmatism. And yet, I know again, intensively in my current parish, just how much resilience and versatility is required in a parish priest. To co-create unpredictable and energizing patterns of church depends on my willingness to risk having my ego transfigured by God and to lose life in order to find it. Renegotiating how to be church with any group requires a deepening connectivity with God and our own selves. What does this say about selection criteria and patterns of priestly formation? What is implied here for the desirability of supervision in various forms as a routine practice? What personal and strategic insights could be uncovered through more frequent retreats, pursuing our creative talents and planning a better work–life balance?

2

What's in your diary?

Many of us long for the church to wake up to its changed place in society, to be reignited by the pioneering zeal of its early days, and to embrace new paradigms and directions of ministry. The more we give expression and shape to this longing, the more likely it is that transformation will take place. But in the end no single conference, book, or experiment will bring about the transformation for which we long – it's a journey, and telling our stories is one important way of encouraging each other on the way.[1]

Owning my assumptions

Most of this chapter will be rooted in accounts of ministerial practice. Those who shun theory often forget that all practice is actually rooted in a theory, however implicit or partial. In my own current work as a parish priest I sense that for the Church to move beyond sustaining a dependency culture requires a compelling counter-proposal, an attractive concept of church, in which all are invited to invest. The advantage of a theory, over a random collection of models, even with unassailable New Testament tags, is that it gives a focus to work towards and critique.[2] A theory also challenges the structures and attitudes that accompany inherited notions of the ordained as the panacea for every kind of problem. It also acts as a counterbalance for when parish priests and churches allow themselves to be blown off course by enthusiasm for a compelling new initiative. Long-term transformation requires that those in key positions learn to *know their place* in developing aligned and persistent planning, practice and review.

I believe the spirit and practice of collaborative ministry (though not any particular form) is more than an optional aspect of church but is inherent in Christian faith itself. Daniel Hardy, a careful and constructive Anglican theologian, developed a theory of church in which the complex relations of church life are deliberately a reading of the content of Christian faith. Its expression in localities may vary but the criteria against which to discern their adequacy can be articulated. Prior to qualitative and performance issues must come root questions, 'Who is our God? Who are we worshipping? What is church? What's it for? Why do we bother to make it happen?' Only then, do we ask, 'How can churches help make a better job of doing God's work in the world?'

In 1850, Edward Monro proposed that a 'clergyman' should give three hours, on three evenings a week, to pastoral visits. He insisted that what is critically under scrutiny is the quality of the relationship between parishioner and priest:

> the visits of a clergyman to the poor must lose very much force unless he lays aside the magisterial air, so very commonly used. He has no right to cross the poor man's threshold with a covered head, nor in any degree to demean himself as superior within the walls of the cottage.[3]

Russell's *The Clerical Profession* provides a detailed and provocative historical study of the development of parish clergy. He documents how they come to identify themselves as competent professionals, in parallel with secular equivalents, and increasingly distribute tasks formerly reserved to their own role. It is common today, in conversation with parish priests on the verge of retirement, to be told 'now I can do what God really called me to'. Further probing often produces the response that the clerical ministry is a blend of leading worship and visiting people at home or in hospital.

Taking stock

This renewed consideration of ministry and clerical identity is rooted in an appreciation of the variety of contemporary ministerial patterns. What energizes, engages and fulfils parish priests and bishops in their work is the central question of this chapter. What are they facing? What inhibits or reduces energy? These are important questions to consider as a basis for any attempt to advance suggestions about further developments of thought or practice. In leading workshops in dioceses in the UK and elsewhere I have often been surprised at the frequency with which very similar themes have arisen in reviewing clerical life. Rather than merely offering my own take on this, I asked colleagues to conduct very simple interviews with priests and bishops. As this is a study especially of the link between parish priest and bishop as sharing *episkope*, from their different but complementary ministries, I decided it would be unhelpful in this context to introduce material from the reflections of deacons.[4]

The interviews: methodology

I am grateful that 45 parish clergy and eight bishops, from the Church of England, Church in Wales, Episcopalian Church of Scotland, the Anglican Church in Aotearoa, New Zealand and Polynesia, and the Evangelical Lutheran Church in America, have helped with this particular aspect of the study.[5] Their responses to the questions of what energizes and what inhibits the ministry they exercise in the Church draw out multiple roles, attitudes, disciplines and purposes espoused by clergy in faithfulness to their calling within the witness and mission of the Church in today's world. Social anthropologists and psychologists have contributed scientifically based research to this field, for example Tim Jenkins, Fraser Watts, Rebecca Nye, Sara Savage, Leslie Francis and Mary Robbins.[6]

What I am offering distinctively, from a phenomenological perspective, is an overview of responses from interviewees, drawn out in structured conversation across gender and age from parts of the world Church. Each person within the space of an hour was asked to speak freely around the appreciative enquiry questions, 'What energizes you in your work as bishop or parish priest?' and 'What inhibits you in your work as bishop or parish priest?' The interviewee was then invited to reflect freely, while notes were taken by the interviewer. Those invited to be interviewed were within the range of bishops and priests who, though varied in outlook, are still positive about their work and usefulness. What intrigues me is how much of the material gathered, although from colleagues ministering within many contrasting contexts across the world, has a very familiar ring. I am aware of how some will lament the absence of data from significant parts of the Church, for example in Africa or India. Deliberately I have disguised the identities of all concerned and am offering a theological systematization rather than a sociological or ethnic survey.

The interviews: introduction to the content

Generally, it is apparent that many have responded to the call to ordination through a burning desire to serve God and others with more explicit 'permission' to live passionately for the gospel but with no specified prior sense of what this will mean. Understanding has grown with practice, partly shaped by inspiring role models, communal language and rituals, reflection and hindsight.[7]

The shape of any particular ministry depends on the human context, the life-stage that person has reached and the range of the other vocations and responsibilities into which they have already entered, for example family, work or locality. Theoretical ideas are probably for most parish priests of less significance than cultivating and enacting a particular kind of culture or energy. The increasing number of women in ordained ministry is complementing and frequently challenging the long-established habits of an androcentric culture.

Maggie Ross, Sue Walrond-Skinner and Una Kroll have contributed to my understanding of how the familiar fabric and power dynamics of the Church and its inherent style of personal encounter are being questioned and turned around.[8] Women, lay and ordained, though often stigmatized and hindered, their concerns ignored, misunderstood or silenced, frequently prove to be navigators of passages to a new way of being church.[9] Despite the many crushing and humiliating setbacks that women separately and together have met, Churches are slowly recognizing the new possibilities they bring for the Church's spirituality and notions of power and task in society.[10] Urgently, women are reminding the Church of the significance of the choice of language we allow to shape our discourse and imagination for the Church and its ministry. They are also challenging the value of binary oppositions in mapping power configurations, personal, societal or global.[11] A trinitarian understanding of divine life as a *communion* of relations, rather than as one absolute ruler, can point to Christian community and ministry that releases justice and full identity for all.

The renaissance of a trinitarian approach to understanding the Church's nature and task, rooted in the work of Jesus Christ and the reflection of the worshipping community, provokes the question of what kind of analogy between God and church, Trinity and community might be authentic. Increasingly there is a desire to find an unprecedented, new practice of church, through the interaction of all who minister, ordained and lay. Its character is reciprocal, as participants do not assume permanent positions of superiority or subordination, but deliberately constitute one another as believers.[12] In the interviews, many clergy spoke of giving serious attention to connecting and interrelating with people and groups and their concerns to make it possible for Christ to be more deeply known and understood.

Increasingly laity, in a voluntary or salaried capacity, are taking responsibility in partnership with the ordained for developing the church in mission that includes ordinary secular employment and life. In the process they are witnessing to an increase in commitment to growth in faith, integrity in building the church, mutual accountability and prayer. Inevitably, though usually implicitly, they are contributing to a further development of ecclesial self-identity. The phenomenon generally called the Local Shared Ministry movement, treated with ambivalence by many senior church leaders, especially, offers a focused example of this process.[13] At the heart of Local Shared Ministry is a deepening conversation around theories and practices of church rooted in 'an intra-trinitarian dynamic' that move beyond a linear or hierarchical approach.[14] The Christian account of the practice of trinitarian community reveals God as *communion*.[15] Constantly reminding ourselves of the need to be tentative and analogical, we shall later investigate how a clutch of new insights about church can be developed into an integrated theory that can be directly relevant to the task and role of priests in the local church.[16]

One of the recurring considerations here will be the extent to which the present ordering and working of bishops and priests releases or generates the fullest identity and capacity within the Church as a whole for serving God's mission in the world. As has been established in many recent theological studies, any enquiry into ministerial identity and practice will inevitably be related to an understanding of God's power and grace permeating all life in the world, and the Church's response to that. Further, as we shall explore, the work of the ordained cannot, in practice or theory, be separated from that of the Church as a whole but rather provides a focus for its unfolding and development.[17]

I give examples of the specifics of contemporary priestly activity, aspirations and frustrations in order to ask how far the threads of God's calling to ordination connect with four essential dynamics or tasks of the whole Church. In Chapter 3, I shall develop these dynamics more fully as a contribution to articulating a credible and attractive ecclesiology rooted in *communion*.[18] I am asking if these tasks add up to an adequate framework for discourse around the characteristics of church and its way of working through every participant. But now in this chapter I shall roadtest this framework through the reported attitudes and working practices of parish priests. I seek to establish:

- To what extent are priests and bishops working within these principles (overtly or not)?
- To what extent are they fostering discipleship and ministries in others?
- What capacity is being lost either through inappropriate structures or the freedom of choice exercised by the clergy concerning the distribution of their time and energy?

In *Models of the Church*, Avery Dulles pioneered the move to discover models alternative to that of institution, 'so as to operate more effectively in the social environment in which it finds itself'.[19] He categorized the many ways in which the Church has functioned and been understood, using the idea of five models: institution, mystical communion, sacrament, herald and servant. Dulles showed how none of these can stand alone, and the weakness of churches when one, for example the institutional, is allowed to dominate the others.[20]

We take for granted that any conversation about working with the dynamics of God's love is limited by the constraints of human speech and by the long domination of an exclusively male leadership. However, as a necessary preface to developing the tasks of ministry, questions of the nature of the Church and how it reveals God's life and work must be pursued. To be true to its calling to share in God's work in the world, the Church has to be intentionally a form of human society that in all its relationships, internal and external, is a deliberate reading of the gospel.

In *Finding the Church*, Daniel Hardy reported and stretched the Anglican debate on the form of church that is most consistent with God's own life and that can best witness in today's world. In dialogue with this seminal work, I shall attempt to develop the notion of church as a *communion* of difference, mediating among others for an alternative world of justice and love. I shall describe and evoke this around four themes:

1 richness – growing into the richness of God's life;
2 range – working with God in every place;
3 contact – deepening contact between people;
4 transformation – a new world beginning.

In the remainder of this chapter and in the one following, on the Church's character and task, I shall further explain and test out these four categories. For now I shall briefly point to the core values of these pointers to the Church.[21]

Richness

First, the call to grow into the *richness* of God's life links with the call and dignity of all the baptized, characterized by constantly growing in knowledge, love and the following of God revealed in Christ through the Spirit. A priority is for the people of God on pilgrimage to be ever more riskily open to transformation, through an ever deepening engagement with the dense disclosure of God's abundance in Jesus through the Spirit. In this chapter, what evidence do we see of this in the accounts we have of the work of the parish clergy who were interviewed?

Range

Second, because the gospel has to be engaged with in every time, place and culture, the Church has a desire to be open-ended, extending infinitely its *range* of contact with people and situations. As history attests, despite its sin and fearfulness, the Church aspires like God to be an infinitely generous movement embracing and intersecting in relation with the widest range of people and issues in the world.

Contact

Third, the Church continually seeks for more genuine *contact*, interest, friendship, interaction, acceptance, companionship and free engagement called out between the life of people and the situations of their work and particular concerns and Christian faith embodied in the teaching and practices of the faith community.

Transformation

Fourth, a compelling understanding of church integrates the previous three elements, as mediating the well-being and final *transformation* of humanity and the world. A key here is the work of bishop and priest, in their different and complementary navigational roles, in bridge-building, gathering and developing a worshipping, baptizing and ministering community of such a character that it can be an agent and a sign of hope for a renewed creation. In this regard, parish priests, especially when presiding at the Eucharist, but also when leading, gathering and animating communities, work for the embodiment of the joy and fullness of Christian hope in the promises of God made real in the risen Christ.

The details of the working lives of clergy show both the immense range of possibilities for allowing the world Church to be a resource for responding to God's mission as well as revealing how great is the limitation on our reaching our full potential. There are internal contradictions and no clear blueprint, but many compelling indications of a Church that shares God's passionate hope for the liberation of all people and all creation. How then do these categories suggested above relate to what we know of the diversity of committed work and the attached feelings articulated by a wide range of contemporary parish clergy? In the remainder of this chapter I shall take each category, asking the two questions of those clergy who were interviewed what energizes and what inhibits the flow of energy.

Richness – growing into the richness of God's life

What energizes?

New developments in adult education have increased the possibilities of learning, which leads to the reawakening, deepening and training in faith and skill of those who already participate in worship and share in the Church's ministry. Parochial clergy interviewed spoke of the deep personal satisfaction drawn from facilitating the searching of individuals and groups. The time and effort invested in nurturing the imagination of the congregation in adult education, especially Bible Study, is recognized as a key to the encouraging, enlivening and intimacy of church members for themselves and for others. A priest described the struggle with Scripture as a vital task for the ordained 'so that its poetry can address us and we are comforted, confronted and sometimes confounded'. Some gave time to developing in others and themselves self-awareness and growth in a sense of personal identity, responsibility and self-acceptance. These are all active signs of Christian people deepening their life with God.

For some, the priestly vocation is mostly activated in sustaining people in a desire to search for God through the routines of enquiry and worship associated with baptisms, marriages and funerals. Baptizing new Christians and enabling God's grace to flow, as a sign of Christ's own hospitality, engages some priests highly. Processes of adult confirmation preparation are often experienced as a vital way of drawing out people's potential. One priest spoke of funerals as a special way of touching 'as many people with the love of God' as he could. Serving the helplessness of people shattered by bereavement and the opportunity for consoling and helping them to express their feelings are all priorities for a significant group of clergy. There can be no doubt of the privilege of being admitted deeply into the heart of a grieving family to design and deliver a service of healing and closure through touching the self-giving love of Jesus. There are those who define a fulfilling part of their calling as being a soul friend or spiritual director, freeing people's hearts and minds so they can listen for God speaking. Generally, helping others to develop new possibilities through intimate conversations about faith is an aptitude and a diary priority for priests.

A bishop summarized his task as to enact a positive model of faith, enjoying life to the full, expressing creativity and 'showing that Christianity works'. A priest spoke of ministry as serving others in Christ's name through the witness of integrating a personal and public way of living out the Christian ethic. There was a general agreement that the God-given gift for such ministries is intensified when a priest deliberately develops his or her own knowledge of the transforming wisdom that comes from openness to God. So an extrovert crucially insists on making regular space for silent depend-ence on God. Another appreciates the privilege of being called to the discipline of daily prayer in an ancient building. Some need to be sustained in this by dependence on others willing to pray together.

Many parish clergy have developed a love of learning and a desire to form mature faith in others through exploring Scripture, people finding resonance in each other's stories, and developing their baptismal call. Priests spoke of finding their own growth in wisdom through the satisfaction and pleasure attached to the demanding work of preparing and delivering sermons. Bringing alive and mak-ing active the three-year lectionary and the daily readings provides for clergy and other preachers a great privilege, joy and delight. A bishop had rediscovered energy through, unusually, being invited by a local church to lead a complete series of meetings with a group of adults wanting to extend their faith journey. Ensuring that learning structures are available in the diocese to stimulate the laity intel-lectually, emotionally and spiritually is now identified as an impor-tant episcopal role.

Clergy who feel fulfilled have learnt to live with ambivalence about the church as institution. Some spoke of how their energy for ministry increases as they learn to live within the paradoxes and tensions of church life. Those who find a vision and an environ-ment that stimulates their own growth are much more likely to experience being 'full rather than empty', however unpromising external circumstances may be. Almost all emphasize the sustaining value of sharing the journey with a spiritual guide. One referred to finding support in a 'like-minded' Buddhist chaplain. Another was passionate about the benefits of a two-month sabbatical, learning to use art as stimulation to worship and congregational creativity. Several had benefited from the challenge of a pilgrimage. To grow in alertness and openness to change, reading and reflection is a vital source of encouragement for some. Reading in the fields of economics and keeping abreast of current affairs and other human disciplines and conversations is a necessity for some clergy. A bishop spoke with enthusiasm of the value of his own study of history to throw light on the present time, and of philosophy to assist the Church to understand contemporary movements of power and culture. Through interweaving various intellectual disciplines, many clergy enrich the quality of their practice.

What inhibits?

Some priests identify problems in dealing with conflict and poor congregational communication, and the apathy of people and groups who are closed in on themselves, as debilitating. Connected with this is the personal struggle in the face of criticism from those who believe the faith of others, often the clergy, to be deficient or misguided.

A bishop finds it irksome that cost-saving measures around administration inhibit his effectiveness to fulfil his true calling. Another bishop reflected on how the demands of the e-mail culture can easily limit his freedom to make choices about how to be proactive in ministry. Intense arguments about the minutiae of church furnishings have eroded the enthusiasm of some clergy. When visiting is a high aspiration it is frustrating when other tasks have to take priority. Another bishop describes the pressure of keeping abreast of unprioritized demands, not least e-mail messages and the mental agility required to make right judgements and to share the responsibility.

One bishop is convinced that when the laity are regarded by the clergy and by themselves as having no gifts for ministry and mission, churches become distracted and lose the chance of finding new possibilities in God. Another laments about times when there is a breakdown of trust and when laity are limited in their spiritual growth by long years of clerical domination or lack of expectations.

The diversity of the clergy themselves is illustrated in the complaint of one of the frustration, for an extrovert, of being expected to be silent at clergy retreats, and of another of being an introvert and being debilitated when prayer routines and silence could not be paramount.

Some priests are discouraged when laity seem to be fearful or have a low level of expectation. A recurring issue for clergy is finding it both expected and impossible to meet all the needs that a congregation will express. Demands seem diverse and too onerous for one person to deliver. Inappropriate structures or limited expectations can also dilute energy for stimulating engagement with God, for example having responsibility for maintaining several worship centres and for being charged with 'looking after' a cluster of rural parishes. To exercise a lone pastoral ministry as a priest, across several churches, can be sustained with difficulty, but leaves many tasks and opportunities for supporting people's growth into God unaddressed.

Range – working with God in every place

What energizes?

The interviews showed evidence of churches deliberately demonstrating God's love for the locality, for example through programmes of social justice, working with illegal immigrants, using knowledge and skill to promote sport among young people or lending support to a farmers' market. Many spoke of enjoying the facilitation of groups of laity for mission in the neighbourhood as an essential part of the Church's character and external influence, echoing God's love. Increasingly laity, often more women than men, have been encouraged to develop learning programmes for children and adults, produce innovative outreach services, engage in sick and bereavement visiting, share Holy Communion with the housebound, communications groups and other acts of service in the parish.

Developing lay confidence in becoming more acutely aware of the people and institutions of their neighbourhood is a growing priority. At the extreme edge of this, one priest interviewed spoke with enthusiasm for preaching on newspapers and comics, rabbinic Midrashim texts as well as the Koran, on the basis that God speaks to the world in a wide variety of ways. Working from an implicit theology that God is here, present in every human event, many parish clergy warm to the task of building the church as interactive community, facing outward towards the neighbourhood and world.

The call to enable more people to broaden and deepen their faith and respond to the gospel is spoken of in varying ways by clergy. One spoke of being 'obsessed' with 'spreading the Word of God' and finding commitment. The practicalities of this in a parish can often include the clergy visiting people at home and taking the opportunity to invite them to a greater commitment in faith. One spoke of being 'a better evangelist than a parish priest'.

One interviewee enjoys expanding the number of local people who are enthused to work together, whether members of the congregation or not. A bishop speaks of the importance of the Church weaving in society rather than separating out. In practice this is demanding, perhaps including people who are disruptive, angry and take up a lot of space. One bishop makes it a priority to engage critically with the justice system and its values, while another enjoys engaging with the local church in its local setting. The continued willingness of some parts of society to make space for the role of clergy meets a strong response among some. Proud to work from an incarnational theology, some clergy enjoy the expectation that they will speak of the gospel beyond the boundaries of Sunday worship, for example at funerals at which over time thousands of people will be encountered. Recognizing God's regenerating newness in unexpected places is how one priest describes his opportunity. A bishop has an image of himself as an agent, opening doors for the local church into the structures of society and government.

Many of the parish clergy are acutely aware that there is nothing within the varied lives of people and institutions that is irrelevant to the parish priest. Bishops generally derive energy from tough engagement regionally and nationally with continuing changes and crises within society and community. One spoke of being fascinated by the capacity of the Church, with other bodies, to foster the movement of God's healing compassion within forces of movement within society. Contact with the arts is the arena for some, notably musicians, among whom the bishop or priest has the chance to relate faith to areas of profound emotion and creativity. The consequences of such encounter cannot easily be measured or planned.

One priest spoke of the peacefulness of slowly connecting her own life with that of a cluster of rural parishes, ever more deeply touching people's daily lives and letting go of any personal ambition to have wider influence. Another highlights the privilege of being expected to be a peacemaker locally between individuals and groups. Many prioritize time to meet people in or near their workplace to demonstrate God's dynamic presence there. A bishop speaks of the importance to him of engaging in dialogue with people, with no idea what the outcome will be, and not shying away from situations of conflict. Some clergy, allowed into people's intimate spaces, have acted as God's instruments with those experiencing great suffering or the death of their children.

Notably, some priests thrive in long-term individual commitment to a local school beyond 'the walls of the church'. Enthusiasm was expressed by many for the wide opportunity to preach the gospel to countless children and teachers, without any concern to measure outcomes. Such priests are energized by the chance to tell stories of faith and to spend a significant proportion of their time in many aspects of a school's life. Models for this include sowing seeds of faith, with no prior knowledge of which will germinate, and Jesus' sacrificial service and emphasis in his teaching on self-donation and loving our neighbour. Showing God's compassion and comfort, especially to people in times of emotional need or in life transition (for example at weddings and funerals) is a key element in the ministry of some of those interviewed.

Others are energized through 'the privilege' of making regular contact with firefighters, police and emergency medical teams, and prisoners, as pastor and listener, especially in times of disaster and public grief. One described his deep involvement in leading and driving healthcare through local institutions, as 'the right place for the Church'.

Significantly, a very small proportion of clergy had enthusiasm for stretching out to work ecumenically between local churches and to varying degrees of real engagement. The same could be said of concern for interfaith and ethnic issues. We shall need to return to this in an attempt at a coherent theory of church.

What inhibits?

Some clergy are drained by opposition from the congregation when they discern and pursue a 'Kingdom' ministry that apparently takes time from the priest's proper care for the congregation. Others are diminished by the constant concern that the parish share to the diocese must be paid and the frequent link made that the priest must spend quality time with those who foot the bill. The lack of money to pay for administrators to release energy in clergy to work beyond the Church's borders is a frustration for some. So spending time arranging church repairs, fund-raising and other maintenance tasks is seen by some as an infuriating waste of their time. This is especially true for those who have benefited from such support in previous secular spheres of work.

Administration, routines and attendance at unproductive meetings saps the energy of many parish clergy. Although the historical process that has created Churches in their present form and the sheer necessity of financial accountability is understood, there is a high degree of resentment around the task of caring for the Church as organization or institution at parish and diocesan level. One priest spoke of hating being desk-bound and being depressed by general administration and answering questionnaires. A bishop is adamant that he is not the Chief Executive of the diocese but is limited when others persist in placing this expectation on him. Another bishop expressed frustration at the time and energy involved in frequent travelling beyond his diocese. A common question is, 'Why do pastors have to do administration and make judgements about building repairs when they are tiring and depleting if this is not your skill?' Despite recognizing the valuable resource represented by a building, priests normally resent precious time for 'the ministry to which they were called' being lost to organizing repairs.

Another describes the weariness consequent on running a demanding parish church with no additional stipendiary staff – leaving him with photocopying, janitorial and mentoring tasks for the whole church. One spoke of times when the administration simply overwhelms and the study is unworkable. A bishop in a fragile diocese also spoke of his impatience with the time and effort expended resulting from a lack of support staff to deal with practical arrangements, such as approving the design of new church notice boards. One referred to the difficulty of having to conform doctrinally to views he personally finds unsound. For some this was linked with the Church being too self-obsessed, out of touch with society and uncritical of its ways of operating. Some experienced a sapping in energy when expected by the wider Church to assume the role of 'leader' when their own priority and personality is at odds with this, preferring to see themselves as a pastor and called to live on the edge of institutions. Unpleasant conflict with colleagues and with the diocesan administration takes up the energy of some.

Unresolved tensions in the wider Church about women in ministry or homosexuality create debilitating frustration in some clergy. One bishop, describing some of the world Anglican debates on sexuality as 'pathological', finds it draining on energy to be patient enough to engage with fears incomprehensible to himself.

A general sense that diocesan structures are in the medium term unsustainable and stand immediately in urgent need of down-sizing, to avoid a crisis later, is a source of deep concern to some. This is linked for one with an embarrassment at the Church work-ing with outdated structures, systems and models of education. One complained at the lack of room for creativity or spontaneity in the liturgy.

One bishop lamented the way the Church at times makes itself look incredible and foolish in the eyes of society. Sexual miscon-duct in the clergy and the way it is dealt with affects not just those directly involved but also the wider environment. A bishop com-plained of the slow, rigid and immoveable procedures of the Church of England, echoing and compounded by those of Parliament. Despite conferences and courses on new styles of leadership, many remain frustrated by the apparent inability or unwillingness of senior leaders to face structural questions professionally. However, the wider Church was blamed by one priest for taking away a sense of priestly vocation through too much professionalism. There is a widespread sense of the absence of openness about ministerial career development for all, linked with hints from those in author-ity that seeking earthly power has nothing to do with vocation. One spoke of the important but tiring responsibility for stipendiary clergy of helping to maintain the wider infrastructures of the dio-cese and beyond. 'Witnessing in an indifferent environment' or to preaching when no one turns up or responds saps the energy of some. One referred to the increasing sense that structured and insti-tutional religion is increasingly mistrusted and frequently perceived as damaging to people.

Contact – deepening contact between people

What energizes?

Several of those interviewed mentioned the pleasure and benefits to the church of extending the quality and range of teamworking and of enabling the work of others. Increasingly clergy showed signs of fostering mutuality and collaboration and recognizing different gifts in others for leadership.

One priest spoke of the exhilaration of connecting through preaching, scholarly training with the minds and hearts and every-day life of people already present in church. Sharing life with and knowing the congregation well is regarded by some as essential for effective preaching. One of those interviewed spoke of the great pleasure she derived from the meetings, over months, preparing couples for the marriage service and married life beyond. Some spoke of the possibility of breaking through the wariness of unchurched people, even briefly, to a more direct contact. One said that in such conversations it can be more likely that he would reach into areas of spirituality than with a regular church attender.

Engagement with others, where the personality of the priest is directly in contact with others, is a common element in what priests believe gives them energy. A bishop told how he thrives on opportunities for close, intimate pastoral work with individuals. Being with people and having a good rapport, in all kinds of situations, brings satisfaction to many clergy. Some say they feel most fulfilled in one-to-one conversations in hospital or nursing home, and when the appreciation is mutual this heightens the sense of contact. Visiting people and getting to know them in their homes is a priority for some. Others speak of being profoundly moved when taking home communion services. Hearing people's stories and helping them piece it all together is a common essential in the priestly vocation.

A bishop speaks of his commitment to interweaving his own ministry with that of the clergy. A number of clergy interviewed spoke of the revitalizing effect of intimate interactive meetings with peers or support networks, sometimes ecumenically. They spoke of the value of being asked to speak in confidence with colleagues about how they are currently experiencing life or about their awareness of God.

What inhibits?

Some clergy feel overwhelmed at having to work with the wide range of individual commitment, apathy and a lack of understanding of faith. The recognition is common that perhaps fewer than 25 per cent of the worshipping congregation is 'committed' in a way the priest can recognize. This is experienced notably in the tendency of some church members to have an investment in control and manipulation of the community rather to act from a genuine sense of vocation or being gifted in the area in which they exercise influence. One spoke of his distaste when the church is full of people, many of whom have only a small understanding of faith and worship, for example at Midnight Mass.

Transformation – a new world beginning

What energizes?

Gathering people and leading worship for groups of all sizes is the point where some clergy are most engaged and have the experience of feeling truly focused in their own identity as well, as fuelled for ministry. A common strand for clergy is the unearned gift, privilege and tremendous personal strength they receive through gathering people in the Eucharist. Here above all they see integrated the neighbourhood and the community of the natural world, in connection with the Church of every other time and place, embraced in God's love.

The amazing privilege of ordination and being placed in the unique position of making God real and present for people is highly energizing for the ordained. One speaks of giving people, through liturgy, a sense of who they really are to become. For another this brought a sense of knowing she was 'in the right place'. Others are awed in believing that, in certain circumstances, it is only a priest who can facilitate for others the presence of God's grace. Many spoke of the difficult-to-express, profound feeling associated with 'celebrating' the Eucharist, of being the one who uniquely draws together many different relationships and human concerns with God. Others speak of the personal joy of 'presiding' at the Sunday Eucharist and the preparation and communication involved.

Small quiet services of Holy Communion are equally energizing for some. Services that 'take off' or where there is a 'breakthrough' are the tantalizing open points where everything connects for some priests. Singing together and a sense of intimate engagement with the congregation are experiences almost beyond description for some. A bishop described how he experiences great joy when preaching about a God of love so that no one is left in doubt of God's true nature. Another bishop enjoyed the response when people engage with him after an occasion of preaching or teaching. Some described the awe, excitement or privilege of preaching so that others can understand and receive the incredible truths of the gospel. One describes how feeding the hunger of those who recognize a need for God and who go away 'full' brings a great reward. One feels strongly that priests should live within the presiding role with sufficient vulnerability to be able to connect in humility and truthfulness many others beyond the Church in a common quest for the world's flourishing.

Some would emphasize the way in which praise and worship illuminate and contribute to achieving their goals in the parish's ministry. One appreciated the possibilities for creating a blend of structure and freedom in liturgy. Another was energized by new possibilities in worship through the introduction of multi-media technology.

The ordained have a clear sense of being called to gather, know and oversee the congregation's life, but the approaches to how this contributes to the world's flourishing vary immensely. The respondents naturally disagreed on how much of this bridging or representative task of the Church is unique to the particular role of priest or bishop. Illustrative of this are the following strong statements from clergy, which will give us material to reflect on as this study evolves. Keeping confidentiality and being 'set aside' and being allowed into other people's lives in ways that are uniquely accessible and acceptable were highlighted as two chief characteristics of the unique role of the ordained. One expressed gratitude for the humbling privilege of being a 'conduit for something transcendent'. A priest admitted that he is 'keen on lay ministry' but is also concerned about eroding the Church's priesthood. Another distinguished between 'being responsible' for leading worship and sometimes being 'free' to be out of role, in the congregation. For another the particular representative role of responding to human situations, as they arise unpredictably, was very important. Being a signpost, helping people to make connections as appropriate, like a General Practitioner, were images expressed by one who was interviewed. There is no consistent view of how far these are essentials of ordained ministry.

Clearly for many the experience and practice of ordained life is an intensely personal one. For example, a bishop told of the personally energizing liturgical experience of confirming and ordaining and the situations surrounding those occasions. Some get a 'buzz' from the responsibility, the demanding hours and practicalities of 'running' the church. The integrating tasks of administration and management give pleasure to some, especially through the use of computers. Some enjoy fund-raising. Several spoke of the rewards of seeing people in difficult circumstances transformed through a one-to-one healing ministry. Simply being present in the community as priest is listed as a key and stimulating role. Attached to this unique role is the chance to live a very private and ordered life, to be available to people and decide what should be the church's priorities. One speaks of ensuring she is not tired and makes time for reflection.

However, the view was also expressed that priesthood flourishes primarily in relationship and community, rather than isolation. There is a strong move towards seeing the role of the ordained as developing the mission and ministry of the whole Church for the world's healing. Stimulating the whole church to work effectively to achieve its goals, willingly using all their gifts, gives satisfaction to some even after several decades in orders. Equipping others is seen as a key element in leadership. A priest speaks of the energy of seeing the success of good relating in community and worship through his own inspiration and efforts, 'seeing God at work when people share gifts, feel trusted and build a different culture and knowing that I helped with that'.

A bishop speaks of the pleasure of working with others in risky theological discussion to seek a deeper truth. One priest spoke of the pleasure of being a catalyst, building up a small group as a 'fireball' to serve the locality or for youth work. Another identified the energy in leading strategic envisioning exercises with the church council.

Another is keen to develop the work of the whole Church through facing realistically the likely transition in coming decades towards a Church in which most of the ordained are unpaid, so that for example the post of full-time Rector will be less and less likely to exist. One bishop is enthusiastic for worshipping and working with others to respond to challenges and find out how to be church in the present time and place. A bishop describes his enthusiasm for enabling other clergy have a lively sense of God and so be always on the move to new insights. A priest spoke of the energy experienced when others were not dependent, 'when I am surrounded by parishioners working in good relationship and can see people growing and thriving'. So there are bishops and priests who are glad to see themselves as leaders in the sense of helping many laity also to recognize their own leadership.

The backdrop is of an overall drastic decline in church attendance and in the number of clergy paid a stipend to be available full time to a parish church. Most expect that the scale of the Church of England's institutional arrangements will be downsized as congregations gradually default on the current level of contributions to the centre. God's newness appears for some in the embers of the old institution, so one bishop is energized by new initiatives that involve risk and empowering others to take new steps. A bishop described being energized by his work with the Church Commis-sioners, where he was often in contention with dominant ideologies and solutions to the Church's financial management issues.

The demanding and responsible work of providing a good learn-ing environment for a reader, an ordinand training on a local course or curate is balanced by the learning to be received by the parish priest. One speaks of the pleasure of seeing a student discovering their own particular ministry within the diversity of the Body of Christ, through their unique gifts. For one this has been enhanced since the beginning of the ordination of women. One priest spoke of the importance to him of part-time working in the diocese on an Ordained Local Ministry training course.

What inhibits?

There are inevitably many ways in which clergy feel responsible for the Church self-limiting itself and serving lesser goals. For example, a bishop blames himself for being too inquisitive. His inability to say no to invitations leads to exhaustion and spreading himself too thinly. But this is a choice and he is not a victim of anyone else. One spoke of being the cause of his own de-energizing by failing to prioritize tasks or spending too much time in administration rather than with people. One speaks of the inevitable weariness that comes with years in ministry, so that the liturgical cycle becomes a burden rather than a source of refreshment. A priest spoke of having prob-lems through an unrealistic expectation of herself in her role. Another spoke of not giving herself enough time to deal with the feelings brought out, for example, by taking a funeral soon after a personal bereavement of her own. Some owned up to choosing to be too busy, stretching themselves too thinly and so becoming a victim on a treadmill.

Aspirations to involve lay people more in worship or service of the community can be frustrated by the pressures of modern life. Some clergy despair that the laity don't have a vision for Eucharistic living or a willingness to put energy into their church, resulting in their spending time in overconcern about detail and in rivalry between local churches. One referred to frustration when laity re-garded the work of clergy as something to be observed passively, when there is no rapport or response during or after worship. This connects with the lonely work of attempting to activate others who don't see the need. One speaks of the tiring task of keeping many plates spinning so that more and more recovery time is required.

One spoke of frustration with laity who wanted to maintain a passive role. After a long time in one post, one priest sensed his capacity for encouraging others to take on a role in the church was considerably reduced. One was frustrated by the lack of openness to the gifts of others by long-established members of a congregation. One mentions the frustrations of dealing with similar problems with individuals over and over again. One speaks of frustration when church members are selfish and unaware of others. A bishop is frustrated when there is no willingness to go forward or even to debate the blocks. One priest spoke of the paradox of feeling a lack of 'priestly satisfaction'. She knows that to make a fulfilling space for lay people in the church, she has to learn to be less often 'in control'. Another described the effects of nastiness and destructive behaviour in churches, which severely hampers the work of mission.

One felt that the Church's ways of making appointments to posts often robs local churches of their proper role and dignity. A bishop spoke of the frustrations caused by the inflexibility of the parish system and its inability to meet current requirements.

Some complained of a sense of loneliness through the absence of like-minded colleagues. A bishop spoke of a sense of being judged against other bishops and by the community generally. A priest speaks of times when her needs go unrecognized by others in the church. Sometimes the life of the church is isolated from the world's concerns. One describes priesthood as not a hat or a skin worn on the surface, but something utterly mystical in which the priest gives up all rights to being a free agent.

A woman priest spoke of inhibition caused by the lack of female role models. Others were aware of the unacknowledged difficulties male colleagues could have in working with women. Patronizing attitudes and lack of equal respect leads to missed opportunities in collaborative ministry and diminishes the Church's authority.

One spoke of the trial of addressing people informally in crowded situations and having to speak, representatively, however he might be feeling.

A priest spoke of the debilitating effect of back pain for himself; another of the draining effect of spending time with others who are suffering. Another spoke of the disappointment at showing his exhaustion instead of 'life in all its fullness' through the overwork caused by lack of lay involvement. Another speaks of illness, stress and lack of personal energy as inhibitors, even though they are a stimulus to clarifying priorities.

One priest speaks of the problems caused by profound changes in society, so that all visiting has to take place in the evenings.

A bishop admitted to experiencing fear when dealing with 'scary things', such as the possibility of presiding over the meltdown of inherited church structures or recognizing the wide range of 'belief' in a diocese. A priest spoke of fear when faced with people different from oneself or trying to communicate in words that people understand.

Frustration was expressed at the times when no one listens or the repairs to the vicarage are not done and the garden is too large to manage.

A number gave thanks that the positives far outweigh the negatives, the energy exceeds the weariness. Recognizing that some hindrances are inevitable, some concluded that when their personality is not required to be engaged they feel most inhibited. There are less exciting parts of being a priest that can't be separated off from the energizing. One recalled that Jesus coped with the hindrances of working with disciples who had limited understanding of his mission. Some claimed that retirement frees a priest from all that inhibits, to be fully a priest.

Conclusion

There are numerous compelling reasons for the Church to re-examine and reconstitute its mission and structures, to be a convincing witness to the freedom and healing brought to humanity and the world by the presence of the risen Lord, through the Spirit (Gal. 5.1). There is a strong case for concluding that present institutional forms of Christianity are a spent force, even though pockets of Christendom persist. It takes a daring maturity to avoid the temptation to become a ghetto, out of which to speak with an anxious triumphalism. Yet there never was a time when the Christian gospel, the 'wine of everlasting joy', more needs to be joyfully preached and lived.[22] The hope and liveliness that the Church can offer to the world's transformation now has to be deeply confident, willing to live in ambivalence in particular situations and tempered by patient listening and waiting. How are we to know the way forward?

As a beginning, we need to celebrate what is so vibrant in often very unpromising circumstances. This chapter has shown how clergy, in so many faithful ways, are assisting connections between people and God, with the neighbourhood and with one another for the transformation of the world. The brief accounts drawn from their own words reveal the amazing tenacity of the Church's clergy in a time when the proportion of society that worships and participates in church is extremely small. There are clear parallels between many aspects of clerical life and work and that of counterparts in education, medicine, the law and management. The informal drift of these interviews, however, is a reminder of the unique timbre of the work of the ordained. Called to be at the interface between every 'level' or dimension of human existence, parish clergy inevitably absorb and carry some very deep emotions and aspirations for the entire community. Many work prodigious hours following their intense sense of calling, responsibility and delight.

Can any common strands be discerned from the testimonies of these rich accounts of clerical activity and attitudes in the opening years of the twenty-first century? I take with great seriousness the many situations in which bishops, parish clergy and church systems lose energy, partly through personal skills not being matched with particular situations or demands. In this review, however, an emerging vision can be discerned, as perhaps a transition stage from solo-performance, professional clerical ministry to a nascent integrating ministry. This interim form of an *episkope* ministry stimulating *communion* may be summarized as the Church:

- beginning to value and learn from the experience of women in their struggle to be recognized and heard and to honour their different approaches to relating and speaking;
- continually being readdressed by Scripture and linking many aspects of its learning and performance to the liminal biblical journey of God's people;
- drawing deeply on God's gift in Eucharist and recognizing the celebration as a unique place of transformation for persons, communities and the world's life;
- recognizing itself and the teams within church community as held by God in times of personal growth, crisis, bereavement;
- promoting learning for its own sake as well as to support the burgeoning discipleship and ministries in congregations;
- letting prayer be the live current that, in connecting the church community with the triune God, releases resurrection energy for hope;
- attempting to be exemplary in accompanying local communities without expecting a return;

- accepting the opportunities of handling disagreement with maturity, so that radically different people and views can connect with respect and creative outcomes.

The dedicated lives of a range of priests and bishops in the Anglican, Episcopalian and Lutheran Churches have provided an essential starting point for this study. However, it would be too thin and predictable to attempt a redescription of mission, church, ministry and priesthood from reflection on experience alone.[23]

Since the ground-breaking work of Leonardo Boff, Colin Gunton, Jürgen Moltmann, Edward Schillebeeckx and John Zizioulas, each in their own traditions, a trajectory of theological thought now makes it truly impossible to speak about the work of the parish priest, and those working in association, in isolation from considerations of God's Kingdom, mission and church as *communion*. Relearning right speech about the mystery of God as an economy of exchange, the ultimate point of reference for considering the interconnected life of the cosmos, inevitably sheds light on the inherited thought and practice of a Church serving God's purpose.[24] Through the labours of Elizabeth Johnson, Catherine LaCugna, Miroslav Volf and so many others in recent decades, we are offered accessible and challenging ways to move beyond merely binary approaches to understanding and articulating the quality of loving relationship at the heart of all theology.

An essential ingredient in this many-voiced movement is the recognition of the lively connection between speech about the God of Scripture, Church practice and the affirmation of freedom for humanity and the cosmos. This is a process of mutual exchange, still in its infancy, and as yet largely ignored by mainstream institutional Church life. The tragedy of this is that the very credibility of God and Christianity is under threat in a society that has only the contemporary Church to observe for evidence of what it means to encounter the sheer aliveness of Good News.[25] Daily assumptions, preaching, experiences of belonging, the work of ministers, the handling of sensitive and controversial issues, approaches to Scripture, the treatment of those whose lifestyles are different and the Church's relationship to society are all under scrutiny within this discourse on the identity of the Church.

3

Church: communal practice of Good News

Another world is possible – *in our practice*. We are only a few, but we are some. We can do little, but something. As we stay with the cadences of our defining utterance, we begin to enact another world. Foolishly we enact obedience to a daring claim, obedience to a possibility; we specialize in cold water and shared bread, in welcome speech, hospitality, sharing, giving, compassion, caring – in small ways – and in setting the world afresh.[1]

The need for a theory of church

You, the reader, may be tempted to skip over this chapter because what concerns you is an understanding of the parish priest's role. I wrote *Transforming Priesthood* in the conviction that it is theologically impossible to understand the work of parish priests, except in dynamic relationship with:

- an understanding of the triune life of God;
- God's purposes for creation;
- the character and task of the local church;
- the particular context in which a church is set.

My belief is confirmed that any discussion of the role of the parish priest has to be on such a broad canvas. In this chapter I want briefly to be explicit about the theory of church within which I am rooting an understanding of the work of parish priests. In Chapter 2, in order to listen deliberately to the voices of those interviewed I avoided any detailed mapping of the theology of the four categories of experience and work: richness, range, contact and transformation. Now I intend to test further whether the four elements of this proposed theory of *koinonia* church and, therefore, of priesthood in the parish, as *episkope*, can bear the weight put upon them. The elements are offered here as a way of describing the Church when understood as constantly re-finding its identity at the intersection of the concerns of the entire world and creation, that is, the arena for the relational presence and working of the triune God.[2]

So the theory assumes no exclusive zone for experiencing God's mystery and God's mission, reverberating in every person, situation, society, culture and part of history. Local churches are graced, but not sole, agents of God's love, working prophetically, in companionship with others, at the creative overlap between religious and social groupings. I explored earlier how the episcopal, presbyteral and diaconal aspects of church are focused in the ordering of bishops, priests and deacons, but are lived out, moment by moment, by the whole Church. The work of *episkope*, given particular focus by a few but in fact the responsibility of all, is to draw out the Church's life through being formed in:

1 richness – growing into the richness of God's life;
2 range – working with God in every place;
3 contact – deepening contact between people;
4 transformation – a new world beginning.

Richness – growing into the richness of God's life

God who evokes awe

In an age when knowing God is widely regarded as unintelligible or ridiculous, our belief is that, through baptism, we may enter into the life and mission of the triune God. This is the bold and frequently announced foundation of Christian faith. This gospel lived out in worshipping communities has the power to de-centre a society built on the prevailing notions of individualism and human alienation from the natural world. The experience of worship, as participative and as an apprenticeship in holiness,[3] has the potency to create a Christian community of the saints together, delighted in and created in truth through immersion in the intensity of God's holiness.[4] Although the holy mystery of God exposes the limits and frequent oppression of human speech, the language we have developed for relationships, such as nurturing, caring, embracing, mothering, sustaining, respecting, compassion, anguish, freedom, personhood, tenderness and love, convey many of our experiences of God.[5] We should not be afraid, however, to hold, in tension with these, our other experiences – of God's seeming absence, anger, inscrutability, terror, teasing, violence, jealousy and unpredictability.

The holiness of the self-starting, regenerative life of the divine mystery, maintained by no external resource, is endlessly described

in Scripture as demanding and untameable.[6] To assert God's
holy name and purpose as countering despair and bringing hope,
Scripture uses metaphor, poetry and human story, awakening and
stretching our imagination towards the consuming, deep, shimmering, multidimensionality of the unfathomable one who creates a
new thing and 'pervades and actuates the whole created frame'.[7]
The trinitarian, *perichoretic* God is known as holy, attracting and
motivating Abraham, Sarah, Moses, Miriam and all who continue
the prophetic task (e.g. Josh. 24.19; Ps. 99.3, 5, 9; 1 Sam. 6.20; Isa.
6.3; 8.13; Exod. 15.11).[8] God is no abstraction but is practically and
inherently relational, a love defined in making room for others in
communion.[9]

As God is holy, God calls a people to be holy, to love God and
be called by God and to work for God's rule in the whole of creation (Matt. 5.48; cf. 1 Peter 1.16). Jesus shows the way of friendship
with God in both awe and intimacy and the special place in God's
communion for those routinely excluded.[10] The Apostle Thomas,
unconvinced by witnesses, is overwhelmed when confronted by
the presence of the risen Jesus in person (John 20.26–29). Paul challenges humans to recognize they are created for *communion* with
the Triune life of God, renewed through faith and baptism into the
triune name (Eph. 4.24).

This triune God is a dynamically ordered community of relation.
This God, who honours difference and is creator and sustainer of
all, desires all creation to come to its fullest possibility.[11] To be holy
as God is holy is to be directed by and radiate God's own relational
being to bring about the well-being of neighbours and the whole
world.[12] The threefold God, source of all being, order and energy,
invites human beings, in relation with all other reality, to blossom
now in a holiness that creates and delights in difference, depth and
infolded complexity.[13]

The language of depth has been ambivalently employed by
Genesis, the psalmists, Job and Daniel and, later, Augustine, to allude
to the blessings of the productive energy that is the boundlessness
of God, always juxtaposed with fear and awe experienced in facing
the deep.[14] Catherine Keller, in her treatment of God's ordering the
world within chaos (as 'chaoplexity'), challenges human determination to deny the deep its potency.[15] In dialogue with midrashic and
mystical forms of Judaism, she poetically celebrates the holiness of
the unspeakable deity as 'shimmering, rolling, dazzling, dark, hetero-
geneous, bottomless depth'.[16]

God's refining holiness is a fire that purifies (Isa. 6) and yet is constantly resisted. Scripture offers images of holiness as a crucible in which all life is generated, healed and brought into dynamic relation. Human beings are uniquely called or expected within this universe, but God's holiness is to be found at the creative boundary of every dimension of the world's life – ecological, political, cultural, legal or economic. In every sphere in which well-being is sought, traces, usually unacknowledged, of God's generous, relational holiness are at work. It is in participation in worship specifically that God's holiness in the world is learnt and performed.[17]

Responding in wonder, praise and lament

A key biblical concept here is that of facing or being faced by God's self-giving holiness in worship that is a response of acknowledgment and often bewilderment, lifting those who praise into their truest being.[18] Israel was urged to attend to the unpredictable God who consecrates, challenges and liberates this people, as a basis for expecting their allegiance and faithfulness.[19] God's holiness is unveiled to humanity through the refining fire of the crucifixion of Christ and especially in Eucharistic worship.[20] The assembly of different people calls down the Holy Spirit on the elements of bread and wine in order that together and separately they may be lifted in their vocation as priests to the world, as a sign of history moving towards God's final eschatological unity and peacemaking.[21]

Ourselves and all other people, in the Eucharist, are no longer randomly together but co-create one another. Through participating in the Eucharist we become over a lifetime transformed into the Body of Christ and the self becomes the other.[22] Through the sacramental eating of bread and wine the Church is nourished by God in the present moment and participates already in the superabundant life that already takes place within the Trinity. That is how Eucharist *is communion* both with God and with one another.[23] Here, above all, God's holiness is enacted as the many-layered features of life in the world intersect with God's intimate involvement with people to make effective the reconstitution or transfiguration of all creation as a home for all, in freedom and eschatological orientation (John 17.17).[24]

Jesus' constant relationship with God, his 'abba', is a reminder of the reciprocity and vulnerability of the identity of the people of God in response to their knowing God in Jesus (Matt. 23.8–12). Contact with the intensive livingness of God in worship draws out the fullest possibility for human freedom, in five ways:

1 as praise of the vibrating mystery of God, as Word, as silence (the *apophatic* tradition[25]);
2 as confession through opening ourselves to the goodness that overcomes sin;
3 as thanksgiving for the stirring of the human heart and the resistance of notions of scarcity;
4 as intercession, that is the involvement with God's desire to have mercy on all creation;
5 as recalling (*anamnesis*) of God's endlessly faithful ways of blessing and forming people in well-being.[26]

Scripture notably invites us to expect more of the amazing narratives of God's transformation, as specifically shown, for example, in the raising of Jairus' daughter, the restoring of sight to Bartimaeus or the healing of those afflicted with leprosy.[27] There can be no alternative except to 'Go and tell John' or 'Let Herod notice'.[28] There is no deprivation or shortage of love, forgiveness or grace that God's excessive self-giving generosity cannot outdistance.[29]

However, one form of loss that the Church experiences comes from ignoring the full range of Scripture and so inhabiting a small place where God is always triumphant, powerful, almighty. We do this by forgetting much of the Old Testament, losing sight of the psalms of lament or accounts of God's prophets and purposes attacked or defeated. Loss, anger, grief and rage are as much part of the response of God's people as joy and hope.[30] Through the dynamics of worship, every interrelated dimension of life, whether in pain, torment or ecstasy, is held, cultivated, freed, given new hope, energized by and raised to the holiness of God, their infinite and abundant source.[31]

A recurring human experience, reflected on in Scripture, is strangely to discover in pain and loss a place in which to know God.[32] The God of the psalms riskily invites courageous conversation, in which the worshipper can sometimes take the lead. Going beyond subservient respect, Israel can enter into face-to-face dialogue on urgent questions of pain, loss and grief. The psalmists explore the transformative potential of expressing anger to God, knowing that the relationship can be later rebalanced through worship. In the Church today this could be a welcome counterbalance to untruthful piety, and a sign of hope offered to public life. No one can blame society for leaving the Church to its own devices if we have not communicated the love of the mutual, passionate, demanding God who asks for our engagement, blesses our wounds, knows the rawness of so much of our existence and uniquely restores us to hope.[33]

Jesus shows God most intensively in emptying himself, taking the form of a slave and dying, abandoned by all but a few courageous women, outside the city wall. Dorothy Soelle has written that all true theology begins in pain.[34] The rending of the temple curtain on Good Friday is a symbol of God's stance with the vulnerable, defenceless, forsaken, a God who cannot always be assuring or rescuing from danger. Friday is the day of the cross. The crucifixion is not an unexpected event in the life of faith, although it is the decisive event. It is rather the pivotal expression of the subversion of the powers of domination that has been practised and insisted upon by the line of prophets since Moses faced up to Pharaoh. As with Moses, Jesus' ministry and passion replace the practice of oppression with the practice of justice and compassion. As with Moses, Jesus' ministry and passion counter the economics of affluence and show the alternative of the economics of a shared humanity. As with Moses, Jesus' ministry and passion revealed the freedom of God to bring life unpredictably, even in the face of death. So although Christian faith is rooted in redemption from evil, it is also, as Anselm and George Herbert explored, a process of transformation that involves an often gradual disclosure of God's glory.[35]

What kind of people is formed by worship of the triune God?

A new social vision

'You shall be holy, for I the LORD your God am holy' (Lev. 19.2) is a succinct statement of the call of the people of Israel to find their identity through responding to God's call for them to choose to be organized 'in human, egalitarian and communitarian ways'.[36] Israel, answering God's call, offers the surrounding nations a radically new social vision. Holiness is more than a good idea, rather 'the daily practice of enacting a distinct identity that is visible in the world'.[37] The Holy Spirit forms not only individual Christians but creates the baptized as relational, a real community capable of and intending to transform all creation with this character of dynamic communion.[38]

In a trinitarian understanding of church, neither people nor community are prior to each other but 'equiprimal'.[39] This is a significant theological antidote to clericalism and rigid hierarchy. Through baptism, forgiven sinners are no longer chiefly identified by their own history but as citizens, already, of the Kingdom that they are committed to help make a reality in the world. The first Christians, breaking bread together, growing in numbers and praising God in the temple, experienced a concentration of God's holiness. The gathering for Eucharist, an event of *communion*, above all offers the congregation a dynamic connection with the extravagant trinitarian life of God. This God is a community of difference in deep relation, in which difference is creative not divisive.[40] 'There is only one kind of exclusion that Eucharistic communion permits, and that is the exclusion of exclusion itself, that is, of those things that involve rejection and division.'[41] 'The Eucharist builds up the body of Christ as one single body which transcends the racial, social, and cultural diversity of its members, and reveals and realizes the gift of trinitarian communion given to the Church by the Spirit.'[42]

The interrelation of otherness in God's being lies at the heart of a true understanding of the different orders of Christian. Paul's teaching on the mutuality between the parts of the body (1 Cor. 12) and the Church's accumulated wisdom demands a ministry of unity. These are key reminders that the practice of church, rooted in God's relational holiness, exists only in patterns of ministry where interdependence is of the essence.[43]

The radically subversive implications of communion

From critique to imaginative action In relation to churches as institutions, there is muted panic that their former life cannot for much longer be sustained, with only sparse evidence of attempts to find radical alternatives that take into account trinitarian insights. It is not enough for most people to sit on the sidelines and be disappointed by the Church's many imperfections, divisions and lack of repentance. This is the work (watching out) of everyone who cares that the gospel is embodied in attractive and transformative community living. Almost everything about how institutional churches function needs to be rethought and reinvented. The task requires that we take as a central truth that the event of community we truly call church is shaped by and emerges again and again within ever new situations. As the Nicene Creed declares, the

Church is holy, attempting to mirror the relation of *communion* and otherness we believe God to be. The institutional Church often falls into habits of acting from its centre, as though local churches are merely branches of a central organization that is ideally monochrome and intolerant of local difference.[44] So *communion* is an essential core of the being of the Church, rather than an attractive possibility.[45] As a consequence, we need to establish that the holiness that is the *koinonia* we address as the three absolutely different persons of God, is essentially the holding together of radical difference.[46]

The uniting of difference as key To avoid any suggestion that such *communion* allows only for homogeneity and excludes difference, we need to re-examine the Church's understanding of the doctrine of the Trinity. The doctrine of the Trinity is that unity and otherness or difference coexist simultaneously in God's holiness. God is not to be thought of as primarily one and then as three.[47] This is because the Father, as one of the Trinity, is also the originator, sole source of life and being.[48]

Crucially, the distinction between the persons, Father, Son and Spirit, is what creates the *koinonia* (*communion*) of the Trinity, rather than what threatens its unity.[49]

It is vital to recognize the absolute difference between the persons in God in order to see the point that there is no confusion of one person with another. Nor is it the qualities or tasks of each person of the Trinity that distinguish and affirm their distinctiveness, but the (ontological) otherness of their separate persons. So otherness is vital to the intimate relationship of Father, Son and Spirit. 'Communion does not threaten otherness; it generates it'.[50] As God is inherently relational and gives to humanity the gift of *communion*, so churches in liturgy, social gathering, distribution of ministries and contact with other churches and parts of society are constituted and resourced by the deep intra-trinitarian patterning revealed in Jesus Christ through the Spirit.[51]

A liberating practice Worship fosters the building of intimate *communion* based on a trusting interaction rooted in freedom that diminishes fear and signals to the world a model of social frameworks rooted in God's holiness.[52] As a witness to how society might be nurtured and reconfigured, churches are called to build sociality[53] rooted in the holy personality of Christ, whose work on the cross was for the sanctifying of the whole of society.[54] Such a way of being church builds up participants in sharing responsibility for the work of being a deliberately shaped gospel society. It assumes an active desire to raise up a culture in which people are given space to develop and employ their gifts, where there is openness, mutual accountability and human warmth.

It is the holiness of God enacted especially in Eucharistic worship that creates such a potent stimulus for creating and sustaining just forms of society.[55] The Eucharist is the central place in the Church's life where this identity is formed through energetic engagement with God and God's work in the world.[56] The *communion* character of the Church is such that there is no intended gap between the intense engagement of the Church with God's holiness and a rigorous attentiveness to the affairs of the world.

Churches need to be constantly de-centred by the confusing gift of God's holiness. It is vital for leaders within churches – and that includes most Christian people to some degree – to stay on the cusp where God the Father continually breathes out new and vibrating possibilities. History shows how easily complacency and mistakes subvert the Church's calling to bring a counterdiscourse in the world.[57] Having the courage, through participation in Christ, to reimagine how to be church for contemporary society is a very particular way of serving truth and helping to define fuller forms of human existence.[58] The task of the Church is the humble one of being itself, not in isolation, but by seeking to be formed in the divine character as shown in the relationship between Jesus and the Father.[59]

The entire laos formed in the dynamics of Christian life

One of the greatest hindrances to Christian mission is the lack of enthusiasm among the majority of church members for profound engagement with the substance of faith, text of Scripture or experience of prayer. Another hindrance is when the local church has no sense of itself or its purpose. It is a constant part of the church's task consciously to struggle to be neither too accommodated to its cultural setting nor too separated, so that it resembles, often proudly, a museum piece. Christian churches in their traditional form are rapidly losing members and credibility. To discover a renewed sense of identity is an urgent agenda.[60] As has emerged in the pioneering work of John Drane, Wesley Frensdorff, Paolo Freire, Ched Myers, and many facilitators in the Local Shared Ministry movement, this comes visibly through the patient facilitation of the learning of the entire church.[61]

It is in worship that this sense of identity is given. Psalm 42 invites recognition of the waves and billows of God's unfathomable being, thundering and vibrating over our daily lives. Abraham's call to worship and obedience is a recurring scriptural pattern, culminating in Jesus being commissioned and then himself calling disciples to the way of the cross (Mark 2.16–20; 8.34–38; 10.17–22). Jesus invites his followers to dare to accept 'living water', to recognize themselves as rich in God's eyes. To be immersed in God's unshakable holiness is the way to displace routine human anxiety and acquisitiveness. Christian worshippers are those who celebrate the generosity of the creator who gives beyond measure. Assuming the abundance of God's life, rather than being overwhelmed by a fear of scarcity, is the basis of Jesus' ministry to be inhabited by his followers through the Holy Spirit.[62] Baptized and baptizing communities are invited to risk their life being intensified and astonishingly reordered, shaped by the Spirit and the life of Christ crucified.[63]

Learning the disciplines and habits of obedience, through allowing ourselves to be incrementally more orientated to Jesus Christ, is a costly as well as joyful and rewarding road.[64] Tenacity and conviction is required to build up a church community in learning the language of Christian practice. An urgent priority for churches is to offer fresh opportunities for different people, at various times in their lives, to become more vividly and courageously what God asks of them.[65]

A trinitarian understanding holds in tension the inherently ecclesial nature of Christian faith and the uniqueness of persons who are not merely part of an amorphous community. As Jesus in John 7 speaks of teaching that is his, yet not his, there is a paradox about Christian identity. To be renewed in spirit and mind, to become increasingly formed in the image of God, is the remarkable wake-up call to each person. The individual does not dissolve into the community but is a person with responsibilities and identity; simultaneously the person is always immersed in relations of *communion*.[66]

A recurrent question is the extent to which church or human society can realistically expect to be an echo of the divine trinitarian life. A recurrent gospel clue to the identity of the disciple is the notion of self-giving or losing life in order to find it.[67] Jesus, teaching his disciples perfection in Matthew 5, invites them to contribute to redeeming the world by loving those who hate them. In Romans 13.12–13, Paul teaches disciples, having put on the armour of light, to live honourably 'as in the day'. This is a lesser standard than the perfect reciprocal love of the Trinity. But in a flawed world, for those who have 'put on Christ', this would be an advance sign of the perfect world to come.[68]

So, regardless of any cause we may have for judging our neighbour, the engagement with the triune God demands and gives grace to us in order that we may 'welcome one another' (Rom. 15.7) essentially as, by definition, we are persons in relation. Christians, crucified with Christ, are called to be generous, engaged and open as they share in God's activity in society and, as a result, give glory to God, showing the world something of God's holiness and passion for the world's repairing. If God is Christ-like in these superabundant ways, Churches are responsible for being part of the answer to the question of why so many people in the world are starving, naked and poor. Embodying the fruits of the Spirit, Christians are called to show the world embodied practice, increasingly like that of Christ and like the life of people in the Kingdom that Jesus promised.[69]

The newness envisaged (a new creation) is available for all human transactions, so that the whole world, abandoning injustice and corruption, might bear the image of the creator (Col. 3.5–11). The joyful vitality brought to this challenge by the renewal of Christian experience of the Holy Spirit and recognition of God as Trinity allows for infinite openness, complexity and depth, and disallows rigid or merely binary patterns.[70] Rather, the reality of God as community of difference in relation draws out, in Moltmann's words, 'at once the most intense excitement and the absolute rest of the love which is the wellspring of everything that lives, the keynote of all resonances and the source of the rhythmically dancing and vibrating worlds'.[71]

Today, many are seeking meaning through a pastiche of beliefs and rituals but remain unconvinced by the Church's flawed performance of the gospel.[72] The myth that God's grace is the privilege of clergy and a small committed 'spiritual' elite has existed for too long. Rather, because it is God's desire to come close to us, we need to regard this growing into the fullness of God's truth and holiness as normal for Christians in discipleship and ministry and necessary for the well-being of each.[73] God's life moves in the whole of creation, including ourselves, and the path of discipleship is to know that and respond actively.[74] God's truth is known not only in specifically religious disciplines but in the entire range of ways in which others explain the world, search for human flourishing and engage in the pursuit of justice and peace (John 3.8).[75] The Church since Pentecost has claimed a particular relationship to the Spirit of God. However, the world needs an increase in existing initiatives for the shared reading of scriptural texts and exploring spiritual paths among Christians, Muslims, Jews, Buddhists and Hindus. The journey to the world's new identity may be known in a privileged way by the Church, but the journey promised by the triune God is itself one of mutuality. The whole of the world is the arena of the mission of the whole of God.[76]

Scripture reminds us of the paradox that salvation is for all people and all societies who will receive it, and also that it is about the closest conversion of heart at the personal level. The scriptural concept of letting our minds be transformed through God being at home in our hearts reminds us that growing in holiness is about the transformation of our entire being (Luke 24.32). Jesus' disciples said, 'Lord, teach us to pray' (Luke 11.1). In this way our hearts and minds can participate in the life of the triune God and be conformed to the mind of Christ. The wisdom that results enables us to grow in the habit of discerning the movement of God's purposes more deeply in a widening range of circumstances. Learning wisdom in this way is to build the individual and corporate Christian capacity to recognize that in a triune grammar, God's Spirit is abundantly at work in unfamiliar places and in expressions of church we don't understand. We need to respond by participating with all our heart.[77] This is to grow stronger in holiness.

Being 'in charge' in a church rooted in communion

The practice of parish priests in 'collaborative' styles of church today has to wrestle with the apparent dilemma, 'How can I be the presiding minister in such a way as to build up and not pull down the faith and interactive ministries of many others?' Contemporary debates about hierarchy within a communitarian church connect with exploring the nature of otherness within the Trinity. A tension exists between the idea of the Trinity as a hierarchy (Father, Son, Spirit) and as a community of perfect love between people who share equally in divinity.

I shall not attempt to rehearse the competing and complex arguments. Opposing hierarchical and egalitarian views are inevitably shaped by history. Hierarchical patterns of church government are widely critiqued today as borrowed from the context of Roman governmental principles, and that in a very different context now they probably need to be set aside in favour of mutual self-giving.[78] In the early centuries of Christianity, theological thinkers struggled to hold together the experience of God as Trinity with the long tradition of biblical monotheism.[79] Today the debate continues vigorously, with a special poignancy in a time when hierarchy of any kind is a notion that has been oppressive and one many would prefer to see eclipsed. Anglican church practice is still mostly guided by a notion of a static and stepped-down hierarchy (bishop, presbyter, deacon and dependent laity). This conception needs to be in full dialogue with the trinitarian implications that the being of God is an interactive community of loving energies.

The notion of hierarchy, allowing the episcopate a mediatorial function in isolation from the body of Christians, was one element in a complex movement in which Neoplatonic tendencies in the medieval period made a strong separation between the perfect Church in heaven and its imperfect form on earth.[80] One of the chief flaws in hierarchical theory and practice is the assumption that one person alone stands at the apex of power. A biblical account of authority draws together, rather than setting in opposition, the incarnational presence of Christ with the creative and relational energy of the Holy Spirit.[81]

A way of avoiding an unhelpful binary opposition lies in recalling the route taken by the fourth-century Cappadocian theologians. They associate God's loving being towards the world with personhood, rather than substance, describing the person of the Father as the 'cause' of the Triune community. How do we hold this notion of communion deriving from the Father with a theology of the mutual constitution of Father, Son and Spirit as *communion*? The priority of the Father has to be understood so as not to deny that the being of God exists in the relation between the persons. Crucially, the notion of the person of the Father was understood by two early teachers of faith, Irenaeus and Theophilus of Antioch, to be about one who is free to embrace, contain and establish a relationship of *communion* and love, so all creation is drawn into the relationship between the Father and the Son. God the Father is Father because he has a Son and also because he holds everything in creation in the same loving relation that holds together the persons of the Trinity as indivisible and mutual community.[82] With respect to a consideration of the relationship between ministries, in Cappadocian reasoning, love, so far as God's personal and therefore free existence is concerned, is not symmetrical. It comes from the Father, the God of Old Testament experience and Scripture, as personal gift, freely offered and freely received. Persons, in love and freedom, are given and receive identity as otherness in union with others. The Father is greater (John 14.28) not in the sense of qualities but as a matter of simple being, 'ontology'. The Father is ontologically prior, as the giver of personhood to others. So it is possible for the Church to see beyond contemporary disillusionment with oppressive hierarchies that refuse to allow the other to develop fullness in loving and equal freedom. The greatness of the Father within the Holy Trinity arises from his creating others, not as inferior but as having a fully equal ontological status. Each person is a full expression of the whole Trinity.[83]

So the Father is Father to the Son in a relationship in which the Son responds in the obedience of his incarnational life and so shares in the being of the Trinity. In a similar way it may be possible to say that the movement of the Spirit also constitutes divine *communion* through expanding the relationship of Father and Son from mutual love to an outgoing and free movement of creative and redemptive work in the world. The self-giving love shown in Jesus' ministry reinforces this giving of identity to another. The self chooses to give itself away in suffering and vulnerability as an expression of the love that is God's life.[84] Such self-giving creates others, not as less or below, but differently, in their fullest potential. This is the cross-shaped identity of the Church that uniquely promises to bring to existence already signs of a new heaven and a new earth. In a trinitarian ecclesiology there is no question of naively linking the Father with the Episcopate as head of a hierarchy, nor is there a vacuum of power or responsibility. What is at issue is the nature of the power relationships. I noted earlier that in a trinitarian ecclesiology, persons and community are 'equiprimal'. A social trinitarian ecclesiology allows for difference of scope and of responsibility within a *communion* of those given identity as the company of the Holy Spirit, giving themselves to one another and receiving themselves back in love. This is a vital insight for avoiding a false dichotomy between the significance of an *episkope* role in a local church and all the other roles that are required. Roles have to be fulfilled and tasks accepted for the work of the church, without any one minister or disciple becoming permanently fixed in an 'above' or 'below' status.

Range – working with God in every place

The world's need of the practice of Good News

The future of life on this planet is in jeopardy. We live in a society that is degrading rapidly and a world increasingly unable to make sense of things together.[85] Paradoxically, the forces of rapid communications and travel combine with those of economic globalization both to homogenize and divide the world's communities. Calculating the extent to which the overt influence of church and theology has waned is notoriously complex. At deep levels, the patterns by which societies understand and live out their lives in the world are due in large part to our theological inheritance. Images of God that were dominating, isolationist and rigid rather than dynamic and relational have left their trace. They are also a primary reason for wariness towards being associated with the Church today. The resurrection hope that the Church can offer as an antidote to despair must now be proclaimed with humility and with an acknowledgement that we have contributed to the current world failures.[86] The Church's calling is to be a credible icon of the gospel. That is, that the Father, through the vulnerable humanity of the Son, interrelates freely with creation and by the Spirit shows already the nature of the world brought to perfection. And *koinonia* is the quality of the relatedness by which the Church in word and action anticipates the fulfilment of all things.

Critiquing power relationships

I have explored how in worship God's life is intensively directed towards every aspect of life in the world, inviting a human response that seeks just love for all.[87] Although it is frequently lampooned or ignored, the Church's claim that the true way for the world's fulfilment emerges from sharing in God's trinitarian pattern of mission of peace was never more urgently required.[88] Re-examining the power dynamics inherent in common speech has been identified by Christian feminists as a vital way of recovering women and any others who are diminished in the world's cultures and economics. Images and rhetoric either legitimate oppression or break open new possibilities for human relating. In a world where democratic institutions protect the interests of the wealthy, we need to imagine the world from the point of view of the poor.[89] What Christianity, amplified by a feminist liberation perspective, might offer to society is an interweaving of power and compassionate love, so that love is recognized as 'the shape in which divine power appears'.[90]

This movement has resonances too with exegesis of prophetic voices questioning dominating power, for example in Moses showing an alternative to Pharaoh's notion of economics (Exod. 1—15), Nathan's challenge to David's invading his neighbour's marriage (2 Sam. 12) and Elijah's indictments of Ahab and Jezebel (1 Kings 21). Brueggemann reflects that it would be easy, within the sophisticated debates on postmodern power dynamics and contextual approaches to knowing the truth, to dismiss the prophetic approach as simply too confrontative and unconvincing. However, allowing ourselves and our world to engage with scriptural texts as well as with the 'texts' of experience and the world situation, 'makes possible a new field of courage and freedom'.[91]

Instead of living out of fearfulness, churches need to be patiently and passionately working out their identity through recapitulating the fullness of life experienced on the day of Pentecost (Acts 2.1–11). In that critical event, people, transformed by the cross and resurrection, an embryonic community of participation in Christ, were re-energized and the benefits of this became extensively available to others. The Good News in the New Testament was experienced as social, rather than private or individualized. In every generation in ever new situations, whenever the Church has flourished, it has been through the intensity of knowing God through worship, practising goodness personally and corporately, sharing a common life and constantly learning. This produces a new sense of church with new expectations, 'a new urgency about sustaining and transforming social life more widely, even "globally"'.[92]

As I wrote in *Transforming Priesthood*, I believe that an eschatological–trinitarian approach to understanding the Church's identity (ecclesiology) evokes ways of being the Church through engaging with pressing issues, and living in responsible, mutual and often critical companionship with the context. Such a way of church does not seek to address the wider community from the moral high ground nor attempt to impose its wisdom from a position of detachment. Recognizing its calling to live the 'longing, hoping, and imaginative anticipation' of God, this Church will attentively and respectfully promote a sense of shared inter-subjective responsibility for the well-being or sociality of all.[93] Living in eschatological expectation places every aspect of the Church's life and work into the fullest dimension of God's character. Paul, in 1 Corinthians, contextualizes the church's relationships, regulations, habits, disputes and aspirations into the process of looking for the day of Jesus Christ (1.7–8). Living in the penultimate time and desiring and intending the ultimate in worship, community life and trust offers a radical challenge to the values and power dynamics of the world.[94]

Eucharist makes a Church for the world's life

In worship, and pre-eminently in the Eucharist, the Church recognizes creation and all people as God's gift. This is not a gift to dominate or to own but in vulnerability to draw out our response without residue. This has no connection with the quality or ethical choices of others. Each in their unique identity (as being) is given to us as God the Holy Trinity's beloved in which we are in relation and, in Christ, are invited to delight in expansive joy (Matt. 3.17; John 1.18).[95] Instead of defining ourselves in the atomic individualistic manner of the European Enlightenment, the attractive alternative of the gospel is that we are given the other as one to love and in loving so find our own true self.[96] The Eucharist is the place where we learn through bringing together the complex relationships of the world and the 'inner dynamic of God's holiness'. This depends not on our capability but on 'the efficacy of God's holiness' among the worshippers.[97]

In the Eucharist we thank God for being God, whose holy name is made known to us in Jesus Christ. Further, we thank God for our being and the gift of all creation. The ethos of the Eucharist is gratitude for the gift of every other person with whom we have relationship. In a culture of exaggerated individualism, this is highly subversive as it is recognized as threatening our privacy and freedom. Jesus' ethic of unlimited forgiveness and of forgiving others, as we are forgiven, denies us any rights of judgement in accepting or rejecting the other. To forgive the sins of another is for us to choose the path of true life.

The offering of thanks for all others in the Eucharist is our way of entering into resurrection now. The sacrifice of the Eucharist is that we lose our desire for self-love through being caught up in the gift of being shaped by the Trinity. The ethos of Eucharistic community is dying to our own will in the way of Jesus wrestling in Gethsemane (Matt. 16.39) and Paul's emphasis on the priority of the conscience and good of the other (1 Cor. 10.24 and 1 Cor. 10.29).

This is the *communion* that the Eucharist creates, where otherness is experienced as *relational* rather than *adversarial* or *exclusive*.[98] Authentic living is relational as its origin lies in God's triune being. Accepting and building up the other is, therefore, at the heart of God's project given to the Church in companionship with all who share in bringing the world to its destiny. The vocation of the entire creation can be identified, therefore, as to become the full expression of the triune relational identity which is the ethos of the Eucharist. This is not a moral question but one of being (ontology), so that all humanity shares in the priesthood that shares God's passionate desire for the fulfilment of creation.[99]

The Eucharistic performance shows dramatically how particular bread and wine is set apart as a sign of the making holy of all creation. Again, it is the relational gift of God that makes creation holy, rather than some abstract principle or property within creation itself. Jewish and Christian faith offers to the world the vision of each part of the creation offering itself in communion to all others, rather than defending its autonomy. Each part of creation possesses unique gifts for the resourcing and energy of others. Human persons, in particular, have the full potential to respond to this awesome calling to reflect God's own personhood. But this vocation is not for humanity in isolation. The human community together shares the calling to acknowledge and draw out the potential for the calling to free relation of the whole cosmos. Dominant ways of perceiving creation and other humans as sources of exploitation or as separate and depersonalized entities are persuasively challenged by this Eucharistic notion of being in relation, endowed by freedom.[100]

Beyond the liturgical gathering, the human person's calling is to touch all creation as the Eucharistic elements themselves. Freeing everyday situations and relationships from the deadness of isolation and into the life of interconnectedness is an essential part of the Church's sharing in God's mission. To take the Eucharistic ethos into the life of the world is to show the eschatological hope for all creation, so that dominion and decay are not the final end.[101] The holiness of God is made present as the refining fire of Christ's presence to each particular people or place and so to others through them.[102] In this way the Church, as sign of a new creation, can navigate towards a new form of identity. This is a way of being with others, drawing 'impersonal nature into personal relation with the creator in an attempt to liberate nature from its mortality'.[103]

In such a Eucharistic ethos, faith is a new status or relation given to us by God for our thankful response. If the other is given to us and to all creation, faith is an act of gratitude and praise to the other and also to God as source of all others. Self-giving love is at the heart of this ethos and the only certainty is trust in the *communion* of the Trinity.[104] Samuel Wells creatively suggests the

metaphor of making the world a Eucharist as a way of highlight-
ing the eschatological task of church as *episkope*, showing the world
its true life. It does this by extending God's invitation to all to
become God's companions, in the continuous practice of Christian
community articulated liturgically in foot washing, blessing and
dismissal.[105]

The Church's commitment to justice

The 'rumour of wisdom' emerges when the freedom and love of the
trinitarian God is imaginatively brought into co-operation with
the complexity of human disciplines and situations.[106] The Church,
in receiving into itself, principally through worship, the movement
of God's life, must learn to avoid the natural tendency to limit engagement with society – or allow itself to be limited by others.[107]
So the Church, built up for its own sake in God's love, must deliberately contribute to shaping and sustaining over time 'the fabric of
sociality in the world'.[108] This requires churches to take a full interest in the world and be present around the globe with a concern
for fundamental issues about community living, distribution of
responsibilities and of benefits.

The ecumenical report *Faithful Cities* (2005) is a recent UK
example of the Church stimulating debate with interested partners
in the search for cities good enough for all to inhabit.[109] This strand
of Anglicanism has a long history. Josephine Butler, born in 1828,
stands among the many Christian women and men of the nineteenth century whose faith inspired courageous and prophetic writing and work to change lives and attitudes. She offers a particular
example of the links forged by a dedicated Christian between the
practice of mystical prayer and the wilderness of prostitution and
prison.[110] Her leadership and speech, which Butler regarded as a
result of her being possessed by the divine, through 'friendship
with God', connects scriptural apocalyptic hope (Rev. 3.7–8) with
structural sinfulness and the practical love and acceptance of individual women enslaved in prostitution. Alison Milbank shows how
Butler's rhetoric 'offers another narrative of self-understanding that
both allows dignity and agency to the woman (and to the male pros-
titute whom a modern Butler would have included equally) but
offers a way out, not into a utopian future but to a kingdom active
yet not yet achieved'.[111]

Josephine Butler serves to illustrate here the complexity of
Christian concern for justice in society when so often the Church's

deep-seated attitudes, for example in gender bias or oppressive understandings of marriage, make the Christian tradition complicit within social wrongs rather than offering pure solutions.[112] However, Kenneth Leech, from his experience of living and working as a priest in East London, gives an indication of the breadth of the Church's pastoral ministry among those of whose work we may disapprove as well as the Christian task of both 'bearing witness to a different set of values' and 'working within the mess and making the best of what we have'.[113]

Contemporary examples of churches concerning themselves with injustice and poverty, across the world, show the necessity of the Church self-critiquing its own language and concepts as an essential part of serving the Kingdom. The potency of images of God and the need to examine them constantly becomes clear when the connection is recognized between them and the relationship between human thought and behaviour. Potential for the Church's response to and support for the liberation of women who have suffered from male domination is given a wider horizon. Rather than being restricted to the texts of lord, judge and sovereign, feminist writers have developed complementary metaphors of motherhood, pain-bearer and friend. In some certain circumstances, but by no means in all, these may give Christianity a more viable and liberating voice in situations where humans are treated as trivial or where natural forces act capriciously.[114]

Contact – deepening contact with people

Church: school for learning the wisdom of God[115]

In *Practising Community* I rooted all notions of priesthood in an eschatological–trinitarian ecclesiology. The key concept I identified for such a Church is that of *koinonia*. At the heart of *koinonia* lies a relationship of identity created through the dynamic of self-giving and receiving. With a trinitarian–eschatological focus, I worked through each of the credal marks of the Church – unity, holiness, catholicity and apostolicity (first formally pronounced at the Council of Nicaea in 325) – in relation to:

1 a notion of church that is primarily defined for its orientation towards the coming of God's reign and as an advance sign of God's Kingdom in action;
2 the quality of relationality in being church that may analogously be 'an echo of the eternal community that God is'.[116]

In the period since then the debate concerning how far practices of community living can be inferred from a doctrine of the Trinity has been under further scrutiny. These debates have emphasized caution in attempting to abstract theory about God as the gold ore from which to mine a theory of church. The precious metal is the life of God, plurality in unity but a life defined in terms of giving itself away in love.[117] The cross is the central symbol of the triune God's engagement with the world in order 'to transform the unjust, deceitful and violent kingdoms of this world into the just, truthful and peaceful 'kingdom of our Lord and of his Messiah' (Rev. 11.15).[118] The marks of the Church are therefore also marks of the way God will draw the entire world to be – in a unity of difference, in openness to God's transforming love, in companionships of many kinds, leading to the final identity of all nations and creation with God's just and peaceable Kingdom.

Unity

In God's purposes, with the particular support of the *episkope* of all Christians and of those whose ordering makes that their special task, the Church must strive for the practice of unity. Especially this takes place through sharing one baptism and gospel faith, and becoming a joyful, inclusive, attractive and Eucharistic community. Concerning the Eucharist, Paul writes of an organic relationship existing between the risen Christ and all who receive and choose to live the new life offered through sharing communion. 'The cup of blessing that we bless, is it not a sharing in [*koinonia*] the blood of Christ?' (1 Cor. 10.16). Christians live in the space between the unity that is already God's gift in Christ's victory through the Spirit, and the total communion that will be when the universes in Christ are fulfilled.

United in love, the Church acts as a pivot between God and the world, the locus of Jesus' own desire (see John 17.20–26). In Christ's body are closely linked the Father, the Son and the Church (1 Cor. 1.22); Christ is also 'our peace' (Eph. 2), through which the unity of Christians in baptism becomes a seed of unity for the whole world; Jesus' death is the way through which God's mysterious life and purposes become available to all people, time and things (Eph. 3); and the church community in its gifts and possibilities has the capacity to show the world how to live God's economy as learnt in the wisdom of Jesus Christ (Eph. 4). Hope for the re-energizing of the desire for unity in and between churches and the world can come only from continually relearning the wisdom of God in Eucharist, Scripture, praise, penitence and anguish.[119] The current scandal of members of Episcopalian churches refusing to recognize one another's struggles and concerns regarding gender and sexual values, or to engage in tough thinking concerning hermeneutics and the use of Scripture, is a sharp reminder of the value of a *koinonia* ecclesiology. It also highlights the lack of understanding that all must bear some *episkope* for the whole and the consequences when this is left to 'the hierarchy' to sort out. Crucially, instead of public condemnation of the other, an ethic of communion should be realized as the inclusion of otherness and uniqueness.

Holiness

I have developed, in part one of this chapter, orientation to God as the primary root of the Church's life, 'the wisdom of loving God for God's sake'.[120] Holiness is the loving invitation of the triune God for Christian community practice to be identified and sustained in truthfulness through *koinonia* with God's relational self. Increasingly, those who guide others in spiritual growth refer to the explorations into the contrast between the *true* and the *false* self of, for example, Jean-Pierre de Caussade, Thomas Keating, Thomas Merton and Richard Rohr. It is through attentiveness that the human person as a whole discovers his or her true identity in unity through deepening identity with the hidden ground of love.[121] Knowledge of God is permitting God to have the initiative in communication with us, leading to 'a glory and love that evokes all our astonishment, thanks and praise'.[122] To be known by God and to respond to God's knowing is, from a Christian perspective, to be blessed or to become holy. The Church knows its true origin and identity as holy by interactive communion with the Trinity. Through the Eucharist and in worship and silence, the Church grows in holiness and is cleansed of all that impedes its share in God's mission. Parishes and dioceses often seem to starve themselves of this vital oxygen, attempting to create church successfully through mere planning or redesigning systems.

Becoming a community of prayer and worship raises Christian people up into their task of being holy as God is holy, lifts God's beloved ones into their callings and offers exemplars and resources of wise knowledge to the world's final flourishing. There is no holiness that does not travel through the quality of relatedness between persons and in society and between the nations. In the present climate crisis a key aspect of this will be the discovery of a new ecological ethic. The particular form of relationality (*koinonia*) that we learn from the triune God is one that teaches us the quality of co-operation that is required gradually to reorder creation.[123] The contradictions in the Church's life that reveal our failure to live up to God's evocative call to holiness require of us habitual repentance and being open to being surprised by God.[124] The Scripture texts associated with Holy Week and Easter recall that the world is not in the long run in the hands of humanity and that God's final purposes for *koinonia* for the universe cannot in the end be thwarted.[125] Every expression of church, when open to the restorative and demanding holiness of God, allows itself to be summoned in its detailed sharing of responsibilities, internally and externally, to be a constant recapitulation of the Day of Pentecost. As a sign of the Kingdom and a reading of all human relational dynamics, it uniquely practises *koinonia* for the world's repairing.

The community whose foundational gift of the victory of Christ is constantly made new by the Spirit acting in baptism and Eucharist is called to show the world an example of redeemed relationships. It finds its vocation, however tenuously, whenever women, men and children begin to communicate with one another in ways that are directly informed by the sociality that is the trinitarian persons in self-giving relation. In the desire for redeemed sociality, the Eucharistic assembly is not a random gathering but on the way to being an intentional, public, community of difference united in learning to serve God's final purposes.

Catholicity

The call to comprehensiveness, like unity and holiness, is fundamentally related to God, who plans in the fullness of time 'to gather up all things in him, things in heaven and things on earth' (Eph. 1.10). As I discussed in *Practising Community*, and as is implicit in considering holiness and unity, catholicity arises as that quality of life that allows itself to be defined as inherently relational. Christ invites members of his Body to be drawn into *koinonia*, that is his own life, and so of the whole Trinity, and simultaneously to recognize their interrelatedness with every universe.

Through the work of the Spirit, navigating by *episkope* in many aspects, Christ enables the local church to embody his own commitment to the salvation of the whole of creation. In opposing all that leads to the fragmentation rather than the peaceful integration

of the world, the embodied Christ that is the local church is sustained in its catholicity by the action of the Spirit. It is the work of
the Spirit who makes possible the victory of the life of Jesus and
the birth of the Church, to make effective the presence of Christ
in the community Eucharist. The local church's dependency on the
Spirit for its association with Christ's work for the redemption of
all relations is a further reminder that neither the structures of its
life nor its share in the Father's Kingdom project can be brought to
fruition by human endeavour alone. The Eucharist as the centre of
the Church's life both demands and guarantees that the Christian
body of believers keeps open to *all* God's invitation to *all*, expressed
fully in the work of Jesus Christ. So a catholic Church is open
to the pains of the world and in co-operation with those of other
faith and ethical communities, is capable of showing God's own
compassion.[126]

Apostolicity

Proclaiming God's activity, past, present and future, is the point of
fusion for the one, holy, catholic Church. It is where the absorp-
tion in God's intensity, commitment to reaching out to all life and
mutual building up in affinity and openness to context, burn into
the real possibility of newness and hope. Joyfully and obediently de-
centred by the Trinity, in the midst of pain and loss, we groan with
all creation for fulfilment. As the first apostles allowed themselves
to be taught, directed, commanded, sent to all, so churches exist to
make decisions that form them as communities commissioned
to assist in the world's consummation. The bridging between one
expression of the catholic Church and the apostolic handing over
of faith is again a crucial work of *episkope*, formally and informally,
through priest and bishop and through the entire community.
Rather than it being the sole responsibility of a linear succession of
bishops (or any other order alone) to carry the content and meaning of faith from one generation to another, apostolicity happens
when a particular community is an episcopal expression of 'the
continuity of the Church's historical life in its entirety'.[127] Disputes
about who can belong, who is important or who can lead cannot
have the final word. Matthew's scorching words (Matt. 25) leave us
in no doubt that loving God and neighbour are inextricable. Any
assay at being church will sit under the judgement of how the poor,
the naked, the hungry and the imprisoned were better off for that
attempt.

Within the worship and life of the Eucharistic community, the apostolic message handed on by saints in every age becomes simultaneously the loving invitation of God to create the future God desires. Truly understood, the apostolic tradition is always in the process of being reinvigorated, through the recognizably continuous stream of inspired life in which, by the Spirit and especially through worship, the local church is constantly reconstituted. Belief is the 'faith transmitted to *the saints*', constantly received and re-received by the consciousness of the 'community of saints' in new forms of experience and with a constant openness to the future.[128]

In summary, apostolicity refers to the Church's intimate connectedness with its past and its future. As the sign and foretaste of God's peace, it has its roots in the events of Jesus' ministry and the rise of the early Church, and also in eschatological wholeness of the Christ in whose hands the Father has placed the world's final destiny. In any particular context, the Church, through the episcopal work of building *communion* in community and in interaction with its environment, should be open, from the past and from the future, to knowing God's Word as its very life.

The local embodies the catholic

The church that is catholic has a diverse membership open to all. Through interrelatedness with others, a Eucharistic community takes on the character of church – ecumenically, with neighbourhoods, with other faiths and with ecological matters. A Church of the Poor includes, rather than patronizes, those of differing gender, orientation, ethical views, culture or race. In gathering for the Eucharist the church experiences an anticipation of the time when all things and people will finally be united in Christ.[129] Neither church nor Eucharist is so much a thing to be observed from a distance but more an event of participation. Paul describes the Church as a dynamic of the 'one' and 'the many'. In the eschatological journey of faith, John says, all the baptized are members of the Servant of God who offers himself as food for eternal life (John 6.27). Later in his Gospel, John (13—17) links the baptized sharing in the Eucharist with the anticipation of the unity of all in Christ's final ordering of the world. The many and the one are united in Eucharistic community and celebration and sharing in Christ's Body.

So the early Church calls itself *ekklesia*, coming together, becoming in each particular church also all that there is of the catholic

Church.[130] In this community there are no distinctive races, ages or status. All human conditions are transcended. So there can be no private gathering in Eucharist, one that excludes or is intended for just one category of person. Every Eucharist is a sign of the kaleidoscopic unity of God's purpose for the cosmos. In Christ, many who are different become united and remain incomplete themselves when they give up on the search for unity and companionship with all other Eucharistic communities.[131]

Really in touch with localities?

Earlier, we explored the Church's commitment to context to the extent of suggesting that Christianity always travels in particular settings. Yet are we really in touch even with those who are already church? The role of the parish church in the case of the Church of England has often been regarded as automatically available and desired for any in the community, especially in times of celebration or tragedy. I argued earlier to maintain a complex relationship between church and cultural setting, neither cut off nor totally accommodated. Perceptible changes in the attitudes of the public towards humanist funerals and a widespread disconnection with basic Christian narratives and beliefs have to be held in a new and creative tension with old assumptions, signalled notably by the Church's connection with the popular mood immediately after the death of Princess Diana. A complex set of factors interplay, and these will vary for readers in different parts of the world. Yet the impression given in Roy Strong's commentary on many centuries of English rural church life is that the church (usually personified by the parish priest) often deeply disdained the habits of local people – while the parishioners themselves could experience humiliation.[132]

Hardy constantly draws out the need for churches to exemplify in their social life the very belief that brings them into existence and sustains them. So the ways in which we do or are the Church build up or undermine the Church's witness in society. This is more than a vague spirit of 'togetherness', rather a constantly reforming dynamic structure in perpetual danger of falling into one of two traps: ossification or assimilation.[133] The danger is, on the one hand, to live in the past rather than fully in the present, and on the other to be so accommodated to local and global cultures that the distinctive character of church is eroded. Hardy describes a circle of interlinked issues that should define the Church's formation 'in accordance with the economy of God's life and work in the world'.[134]

The Church then is called to be a people living in localities, called together specifically by worship, the ministry of all the baptized according to their God-conferred gifts, with a clear pattern of organization in which tasks of pastoral care, teaching, service, evangelism and so on are distributed for the common good. Such a Christian community exists specifically to be a sign of God's unity, of God's own holiness, always linked with other churches and focused on sharing in God's mission in the world. Such a church will be drawn to the service of those without food, shelter, mental stability or emotional security. These purposes will be sustained through constant opportunities for learning by all, through the ordained ministry and through continuing theological research. This deepening spiral of ever greater participation in the work of God's world is the common calling of all Christians. This circle is lost when education and training is focused on just a minority of special Christians or when clergy are treated as a religious aristocracy of experts, substituted for the whole body.[135]

Challenging the dominant myths of society

In the inherited ministry models, people were held to their local church in their individual selves – through attraction to worship of a particular kind, through respect for who was the Vicar at the time, out of loyalty to family or history with a building, through receiving pastoral care or other benefits for themselves and their family or common agreement on projects. In a church rooted in trinitarian *koinonia*, what are the elements that hold people together in their different roles and callings? How can the life of the church touch the hearts and minds of all concerned as they are in all their variety? It is a formidable task.

To keep in full awareness an understanding of how the triune God invites us to constitute everyday life as relational, could enable churches to make a considerable contribution to countering the pervasive individualism. We form ordinary societies appropriate to our need in diverse patterns of complexity. The particular configuration of social relationships we call 'church' sets out to be a deliberate but variable disclosure of God as community of difference in *communion*. Instead of regarding theological traditions as stable, reliable or universal constructs for supporting Christian identity and order, we recognize the choices from within the tradition that at any time support our preferred understanding of Christian identity. A key question is that of who controls the interpretation of the past so as to authorize our strategy for doing church now and in the future.[136]

With humility we need to start by reordering the internal practices of the Church. This is, notably, to live out the truth that it is never possible to consider the life and work of the parish priest, except in close connection with all that has to be said of the Church as a whole. At one time we mistakenly gave the impression that churches are collections of passive people who mainly needed pastoral care and prayer. 'Say one for me, Vicar' is the kind of church we have been for too long. Now, increasingly, we recognize that all, usually in their daily responsibilities at work, at home or in the neighbourhood, must take their part in the work of God's Kingdom. For this, all need to know the joy of the Holy Spirit and Jesus Christ personally as the centre of our being.

Animating one another through our mutual gifts is the key to a new way of doing church together as an offering to society. In the *Common Worship* marriage service, bride and groom say to one another, 'All that I am I give to you'. Within the Church's life generally we are learning how to receive the gifts of one another. Much of this will be enhancing; some will bring problems of communication and even fear. It is a huge step to move from a congregation of occasional worshippers to being a mission community.

Our animating one another is in the spirit of our diving into the holiness of God and participating in God's life in society. Especially in the Eucharist we give thanks for what God is doing through and in us, but also give thanks for one another. To give thanks changes the quality of our living. We also come to worship and to the life of the church as a particular people, rather than as pew fodder. We have our journey of life and faith, our experiences of work, family and leisure. We bring our skills and insights and we bring concerns for the world's life. We belong to church with all this 'information', and we go back to the places where we 'live' as witnesses to the power of resurrection. We are bridge people, living between the life of God in the world we inhabit physically, intellectually or emotionally. We are an embodiment of 'church' wherever we go. Our ministry, whatever it is and in whatever context, is infused by our involvement in church and worship. We connect them through our person and faith.

Further, our life together in church carries the meaning that we find in God through worship, Scripture, prayer, talking together and mutual care. These elements create us as a community of character.

We are more than we seem. The small and vulnerable church that is our spiritual home is an embodiment of the one, holy, catholic Church through time and space. As we become one in Christ through the Spirit we receive an aliveness that goes beyond our own efforts and a 'peace which passes all understanding'.

Helping one another truly to belong

Now is the time for a grown-up church. Loyalty to a brand is far less important to most people now than the quality of the experience of church they take part in. This sounds perilously close to consumerism. Is the customer happy enough not to desert this company for another supplier? If we are honest, that's part of the scene today. People's loyalty shifts more easily than in a previous era. The perseverance of even the most committed Christian can be tested by severely disappointing or limited experiences of Christian community. Communicating, on websites and through newsletters, that of which we are proud and that we wish others to know for themselves, is an imperative for church life now.

However, this is not to regress into looking after the customer as a model of ministry. In the 1950s, the card-index of parishioners combined with the assiduous visiting of the priest led to the slogan, 'A homegoing parson makes for a churchgoing people'.[137] Now the test of affiliation is whether the 'members' of the church are able to participate as both givers and takers; can grow in faith and love and become witnesses and missioners. Is there a richness and depth to the experience of being church, for all concerned? This is not a hierarchical responsibility, as if the parish priest or bishop were merely the Managing Director. As we have explored earlier, the whole Church bears responsibility for being *episkope* for the world, even though the parish priest and bishop share a unique navigational work of holding the Church together and guiding its journey. Origen, commenting on the Song of Songs, likens bishops to 'rafters' stretching across the walls, sustaining and protecting the whole building from rain and sun.[138]

A church (or group of churches) with 'competitive advantage' will be far more than an organization. It will celebrate worship of many kinds for different people and times, will offer various opportunities to celebrate life-passages, will offer support in making complex decisions about caring for the young and the elderly, be reaching out corporately to situations of 'poverty', locally and across the world, have a congregation where anyone can tell you its current purpose and strategy, where anyone can offer you a word or gesture of loving encouragement and where it is clear that many are growing in faith through prayer and learning.

The power of communal ritual

When families and congregation have been made to feel welcome and prepared, the celebration of a baptism at a Sunday Eucharist can be a sure way of renewing the vigour of the congregation itself. A proudly baptizing community is growing in corporate vitality. When temporary banners are created by a small group or a workshop and displayed for a festival, there is a cathartic power of corporate storytelling: 'This is our faith.' When musicians are persuaded that their playing, and not just their skill-level, enhances worship, what a deep knowledge about the encounter we call community is signalled. When, against their better judgement, a congregation is persuaded – and sustained in – experimenting with worship in a face-to-face manner, it ceases to think of itself as an audience with a minimalist task.

There has also to be a willingness to be disposed to follow the way of Jesus Christ. To avoid a merely narcissistic, ego-massaging or adaptive experience of community and worship there has to be the acceptance of the full-strength wine of the gospel in celebration and penitence. Liturgy that subversively teaches, kinaesthetically, how we are *koinonia*, needs to involve the voices, eyes and bodies of all.[139] 'Knowledge is not only the affair of the intellect: it is born in the marrow bone.'[140] This kind of imagination is required if we are to make a Christian counterstatement in an individualistic, consumerist Western society. Increasingly within traditional churches, new energy is discovered when a few commit to saying together a daily office, studying Scripture, sharing a simple Eucharist, spending time in silent prayer together or planning and leading a healing service. Stimulated by Scripture, sacraments, prayer, theology and ordained ministry, all become Jesus' disciples and missioners – healed, restored, forgiven, summoned and on the way to the love and laughter of heaven.

Transformation – a new world beginning

One of the chief ways in which the Church contributes to showing the world its true life is to live out in practical community life the meaning and goodness it finds in God, as security, freedom, love, peace, well-being and friendship.[141] In the sacraments and in routines of communitarian living, the Church should exemplify the sharing of the peace that is now established as such a central part of the Eucharistic event. So the Church is a visible practice of the gospel faith and the world may become a Eucharist. The way in which baptism and the Eucharist are celebrated liturgically can bring healing to each participant through knowing in our bodies the untiring love that God has for us. In this movement we grow in closeness to one another and help to reform the social networks of the world.

The practical ordering of church community, 'the social fabric', including arrangements for the distributing of responsibilities and sharing of benefits, can often be undervalued when the interior 'spiritual' life of participants is allowed to take priority.[142] It is Christian belief that in the resurrection lies the real power to transfigure all nature and every human disorder. Churches are more than the result of historical, economic, cultural or social crises, but are deliberate attempts to embody the trinitarian mission towards the world now and in openness to the final purposes of God. In other words, Christian faith itself is the content, shape and practice of the Church.[143] Through this intentional practice of community as a participation in God and a reading of the gospel, churches contribute to the web of possibilities for nurturing human life within the world's ecology.

When I come, in later chapters, to explore the specific role of parish priests, who in a particular way share *episkope* with the diocesan bishop, a significant question will concern what kind of person and role can best enable the Church to be ordered for the world's healing.

Traditionally, we have recognized the church's extensivity in its concern for the whole of a locale or parish. In today's complex world the Church, abandoning its own neuroses about the survival of its previous forms, must show to the world the attractiveness and hope of community living that is a response to the self-disclosure of the one true God. It is a mistaken humility to hide from the world the amazing possibilities for human living together, not only of the New Testament but in Scripture, taken as a whole. Often this is mistaken for ideas or theories about how to live well. Rather, through the Holy Spirit, we have an event of God's communication and invitation to be part of the divine life. Paul speaks passionately of humans being 'in Christ'. Christ has both died for us and covered ours sins, but also, now subsumed in Christ, we live in and out of his life and are transformed.[144]

So an authentic, new humanity works against power misuse, greed and violence, both at the personal level but also at the communitarian. The renaming in Matthew's Gospel of Simon as Peter offers an icon of the miracle of new possibilities for humanity. Through a discerning Church – having eyes to see and ears to hear – the world can be re-formed in the person of Christ as the presence and purpose of God.[145] Always in fragility, the Churches of the crucified God have taken a hand in ending the myth of racial superiority in many places, in opposing oppressive control, in turning hate to co-operation, in supporting immigrants and asylum seekers and reaching out to young people detached from families or lost in a world of consumerism.[146]

The Church bears the unique task of helping the world navigate towards true life. The world (and the Church) often misunderstands the Church's watching-out (*episkope*) responsibility when it shows itself too much in terms of demand for an obedience associated with contract or condition, rather than as companionship and covenant. The obedience to God's will proportioned by scriptural covenant is rooted in relationships of *koinonia*.[147] Echoing God's chosen covenantal neighbourliness with God's people, the social obligations and responsibilities offered to the world in Jesus Christ are inherently relational, rooted in an assumption of the given, ontological relationship between all people, regardless of any other condition or quality (see Exod. 20.2ff.; Luke 1.53 and 1 John 4.9–10).[148]

Jesus, in Luke's account of his healing ministry, demonstrates God's life in all people. He freely puts himself personally at risk (8.29); is willing to be confronted in a stormy conversation (8.30); is hemmed in by the crowd (8.42); does not separate himself from others in the chaotic street meetings (8.46 and 50); and is not concerned with the moral status of any of them. In this way Jesus subverts the social norms of his day, as many HIV/AIDS workers beg the Church now to offer to all more than 'contractual compassion' or 'mere tolerance', but rather 'radical affirmation and hospitality, where the first truly becomes last and the least are made first within the communal practices and ways of being the "Body of Christ"'.[149]

The Christian invitation to love, and the foundation of the Church's structured shape in mission, is rooted in the reality that we worship God's passionate commitment to us, inviting us to welcome and be reconciled to one another.[150] The gift to the world of embodied Christian hope in particular situations, though personal, is essentially communal; 'loving and forgiving one's enemy would clearly be seen as a regulative "structure" of ecclesial participation'.[151]

Also, as experience is always particular, the risky work of discerning God's purposes for contemporary living will always be one of navigating open waters rather than reaching for predetermined certainties. The Church most profoundly serves God's mission for the restoring of the world when it courageously chooses to be nothing less than the Church. Conversely, 'the church is never more *irrelevant*, than when it tries to establish and justify the foundations of common existence outside that *koinonia* from which alone it derives its existence as also its conscience.'[152] The Church cannot live in isolation, but in and towards the whole world, through its participation in the life of Jesus, the one through whom all human barriers are destroyed and all marginalization of the weak and the different is disallowed.[153]

A fundamental challenge for the will of the Church to engage with God's mission now was spelled out vigorously at the Campbell Seminar 2000, 'Mission as Hope in Action'. This Seminar, initiated by Colombia Theological Seminary and now an annual event, was constituted by five international church leaders, lasting for eight weeks of uninterrupted interaction. Exploring biblical and strategic options for a new shape of church, the Seminar invited the world Church to take up its responsibility to counter all that stands against hope in every aspect of the world's living. It stands as a vital invitation to churches, and in the argument of this study it profoundly links the first of our two ecclesial strands – the intensivity and holiness of God with the extensivity and reaching out of God's people in every place.[154]

Christian faith and worship offer the capacity, imagination and energy for this hope to become real for the sake of a limited and fearful world. Christian faith, not just an idea, but the embodiment of the triune life actively, means we have the resource to act now *as though* the new rule of God had come into effect. As the claims of 'the technological-therapeutic-militaristic-consumerist world' ultimately fail, we are invited to be ordered differently by the 'new governance of the God who is back in town'.[155] There is vital work for a Christian Church in this situation, though this includes reviewing its own grandiosity and the nature of its structures and relations in the light of trinitarian faith.

God-centred desire for the world's wholeness

Jesus and the early Church expected from God a healing that linked outward need and inner peace. The Word of God, Jesus, healed the sick, evoked repentance, raised the dead, released those who were tormented and brought hope and joy to the poorest. Already in Jesus people recognized the fulfilment of God's project, the Kingdom in which the earth would finally be fully obedient to God. The Church of the Poor reorientates human desire around those in need of forgiveness, freedom, sight. It embodies in its life a 'wisdom of desire' that includes reconciliation, forgiveness, compassion, generosity, expectancy, hospitality, readiness, and faithfulness.[156] Luke reminds us of Jesus' invitation to lose rather than save our life so that the world is transfigured by the desire to follow Jesus being stronger than the desire for life or for the whole world (Luke 9.23–25).

The Vatican II document 'Joy and Hope' (*Gaudium et Spes*) spoke of the Church, the people of God, building a new world, collaborating in the maturing of the world's people. Others since have reminded us that God's final purpose also includes the entire ecology of creation, of which humanity can be the most problematic part. The Church is merely a light and temporary scaffolding for the building of God's Kingdom. Helping to bring the world round to God's way, through the practice of the Gospel, is the permanent, transformative task of Christian community prayer, worship and life (Eph. 1.15–23). In his appeals to the Corinthians, Paul calls them to dare to dive deeper into the heart of the gospel, conformed to the 'mind of Christ'. Through weak power and foolish wisdom, dissension will be outflanked by 'a God-orientated "ecology" of belonging, embracing oppositional confrontation in a higher inclusiveness'.[157]

Such a Church will need to have the closest contact with those among whom it is located. It will need to foster the interaction of its many different participants, and of them with the wider, catholic Church. Church erupts from the intense engagement with God that draws it into the fullest involvement with God's own presence and work through creation. These deepest points of connectivity are the way in which the Church mediates the transformation of the world.[158] There will be evidence within such a community of heart-to-heart relationships that are real and tough rather than sentimental or conditional on our behaviour, even though through the Spirit, repentance and hard work is demanded of those who witness to God's life-giving power.

The work of living in face-to-face community leads to a profound change. A life conformed to the birth, life, death and rising of Jesus, a community marked by the cross, will be a sign to the world of its final changing, when death 'is swallowed up in victory' (1 Cor. 15.52–57). Churches are transformed and become agents of transformation through living out of the inexhaustible and abundant wisdom of God. The person of Jesus shows us how to centre our life on God, the wisdom of the prophets and the loving practices of the Kingdom.[159] A transformative Church is learning in mind, heart and body how to practise and perform this wisdom. The central work of churches is therefore to enter into the same relationship with the Father and with others that Jesus demonstrates. We do this through sitting under the texts of Scripture and learning that desire to embrace the Kingdom for ourselves, for one another and for the world's fulfilling. Endless openness to ways of growing in this desire is our human response to the Jesus God sent in the Spirit.[160]

The worshipping community: amplifying the world's desire

Across the world in praise, confession, Scripture, meditation, rehearsal of faith, intercession, breaking bread and sharing wine, churches have to decide how to worship. What words, gestures, space, music, silence and questioning will best reveal and be a response to the distinctive triune Christian God? A renewed fascination with identifying God as Trinity shows how in baptism, Eucharist and the dynamics of church life, we are offered the indwelling Spirit that 'conforms' us, the saints and the whole creation to 'the image of the Son' (Rom. 8.9–30).[161] Just as doing church itself, as a deliberate act of social interrelation, reveals who is our God, so the way we decide and make appropriate arrangements for praise, Eucharist and remembering and bringing into the present Jesus' words and actions will shape, or not, the intensity of our incorporation into and transformation by the life of God, as redeemed daughters and sons. Both the way we choose to be church and to make the Eucharist are crucial, as they have the potential to be freighted or load-bearing with Jesus, with God's wisdom. Eucharistic life, Sunday by Sunday, has the capacity to form us in a *habitus* where Christian character is forged. The processes of learning of such community can deepen our understanding of God as Trinity. Here we are re-formed, together as a sign of the world's transformation. Christian tradition, drawing on Jewish roots, invites us into a constantly recapitulating complexity of poetry, prose, debate, attention to suffering, compassion, testing, possibilities and transformation through God at work in us.[162]

The Gospels show us Jesus, in his relation with John the Baptist, at the Transfiguration, and at the Last Supper, as transmitting and recapitulating the Exodus, prophetic, looking to the final consummation of God's purposes. The many strands of Eucharistic gathering – listening to Scripture, blessing, breaking and sharing food – stimulate our identity to be intensified, as were Jesus' first disciples, immersed in a new way of life, and so centred in fresh ways and decisively expecting innovation. This wisdom tradition requires to be carefully nurtured, beyond the mere repetition of a tradition. Liturgy carries the meaning we find about God in Jesus in ever new situations, and so carries inevitably a self-critiquing element to its performance. We have constantly to ask ourselves what this worship is telling us and therefore the world about who our God is.[163]

The task of *episkope*

I shall conclude this chapter by summarizing the link that has been implicit throughout, between this theory of church and the concept of the parish priest as *episkope* within a *koinonia* community. This will pave the way for discussing specifically the vital role of the incumbent or parish priest and how this ministry can be truly an agency for this quality of church to happen for the world's fulfilment. Then in the final chapter I shall offer some reflection out of my experiences with people in the parish in which I am currently the Vicar.

In *Transforming Priesthood* I described the theological fault in which the mistake is constantly made of substituting the work of the parish priest for that of the entire church. What became clear also was the self-limitation of deriving notions of ordained ministry principally from the person and work of Jesus (often with an emphasis on the God-ward, transcendent side of the incarnation) and a corresponding neglect of reflection on the work of the Spirit.

My point is that a central focus of the understanding of the work and life of the parish priest in the local church today can be drawn from a redevelopment of the concept of *episkope*. The bishop is to be one in whose person, always in relationship to the entire Eucharistic community of the Church, the local is tied together with the universal, the historical and the eschatological dimensions of apostolicity. The 1988 Lambeth Conference Report, taken as the basis for the Eames Commission of 1989 on *Communion and Women in the Episcopate*, summarized the key elements of the work of a bishop as:

- symbol of unity
- teacher and defender of the faith
- pastor of pastors and laity
- enabler of the preaching of the Word and administration of the Sacraments
- a leader in mission
- an initiator of outreach to the world surrounding the community of the faithful
- a shepherd who nurtures and cares for the flock of God
- a physician for the wounds of society
- a voice of conscience with the local context
- a prophet proclaiming justice in the context of a gospel of loving redemption
- a head of a family in its wholeness, misery and joy.

These largely missionary and evangelical elements carry rich possibilities for the person and community characterized as *episkope* for the world's healing. Kortwright Davis comments wisely on the difficulty of combining prophecy with inherited expectations of the one carrying the episcopal role:

> Whom do you think you were going out to the wilderness to see? If you were looking for a man dressed in cope and mitre, and golden ring, you should have gone to the Bishop's palace (or court, or thorp, or manse or penthouse). Prophets do not dress like Bishops. The prophet stands over against the institution, even if the prophet might be committed to the highest ideals to which the institution also ought to be committed.[164]

We have discussed how all God's people share in all three elements of the Church's work (episcopal, presbyteral and diaconal), and yet this in a relational ecclesiology takes nothing from the particular ordained roles of bishop, priest and deacon. Rather they animate one another. So the presiding priest in each local church shares in the distinctive episcopal ministry of the diocesan bishop. Catholicity requires this mutual bond. It is not possible to read off simple connections with the New Testament churches, which had no consistent usage concerning this role and office.[165] Varying 'overseeing' responsibilities are differentiated, but the overlap with presbyteral roles offers no clear direction.

The notion of watching over (or better, 'watching out for') individuals, faith content and progress of community life in the manner of Jesus, provides us with strong material on which to build.[166] Apostolically, there are also role models and memories from 2,000 years of church life, some very positive and some embarrassingly crass. In early conflicts with heretics and schismatics, the early Church Fathers, such as Irenaeus, came to recognize in the bishop one who was legitimator of orthodox belief. Living apostolic faith is more than a recital or repetition of the past. As resurrection eyewitness, it is always past and future orientated, crucially discerned at the point where the Scriptures and apostolic witness from the past meet with the work of the Spirit in the churches at the present time and in the particular circumstances of a given place. Medieval and nineteenth-century (ultramontane) distortions of episcopal authority, too much coloured by unscriptural notions of domination, need not be illustrated here.

I suggest that the renewal of the Church (in richness, range, contact and transformation) requires the *episkopos as navigator*, walking the boundaries, building bridges or standing at the crossroads, enabling the whole community to take on these values and characteristics. This is the work of all God's people at various times and in general attitude. It is the special responsibility of those called to *episkope* in the local church (whether the parish priest or whoever is called to that task in any given situation), in their person, to help the church to come to know its character and how to live it out in the shifting particularities of that situation. It will call for imagination, courage, effective teaching and communication for an appropriate *episcopal* ministry to develop and blossom against prevailing expectations within individuals, churches and society generally. The ministry of *episkope* understood within an eschatological–trinitarian ecclesiology has the capacity to build the Church in its apostolic character and in the condition of *koinonia* that are the only authentic dynamics for a Church serving the mission of the trinitarian God. Only such a Church can offer to the world a sign of its destiny in Christ through a critique of culture, language and power dynamics that fail to be an embodiment of the *communion* of difference in relation that is God's eschatological pattern.[167]

4

The navigator: *episkope* of the local church

In the time of their visitation they will shine forth,
and will run like sparks through the stubble.
                                              Wisdom 3.7

Episkope in the New Testament

Of the variations of meaning associated with the Greek verb *skopeo* (to be concerned about, to watch out for, pay attention), only four references in the New Testament with the prefix *epi* (*episkope, episkopos, episkeptomai*) refer to one particular person as leader of a community (Acts 20.28; Phil. 1.1; 1 Tim 3.2; Titus 1.7). Jesus is described as shepherd and guardian (*episkopos*) of your souls (1 Peter 2.25). Other references to church development indicate that communal care and oversight are the mutual responsibility characteristic of the congregation (Matt. 25.36; Acts 6.3; 15.36; Heb. 12.15; James 1.27). It would seem to be a faithful development of the meanings of *episkope* to include, not just the one ordered to ensure the Church keeps true to its character, but the entire body as a corporate episcopal personality.

In Acts, when Paul is warning the Ephesians of threats to their identity, internal and external (20.17–38), he instructs the elders to be *episkopoi*, overseers, shepherding the Church of God created from the death of God's son (Acts 20.28). In other words, the elders are to be Christ to the Church (see 1 Peter 2.25). A monarchical *episkopos* only emerges as an office holder in the time of Ignatius (early second century). Moving beyond asking merely whether two words (*episkopos*, overseer, and *poimen*, shepherd) are being used of the same kind of church office, I suggest that *episkope* is a basic requirement of the Church, taking different forms in varying contexts. *The Archbishop's Group on The Episcopate* (1990) maps out systematically the Church's experience of bishops and ecumenical insights of the twentieth century. Notably, the New Testament gives fragmentary evidence of the precedent of James in Jerusalem, Timothy and

Titus. The Report is confident that 'a ministry of personal oversight' was emerging in New Testament times for the support in mission and coherence of the early Church.[1] The discussion that follows in this chapter gladly appreciates the long history of personal *episkope* that has been a corporate expression of the Christian community, of which Ignatius and Irenaeus were prominent exponents.[2] Nothing in this book should be considered to disregard the countless examples of the exercise of personal *episkope* that has been formative for the pastoral, liturgical, theological and spiritual development of the local church's mission.[3]

Episkope for the local church

In this chapter I shall explore how, instead of considering *episkopos* exclusively as a personal office as the head of a hierarchy, we might perceive the role of the priest presiding *within* the *communion* of the local church as also a full expression and 'salutary visitation' to that community of the universal Church's eschatological task. The notion of *episkope*, borrowed from secular usage by early churches to identify those who were overseers, supervisors or guardians of the tradition, has the potential to evoke an interrelational, corporate understanding of church and leadership far beyond many inherited notions of 'bishop'.[4] I am not here making prescriptive suggestions about the work of diocesan bishops. But there are implications here for how bishops, in the way they function and in their attitudes, might share the responsibility for lifting the Church into patterns that are interactive and foster *communion.*

Engaging with clergy at conferences and retreats over recent years, I recognize both the urgent need for a greater clarity in defining the 'it' that is the priestly task of presiding within a local church, as well as the turmoil, internal and external, when such clarity is pressed, as inevitably it involves making difficult choices. Ecumenically over recent decades, co-operation has moved ahead when there has been a deepening of debate beyond the skin-deep inherited historical concepts and language of varying denominations. The wider debate concerning the nature and functioning of organizations in society today also acts as a reminder of the many overlapping ways of effective organization that have been developed among a diversity of cultures.[5] Those reflecting on the current needs of the Church in terms of unfolding identity and readiness for mission have often highlighted the need for forms of local church leadership that are both appropriate and of the character of the gospel.

The theory of church, outlined in Chapter 3, provides the 'information' that glues the Church together in its particular business:

1 richness – growing into the richness of God's life;
2 range – working with God in every place;
3 contact – deepening contact between people;
4 transformation – a new world beginning.

I suggested how this might be drawn from a trinitarian reflection on the mystery of God. Concepts of God and of God's desire for the world's fulfilment will inevitably shape the character of the community of co-workers with God in this project. A *koinonia*-inspired church, assuming the gospel to be inherently relational, is one in which all distributed tasks, ministries, authentically flow in close relationship to the whole body of God's people. As we have explored, the roots of this approach lie in readdressing the question of God – not only what God has done for us and who we are becoming in Jesus, but what we have, analogously and tentatively, come to know of God's inner being and purpose.

I have described God's mission, shown in Jesus, imaginatively described by Paul, as to bring to fruition in kaleidoscopic patterns of unity, the end of creation. The eschatological destiny of creation, animate and inanimate, is to become fully attuned to the trinitarian life of *perichoretic* interrelationship, in patterns of mutual deference. Only in these terms do we have adequate concepts with which to understand what kind of church is required to be the first fruits of that destiny of love.

Parish priest as *episkopos*

Lutherans always call all their clergy 'Pastor' (rather than Father, Vicar or Rector); the shepherd metaphor is universally known among Lutherans. Sometimes the image works against shared ministry, but it also has a positive aspect to it. Lutherans sometimes refer to the office of pastor as being that of the 'bishop' of a local area, and refer to the bishop as the regional 'pastor' or 'pastor to pastors'. I am advocating that an appropriately understood concept of *episkope* could offer to our understanding of the role of the parish priest different tasks and gifts, according to context. The *episkope* person (and team) evokes and fosters attitudes and practices of church rooted in *koinonia*, a distillation of the self-giving ministry of Jesus Christ, which is itself an advance demonstration of the relationality at the heart of the triune God of love. It would be naive in the contemporary situation to assume that working with notions of 'overseeing' will be straightforward. Convinced of the need of an alternative *episkope* ordering within a church of *communion*, I shall now offer a brief survey of some of the painful hindrances.

Being 'in charge' among reciprocal ministries

One of the key tasks of this study is to assist parish priests to be confident about being 'in charge' in an episcopal role, without cancelling out the contribution of others to being responsible for the church's share in the triune mission. The concept of *episkope*, routinely considered as 'oversight', problematically conjures up long memories of patriarchy and elitist privilege. Contemporary concerns to promote equality and to counter power abuse are at odds with the use of any term beginning with a superordinate prefix (such as 'over'). The word 'bishop' itself carries sufficient negative freight to make it a concept on which many today can place too much trust.

In her seminal reflection on *episkope*, Penny Jamieson reminds us of endemic male abuse of power. She illustrates her thesis especially in regard to the Church's struggle to recognize the power imbalance implied in handling cases of clergy sexual abuse. Jamieson concludes that 'a Church that cannot put an end to its own abuses of power has no place as a critic of power'.[6]

Parish priests are admitted, after a 'vacancy' or 'interregnum', to roles and tasks, employing language and liturgical acts of being 'in charge', in isolation from the language and drama of co-operation and diversity. The *episkope* role is both part of the Anglican tradition and an essential means by which the local church holds together. What are the key tasks of the loving guardianship of any church? A bishop or parish priest or group appointed for the *episkope* of a local church (in richness, range, contact and transformation) will need to:

- be able to separate important from the urgent priorities;
- ensure that all are growing in Christian wisdom;
- ensure that tasks are well devised;
- order people in relations of trust;
- differentiate between different tasks;
- differentiate between roles;

- differentiate between personal and corporate decisions and actions;
- ensure the pastoral care of the sick, bereaved and of minorities.[7]

The priest and people together are responsible for seeing that the contents of these pointers are realized in practice. But if one is 'in charge', how is the *episkope* authority of everyone else to be articulated? Traditional rhetoric within the process of appointments to tasks in the church is related to the God under whose authority all serve.[8] In Chapter 3, I discussed the theological basis for avoiding conflict on this issue. Church practice generally has not caught up with eschatological or trinitarian ecclesiological insights. Feminist theologians, in diverse ways, have challenged church practice as irredeemably androcentric, pushing women to the edge of being persons at all, while others point to the relentless male bias that continues to shape theological discourse. There are equally those who would entirely resist all feminist critique of monotheism in favour of traditional presentations of faith and authority.

The contemporary contribution of women

Recent studies by women of scriptural and traditional texts cannot but subvert earlier so-called 'natural' readings that assume God's maleness to be an article of faith. Even when women are accepted as ordained ministers there can be a pressure on the grounds of equality to take no account of the differing lifestyles of men and women, for example over pregnancy. The logic is to explore how exercising priesthood, and being a congregation, as *episkope* can be redefined in categories that do not exclude one sex from participating.

I have explored earlier how the society we call church is one that deliberately chooses to work in intimate response to God's authority. In working for the final establishment of that *koinonia* that God desires for the cosmos, a church discerns how to live and relate as a community only in the self-giving practice of *koinonia*, exemplified by Jesus. There is an assumption here that the one 'in charge' will facilitate the church in its quest to be an advance sign of the reign of God and that the character of this facilitation will itself be characterized by recognizably Kingdom values.

Elizabeth Johnson argues persuasively that the Church should recognize that God's reign assumes neither the maleness of God nor the superiority of maleness. She claims that there is no timeless speech about God and that in our society and through the experience of so many women, the metaphor of God as 'Father',

'Son' and 'Holy Spirit', especially when considered literally, subverts *communion.*[9] Mary Daly and Daphne Hampson are among those women who have described this God as setting the pattern for patriarchy, violent and coercive, set apart from creation and inconsistent with today's world view.[10]

Another approach is to go beyond the language about God debate and consider an 'imaginative' rather than strictly verbal approach to the Trinity as better serving the personhood of women.[11] Emphasizing that all language about God is necessarily metaphoric, Bacon draws on the work of Luce Irigaray to invite women to move beyond the previous thinking of men, and imaginatively to consider God as Trinity in terms of self-love and wonder. Here are seeds for challenging patriarchal understandings of God and to 'undermine . . . phallocentric accounts of subjectivity'.[12] Each centre of personhood in God may then be understood as difference in a mutual relationship of love.[13] Love is a real possibility because 'thinking the Trinity' provides a model of mutuality where violence or possession are not included. Bacon is at pains not to confuse mutuality with sameness and to suggest that her argument makes a contribution to finding models or mutuality based on a *communion* of wonder and space. So God is no distant tyrant but one who beckons the other into nearness and encounter, challenging all male *over* female relations and patriarchal assumptions about God's being.

This discussion has recognized that current language, experience and patterns of church authority, experienced by some as abusive, are certainly not universally welcomed as liberating and energizing.[14] I have shown how a possible bridge of reconciliation lies perhaps in challenging overliteral understandings or language for God, all too frequently connected with previous civic or governmental institutions. At best all speech about God can only be analogous. The link between an image of God as a single ruling male and that of a man as the apex of a hierarchy is easy to recognize. Equally, it is frequently the case that in the interest of polemic we make general criticisms of those exercising office that ignore complex realities. So, for example, although the papacy is an easy target for journalistic criticisms of top-down power dynamics, a careful reading of the encyclicals of Benedict XVI does not bear this out.[15]

Johnson argues that the historic maleness of Jesus (also Jewish and Aramaic-speaking) is not what defines his 'redeeming Christic function', nor should it encourage the notion that men are somehow closer to God or that women cannot represent God.[16] The awareness that all three monotheistic faiths (Judaism, Christianity and Islam) have been profoundly anthropologically shaped at defining moments in their history does not bind them or prevent them from changing in the future. Indeed, so far as this embodies practice of the good, whatever has happened so far is of vital interest and information, but the true task is to discern God's calling now.

The presiding priest

So how does this relate to holding in tension the *episkope* that is the presiding role of the parish priest with the common wisdom of the people, the faith and responsibility of all? In Chapter 3, I carefully noted the particular kind of ordering that evolves from contemplating the Father as cause of the trinitarian persons, equal and forming one another. Zizioulas, with reference to the Cappadocian Fathers' understanding of personhood, developed the concept of all personal relations as ontologically asymmetrical, 'since persons are never self-existent but in some sense 'caused' by another who gives us our identity, who is ontologically 'prior' and in a sense 'greater' than the recipient. If we place in tension with Zizioulas' insight the work of reformed theologian Miroslav Volf, we recover the provisional and relational character of the Church and its forms of organization.

Volf's perception of the charismatic nature of church and ministry seems especially relevant to wrestling with how to understand *episkope* within the body of the Church. The notion of difference in *communion* provides a way of conceiving how one may be responsible for the local church's flourishing in a way that promotes community living that is inherently reciprocal in character, recognizing the differences in gifting and scope of various callings. Volf argues:

1 First, that it is Christ who acts through the gifts of all disciples, so that God's grace is enacted through the Spirit in each reciprocal act of ministry.
2 Second, that although some individuals respond to the call to ministry and many remain passive, nevertheless the Church together is responsible (*episkope*) for its work. Within common responsibility lies mutual subordination in obedience to Christ.
3 Third, that all gifts and forms of service create community that is interdependent and mutual. Office holders and the whole church are held together so that each one in their own gifts is a

representative of Christ. So at some point every participant *both* acts and receives ministry within the life of Christ.

4 Fourth, that gifts of the Spirit do not occur simply within the individual but through the interaction of their distinctive gifts and abilities and the circumstances of their common life in given situations.

5 Finally, that gifts of the Spirit are just that. Within the dynamic of ecclesial life they may not be given to someone for a lifetime, some may be more prominent than others and some may be given several at once.[17]

Dismal images of hierarchies that impose regimes through violence of various kinds seem very far removed from the mutual love of the Trinity and rightly receive negative reactions today. We have previously noted that the particular sociality or *koinonia* that is God has not been allowed to make a great deal of difference to understandings of church.[18] 'Shared ministry' certainly means for many that no one is allowed to be in charge, and there are churches that allegedly manage their affairs on that basis. A visitor to such a gathering will quickly identify those who, in a power vacuum, just know they are in charge. There is a real danger when such persons are not the ones most caught up in the life of God, or in the disciplines of Jesus' self-giving love and the work of the Spirit. Experience shows that lack of clarity about the ways in which roles and authority – hopefully in proportion to faithfulness – are distributed inhibits and weakens the local church's energy and effectiveness.

In a truly ecclesially rooted understanding of ordained ministry, those called to particular office can never be conceived of apart from the church that is all that is locally visible of the one, holy, catholic and apostolic Church.[19] So, essentially, whatever else she may be, the parish priest is relationally one of the baptized disciples of Jesus Christ. Those who share ministry with the presiding priest are all primarily members of the missionary community that is the local church. There is a danger here of assuming that equality, predictability and sameness are keys to the church's authenticity. I am reacting against the burgeoning local ministry movement of the 1980s and 1990s which, though breaking new ground, was probably limited in this way. A common image portrayed identical androgynous figures holding hands and dancing in a ring of bourgeois delight. Some more recent careless descriptions of the predictable and perfectly ordered round dance of trinitarian *perichoresis*, as a model for church, also miss the mark. The untidy, angular and liminal ecclesiology that does justice to a trinitarian concept of God recognizes otherness and difference in relation as pivotal to church ordering.

There is an incipient misunderstanding to be confronted that polarizes the issue: either the priest is so much in charge that all other ministries become fixed in a hierarchical and immature dependency relationship; or the priest has no more authority or power than anyone else, and so is limited to exercising cultic and 'spiritual' roles. How can these extremes be avoided? Parish priests certainly need a theological concept that allows for the holding of all disciples and ministries in mutual respect. They vary immensely from one another and in scope and power, depending on the *charismata* of the office holder. But also within an eschatological *communion* there is a distinctive, though always related, place for one to be first among equals. This *episkope* role has to be characterized by the kenotic, self-giving love of Christ.[20]

As the word 'hierarchy' has such a dark history among us, I would prefer to put it to rest for a while, in favour maybe of the word 'ordering'. Trinitarian eschatological ordering exists in the relating of giver and receiver. The generation of otherness arises from the particular form of giving and receiving that God has placed at the heart of reality and therefore of the Church. Trinitarian life is performed when, as one preaches, another hears or one baptizes and another is baptized. Giving and receiving also occurs when one believes in another enough to spend time patiently summoning them to become the person God invites and graces them to be.

Relational priesthood

The debate continues as to whether ordination is purely functional or has an ontological character. Some churches rigorously allocate no permanent roles to their ministers and so the relationships of giving and receiving, though asymmetrical, are purely provisional and functional. In a trinitarian ecclesiology there is a strong argument that the ordering of ministries is more than a haphazard pragmatism. A relational ontology, rather than one of substance, will place the parish priest within the *communion* of all.[21] So, paradoxically, although the practice of priesthood can be a lonely experience, the ordained life is never one possessed privately by the individual to be dispensed at will.[22] Humanly speaking, the preparations for and celebration of an ordination and subsequent anniversaries reveal a natural excitement that focuses on the challenge and privilege given to the individual. But this has to be held within the complexity of ministry, as both given and received, within *communion*.

Detached from the neoplatonic and the substantist approaches to ordination inherited from the nineteenth century, a deliberately trinitarian ordering distances itself from rigid pyramidical structures, even the inverted ones, popular in recent studies of ministry.[23] The parish priest as *episkope*, rather than being the central focus of the parish's ministry, is a lively stimulus for the building up of the whole body.[24] The Church's ordering images the *perichoretic* reciprocal movement between Father, Son and Spirit. Such a relational community, characterized and constituted in open vulnerable self-giving, will be the Church of the Poor. It will not merely reach out to the poor ones but recognize each person, indiscriminately, as both giver and receiver at different moments as a fresh sign of who God is.[25]

Together with their fellow Christians, the parish priest, always in personal relation with their local community, is called, and in different ways commissioned, to share in bringing about the wholeness and reconciliation that God wills now and in the future.[26] There is tough thinking required surrounding the question of how the Church simultaneously affirms the ministry of all the participants in the local church and at the same time recognizes the specifically essential work of the priest. A dichotomy between ontological and functional is unproductive. *Communion* is the qualifying term for both function and ontology. Gathered by the priest, in the Eucharist the church receives the gifts, 'the bread from heaven', from the Father (John 6.32). As the priest is given by God, the bishop and the people, so he stands as presider at the Eucharistic assembly. The mutuality of this dynamic makes it impossible to interpret this ordering with an overlay of legalism, or sexist or patronizing attitudes. Rather, what is happening here is regeneration and rebirthing as the Eucharistic event recapitulates the life of God in ever new moments of the community's journey. As Jesus standing in the Jordan is recognized as God's beloved, so the participants at the Eucharist are birthed again as daughters and sons of the Father.

In an eschatological–trinitarian ecclesiology, bishop, priests, deacons, readers and laity, in many forms of ministry, enhance one another in a constant movement of mutual expectation and self-giving.[27] Trinitarian uniqueness-in-relationship potentially avoids stolid dualisms and adversarial arguments about clerical superiority. What emerges – and rings true for my own experience over almost 40 years of ordained ministry – is that carrying out functions in the kind of relationships we have been considering inevitably has its impact on the person. This is true of all tasks performed in a creative environment. Observation tells us that office holders who have the calling and potential giftedness to fulfil a role, once appointed to it grow through grace and experience deeper and deeper into that role. This is true of churchwardens, youth leaders, teachers of the faith, those who offer a ministry of welcome, as well as readers, deacons, priests and bishops.

In summary, letting go of monist-inspired ecclesiologies, we regard each member of the church, whatever their particular ministry, as part of one another as disciples of Jesus Christ. The parish priest has no existence except in relationship with fellow members of the baptized community; their own unique contribution is created and sustained within relationships of mutuality with their fellow ordained ministers. Eucharist and worship, generally, is more than a random and occasional assembly of individuals for celebration and learning. The Eucharist is like being immersed in the Jordan and 'in Jesus' and through the Spirit, hearing our names also called as 'beloved' sons and daughters. In worship we become formed in the permanent giving and receiving that is the trinitarian ordering.[28] In a trinitarian church, order is not imposed by one all-powerful force. In an eschatologically ordered church, hope and salvation for all are intrinsic to the agenda. Any church that introduces permanent states of above and below, important and not important, as if some always are givers and some always receivers, has not sufficiently considered the mystery of the Trinity.

Episkope: the navigating task

As I have argued, parish priests are nothing in themselves apart from the call of God, the bishop and the community, and possess nothing for themselves alone. The parish priest certainly does not provide a church for the laity to belong to. The interaction of the collaborative ministries of the whole Church provides a graced vehicle by which the reconciling and costly work of Christ, in and through the Father and the Spirit, is made available to the world.

What language will best enable parish priests to understand about being both a member and being in charge? There is so much to be learnt about giving impetus to the releasing of the gifts of the whole *laos* and the sharing of authority in a dialogical way. This is the greatest issue to be faced about the future of collaborative ministry.

I have explored at some length the various intra-trinitarian approaches that move away from linear hierarchies. I have shown that a social trinitarian understanding of God means we live only as beings *in relation.* It is impossible to understand the truth entailed in addressing God as 'father' without the truth that this divine person is identified as 'father of the Son'.[29] The understanding of God as a *communion* of personal and diverse relations, in which none is ever in a permanently dominating or dominated role, offers a vision for priests to be 'in charge' without becoming merely separate or superior. But the frequently painful, practical experience when such relating becomes distorted is a reminder of how much more we still have to learn.

It can be considered perhaps as an unwritten mandate between priest and people. The priest is saying that the people must not forget that she is essentially one of *the laos*, a Christian like themselves, by baptism. Thankfully the people respond that they are glad this is her primary self-understanding, but in fact they are asking her for the time being (in harmony with the will of God and the bishop) to be *episkopos*, the one who persuasively draws together and holds the values of their community. The profound mutuality within difference in all Christian ministry is nowhere more clearly expressed than in the liturgical response to the blessing, 'The Lord be with you', as the people energetically respond, 'And also with you', or in the dialogue in preaching when the speaking and hearing are both essential and mutually generative. The preacher must first hear the life of the people before responding with commissioned, authoritative public speech; also the people in their own hearing of the words spoken are seeking and calling for something new to occur. The positive place given to the deacon in liturgy also lifts up the trinitarian understanding of God, mission and ministry. Bishop, laity, priest, deacon, reader, publicly and creatively showing the mutuality of charisms, makes a subversive counterstatement to inherited ecclesiological theories.

In *Transforming Priesthood* and *Practising Community* I explored the roles and qualities of the parish priest as one who '*presides*' through the threefold processes of discernment, blessing and witnessing. I shall revisit and revise this cluster of metaphors now, in the light of the theory of church developed in Chapter 3 and my own recent experience as parish priest. The tests of the appropriateness and durability of metaphors for the ordained must include their simplicity, accessibility, clear description of both role and activity, and inherent relationality.

The call to any ministry is always two-way. No one has an authentic calling to which the Church has not summoned them, often against their better judgement, because in that role they are competent, trustworthy and credible. Equally no one is entirely free to construct the nature of a calling. The Church in different times and situations has need of different tasks to be fulfilled and the freedom to call those most suitable. So a nostalgic memory of what once was 'truly' priesthood in the Church cannot be foisted onto the Church in a new era by any who simply choose to ignore the *sensus fidelium*, the emerging mind of all the baptized. When huge paradigm shifts are occurring in turbulent times, a test of trinitarian generosity must be the extent to which all, clergy and laity, may continue to find a place within a Church unified in diversity. However, unity needs to be held firmly in balance with the involvement of the whole *laos* in speaking and listening within the flux of conversation on: the sustainable and appropriate mission of the Church here and now; contemporary limitations in communicating the gospel; and how to use wisely limited resources of people, education, buildings and finance. No one can claim to be 'ordered' as deacon, priest, laity or bishop, unless they are displaying an intense desire to engage with synodical and ecumenical processes by which the *episkope* of the whole Church is constantly rediscovered in ever new times and situations.

However, this has to be held in proper tension with the Church's need to include in vocational discernment processes those who can speak prophetically from various 'places' within the body of the Church.[30] Penny Jamieson identifies that precisely when women in particular, but not exclusively, present themselves as priests in ways that will be likely to gain most acceptance within the culture of domination, then Christian identity, as a hallmark of vocation, may be diminished. Parish priests have the demanding and often punishing task of showing the world gospel values, sometimes therefore not bringing peace but a sword.[31]

The theory of church that I articulated in Chapter 3 requires the presiding *episkope* ministry to be a stimulus for deepening the Church as a community formed out of intense engagement with the triune God, constantly reaching out further into the whole of the life of creation, bridge-building so that many who are different are held together in mutual respect, in order that they and the world may be transfigured by Christ. Revisiting *Transforming Priesthood's* discussion of the presiding ministry, a decade and half later, I shall now draw out theologically the task of *episkope* for the local church under the overall notion of navigation.

Discerning

In the context of a range of human disciplines

The term 'navigator' features strongly in contemporary debates on economic management strategies. In a complex and bewildering environment, software programmes, databases, search engines, editorial teams and small businesses have dramatically contributed to recent fundamental power-shifts and how to reflect on them. In *Blown to Bits*, Evans and Wurster describe navigators as 'critical de-constructors of previous hierarchical chains of supply and demand'.[32] Before the present constantly expanding explosion of interconnectivity we associate with the worldwide web, the delivery of information assumed expensive links between 'rich information' and its physical carrier to many people.

> The traditional link – between the medium and the message, between the flow of product-related information and the product itself, between the informational chain and the physical value chain, between the economics of information and the economics of things – is broken.[33]

Notice the parallel here with our earlier discussion of the role of priests in a Church where living in the intensity or richness of God's life is one of the four key elements. Evans and Wurster describe how, replacing expensive providers of 'richness' for a limited few, navigators can cheaply enable the diverse flow of 'information', a word used to describe what businesses are in the market to sell, across extensive fields of communication. Navigators provide welcome strategies for others to access rich resources, to reach out to many contacts, build networks, and are then potentially agents of the transformation of network-based business. Those businesses that continue to rely on expensive hierarchical chains for communicating 'information' are deeply vulnerable to deconstruction, whereas the navigator within the new economics of information can potentially release tremendous energy and value for many.[34] Again the echoes for the often-failing and expensive running of a diocese, based on hierarchies of clergy as providers of 'information', are clear.

As I mentioned at the start, visits to Australia and New Zealand in recent years awakened my long fascination with the extraordinary voyages of settlers from the Polynesian islands as well as expeditions from Britain. What connected for me in reflecting on new possibilities for parish priests as navigators was the daring and resilience of those early travellers. They navigated with just an intuition that they knew where they would find their goal, with internalized 'maps' of the interrelationship and distances between islands and land masses, constantly taking back bearings from landmarks and watching the prevailing winds and swells, land clouds, the flight paths of land-roosting birds, the direction of the wind, debris floating on the waves and the varying colours and depths of the ocean. The role of 'redeye' the navigator, on watch many hours out of every 24 to keep a sense of position, was definitive and could never be abandoned, but was never in isolation. No metaphor says it all, and I can see how the last sentence could easily be seen to justify the overwork to which many church leaders have become attached as essential to the role. I believe the overall concept of the navigator still makes a powerful contribution to the discussion on the work of parish priests today:

> Voyages of exploration were often sailed upwind or using wind shifts, allowing a safe and rapid downward journey home. In unfamiliar waters, a skilled navigator could recognize and name new swells by studying the sea hour after hour, and the star-path (or succession of guiding stars), the wind and current patterns and numerous other items of navigational information were memorized for the return voyage. During such expeditions the navigator slept as little as possible, ceaselessly scanning the sea and the night sky and keeping watch for land clouds and homing birds. It was said that you could always recognize a star navigator by his bloodshot eyes.[35]

The navigator's vital skill and commitment gave the crew essential information and confidence for their survival and success. Equally, he was dependent on those who collected food, cooked, made decisions about the direction and speed of travel, attended to discipline or maintained the ship's fabric. I suggest there is an imaginative connection here for describing the public ministry of the parish priest that evokes wisdom and promotes the idea of purposeful, reciprocal *communion*.

There is evidence of this concept being widely explored. Len Sweet, Professor of Evangelism, training leaders for a postmodern culture, is President of Spiritual Venture Ministries and a prolific writer and lecturer. In *AquaChurch*, 2008, he writes of leaders 'piloting' churches in a fluid culture. He describes the traits of leaders (as arts, not techniques) who know that maps can be unreliable and that true places do not appear on maps. Being anchored in Christ (Heb. 6.18–19) is not about being safely moored in harbour but deliberately running into the storm. He describes the navigational arts of the church leader as: orienting by the North Star, studying our compass and feeling the wet finger in the air. Sweet focuses on the role of the pilot as one who takes risks in an entrepreneurial lonely style, but the book contains a section called 'the captain's logbook', which bears testimony to his willingness to enter into personal dialogue to facilitate collaborations and teamwork.

A parallel concept is that of 'executive function' described from a multiple-intelligences perspective and currently being debated vigorously among educationalists. Expecting students to take responsibility for their own learning, and regarding leaders as learning facilitators, requires the sophisticated navigation of varied types of information. In performing everyday tasks we all exercise 'executive function', 'the mental process of planning and organizing flexible, strategic, appropriate actions'.[36] Executive function is a way of describing the way someone contextualizes future plans in the light of past knowledge and experience, triggers in the present situation, expectations for the future, and relevant values and purposes. The keys to this intuitive approach are a sense of alertness, agency, flexibility and coherence.

People vary greatly in their ability to integrate in a complex way the establishment of a clear aim, the necessary abilities and techniques and the volition to start and the resilience to continue until the goal has been attained. As intrapersonal intelligence varies among people, some have a searchlight ability to hold in balance a range of information of varying kinds, while the creativity of others is composed by a laser profile composed of just one or two sources of intelligence. Inevitably parish clergy will vary in their development of executive function, but they do have the opportunity through the contribution of others to ensure that the local church is enriched through its corporate capacity to navigate a constantly new situation and innovative tasks through God's gift and invitation.[37]

Or again, in discussions of medical professionalism and changes for general practice, the evolving role of the GP has some parallels with that of the parish priest. Doctors have gradually relinquished the notion of 24-hour, 365-days-a-year responsibility, and the relationship with patients that implied has shifted as a consequence. Teams, specialist roles and health centres are all indications of this. Many parish priests remain ambivalent in this regard. But the invitation of this study is for parish priests to have more of a sense of *episkope* for the development and mission of churches, than one of a largely individual priest-parishioner pastoral model. It would not fully do justice to the communitarian approach to church and priesthood simply to liken the relationship between patients and doctors with parishioners and clergy, but the resonances are worth noting. In particular, I refer to the remarkable suggestion in 1968 by Cardinal Heenan, Roman Catholic Archbishop of Westminster, that the medical profession are 'the new clergy, you – and especially the general practitioners amongst you – are the modern priests'.[38]

Significantly for the concept of navigation, Sean Hilton, Vice-Principal at St George's teaching hospital, University of London, and a GP in Kingston upon Thames, suggests that professionals no longer have what it is perhaps assumed clergy claim, namely 'moral, sapiential, and charismatic authority as of right'.[39] Quoting Palmer's *The Courage to Teach*, he emphasizes that the GP's identity and character evolves from interaction with the patient:

> When we are willing to abandon our self-protective autonomy and make ourselves as dependent on our students (patients) as they are on us, we move closer to the interdependence that the community of truth requires.[40]

Hilton quotes Palmer's discussion-starter, 'When I am teaching at my best I am like a . . .', suggesting that his own metaphor is that of sheepdog, 'maintaining a space, protecting the sheep, guarding the boundaries, and moving them on when ready'. Alternatively, Hilton describes himself with patients as 'a mountain guide, patient and not too ego-driven'.[41] The navigating GP, albeit mostly working one-to-one with patients, has some powerful connections with the navigating role of the parish priest, who as proto-bishop in humility communicates well, is interested in my climbing, my goals, advising me expertly, judging difficult circumstances in ways I can trust, and being 'prepared to go out on a limb for me'.[42]

Exercising right judgement

A parish priest has to know her navigational role within the web and field of the local and wider church. She has to know that this is her unique place, rather than some other place, and that if she fails to fill it, the community is at a loss. As Penny Jamieson said of herself, 'I am never not the bishop', concluding that the power this gave her was to hold the community to searching 'their own hearts for the will of God and for the strength and courage to speak that will, and to follow it as it emerges in the process'.[43] The deep implication is that although the priest is deeply involved in discerning and communicating the vision, the direction and flow of the community's journey can never be just in the hands of one person.[44]

Personal freedom in church ordering is voluntarily related to the body of Christ, the Church and to the triune God. An essential part of remaining ordered is to be not only a liturgical functionary but to be authentically a witness to gospel values and to promote right judgement of the local church. This being held in an ecclesial framework is true for all baptized Christians whether or not they are aware of it. It is true for the ordained because they have accepted a call to be part of the networks of mutual respect and the committed following of the gospel and to help others discern that path also. This needs to go further than a personal relating to God through spiritual practices. In today's developed societies, the Church that God needs must be able to confront the poverty of an individualist and superficial culture. The world needs the Good News that each person's life is of infinite value and that churches have the capacity, through God's Spirit, of assisting us to discover our core identity as God's beloved, called to share in Jesus' own character and work. Communally and personally, the call to be ordered by Jesus and the Spirit must involve whatever tough maturing and integration, welcoming and integrating of our weakness remains to be done, both in ourselves and in the other. For many this may be a greater recognition of their true power rather than a phoney pretence at obedience to institutional regulations and to damaging patterns of leadership (see Matthew 5.3–9).

Self-awareness

If the local church is to be maintained in wisdom or right judgement, the discernment work of the parish priest (and the extended *episkope* in the team) will be constant. For the priest to be more than a guardian of traditional conventions she will need to be personally committed to ways of growing in maturity as well as stimulating this in others. Personal and relational authority are essential characteristics, and in working for the Kingdom can only exist as a matter of giving and receiving. The first of the strands in our theory of church insists that spiritual and relational identity, learnt through closeness to God, is a pivotal focus in renewing the Church.

Part of the effectiveness and role of the parish priest comes through serving as a catalyst in helping people encounter the holiness of God in the fine detail and confusion of everyday church life.[45]

There have been centuries of collusion that looked to the priest as the fount of all wisdom and as somehow closer to God than the rest of the church – even though reality never really bore this out. While the mystique of a holy clerical elite who are observably remote and 'spiritual' on behalf of others may for some be re-assuring, it is an inadequate portrayal of priesthood. Those selected for ordination certainly need to be drawn from those with an observably deepening personal relationship with God and who are unostentatious in this practice. But the expectation that holiness somehow excuses incompetence in other aspects of work directly impedes the development of the *episkope* function. An essential part of the mutuality of the ordained will be deliberately to make space for their own growth in self-awareness and to allow for the vulner-ability of listening to feedback and being influenced by the percep-tions of others.[46] *Episkope* will require a personal effectiveness in those called to priesthood as builders and guides of the spiritual maturity of the local church itself.

A life-long learning approach that integrates initial and con-tinuing training and in which clergy, readers and laity – not to mention local ministry teams – frequently learn together, is already fostering a church culture very different from the days of semi-monastic theological colleges as the place of formation for 'the' ministry. This is not to set up a polarization here between past and present. There were immensely valuable fruits in previous patterns of training for priesthood but, in those forms, they cannot serve individuals, families, churches or neighbourhoods now. In a new environment, when many recognize different expectations in them-selves, the Church needs other agendas. In short, because some parts of the picture have changed, everything has to be worked out afresh.

This process will not take place by chance and not with every-one's approval. In practice there are ordinands and indeed educa-tors whose own clerical role models – which triggered their sense of vocation – are looking to fulfil traditional expectations of self-sacrificial solo ministry.[47] Transitions take many decades, and other priorities will come well before one transition is complete. How-ever, the present need is to move from a notion of the parish priest shaped predominantly by a high Christology to one that includes the work of the Spirit. An eschatological–trinitarian ecclesiology and view of all priesthood will require dioceses to make deliberate and aligned choices about vision and policies that favour mutual respect and the imperatives of the gospel. The impact of the discernment of the ordained is very publicly in view through our choices of behaviour, language and the shaping of relationships.

Social and historical context

A Church committed to being a sign and foretaste of God's passionate desire for creation will need to have its eyes and ears open to discern the nature of the place in which it is set. Since the 1970s, contextualization has increasingly become a key to a theology of Mission.[48] It is one of the most frequently expressed ideas in discussions about mission today that there has to be listening attentiveness to a particular situation before any community or person may presume to formulate plans for the Kingdom. There are churches that by design or accident live in isolation from their locality – on grounds of purity of doctrine, lack of confidence or of resources.

The local church must ensure that somehow or other, steps are taken so that it knows in detail the concerns and aspirations of the neighbourhood and is recognized as sharing and serving the concerns of local people. This attitude of companionship may be fostered through those members of the church who have time, energy, local knowledge and the ability to know where to ask appropriate questions. Statistics about levels of deprivation are available through local authorities, and a basic understanding of local demography is a necessary tool for any church sharing in God's mission for human wholeness.

Parish priests (and colleagues) also need the insight and courage to recognize and confront tendencies in the local church towards aims that are probably not Spirit-led. Sometimes the priest himself (rarely without others) will be led to say, 'Wait, let's examine whether this really is God's will for us here.' It is the parish priest's responsibility to build up the whole church's desire and skill in examining the effects of its policies and strategies and response to its findings. A severe test of her presiding gift comes when the parish priest is required to enable the church to wrestle with conflict and make a decision that will inevitably leave some members feeling angry or powerless. A maturing church will be struggling to share responsibility, including both the pain and the pleasure, for the evolving of the missionary task and of the internal relatedness of the local church. This is the corporate *episkope* we discussed earlier, of which the parish priest is a notable agent and mouthpiece, but not in isolation.

Awareness of the Zeitgeist

Navigating God's desire for the relationships, business and future of the Church requires God's guidance and vitality. To know this is no simple matter, requiring structured time for prayer and reflection. Parish priests need to acquire the skills of adult educators and to be ourselves regularly engaging in appropriate disciplined study. Not all clergy will pursue biblical interpretation or theological understanding – though many more should than probably do (theology everywhere and in everything – in reflection on a street full of people or on the day that is past; in the study of music, poetry, drama, history, politics, psychology, science and mathematics). Models from further education could often be more helpful to some than from the world of higher education. The presiding priest needs to make systematic space for study, along with time for family, for friends, for self – in short for being human. If God is allowed constantly to reframe priests in knowing who they are before him as a person, the rest will fall into place.

In the understanding of church in this study there is a need for discernment to be more than on an individual basis. How does the navigator assist the body of the community to know its way and to follow it? It is not the task of the parish priest to take many decisions but to create a healthy environment in which those who have a growing faith, who walk with God and have an awareness of the leading issues, can use their skills appropriately (hearing and articulating the common wisdom of the people). The priest cannot simply opt out of areas in which he or she has no expertise, such as administration or finance, as though God were not concerned or involved with such trivia. The task is to check what intellectual, spiritual and emotional resources the local church (probably networking in a deanery or ecumenically) needs in order to keep up its energy-flow in consultative policy-making, planning liturgy, preaching, teaching, caring for the needy and evangelism.[49]

The parish priest, as the bridge between the local and the catholic Church worldwide, must be the navigator, ensuring that there are open channels to keep the local church in partnership with the movement of the Spirit in sister churches. A result of such developments will be that the reflective practitioner in ministry will enable the whole community to relate their daily responsibilities and hopes to the Word of God, the Eucharist and to *communion* with God in many kinds of prayer and concern for social action. The often inarticulate but ground-bass theology of the laity needs to be brought out into the open, put into words and symbols and put to use as a vital resource.

The perennial question of how far the parish priest should expect to promote his own ideas and how far to listen to other viewpoints in matters of strategy is strongly related to the faithfulness of the church and his own developing spiritual and intellectual quest. The corporate decisions and holistic agenda of a Eucharistic community should be made out of the reflection and prayer of a local church that is prepared to give sufficient time to arriving at a consensus, so that neither the priest nor a nostalgia lobby within the church seeks to introduce a dominating authority by which to impose their views.

Prayer and worship that embrace diversity

The Eucharist is the Church's crucible of learning for the growth of all in Christian maturity, so as to be journeying into the full *communion* with God's life that is our baptismal birthright. In *Self and Salvation*, David Ford uncovers some of the benefits of this Eucharistic way of living. Ford, in parallel with Samuel Wells and Stanley Hauerwas, offers life-changing drama as a primary model for considering the Eucharistic event. In the performance of the text of faith and the Pentecostal improvisation of word, preaching, intercession, reconciliation, peace, taking, offering, breaking and sharing bread and wine, reflecting and being sent out, the local church especially learns to be its true self. The ways in which the Eucharist is celebrated as an event – the space, the furnishings, the human postures, the relationships, the voices, the vesture, the hopes and failings expressed – articulates that local church's mission. Every new Eucharistic moment is a fresh outpouring of God's superabundant blessing.[50] Imaginative improvisations of poetry, drama, music and colour can make real the Spirit's activity in different contexts, giving the Eucharist a 'superabundance of meaning'.[51] Paul refers to this as discerning the body. The church's habits of prayers, Scripture-reading and life together, characteristically but not exclusively in the Eucharist, enable it to reveal and act out that peace that is God's final choice for the cosmos.

A core of the identity of the parish priest is increasingly to be supporting others in planning for and leading liturgies that will draw people further into the mystery of God's life, into deeper friendship with each other. It will give them a place to ponder together the complex and often broken relatedness of human existence in the light of God's saving love. One of the imperatives is to struggle to hold in uneasy tension the closeness and immediacy of God's life among us with the mystery and unknowability. Effective management and awareness of power dynamics must not lose sight of the utter mystery of the sacramental life of the Christian that it is particularly the priest's task to foster and open up. This is illustrated especially well for me in R. S. Thomas' poem, 'Hill Christmas'.[52]

Hiding anonymously behind the formalities of clerical role hinders the development of eschatological companionship. Authentic and vulnerable church instead offers space for attempts at the fullest integration of people. An important contribution by the parish priest will be honesty about her partly redeemed and partly unrealized communication with God. Rather than being just a professional minister towards the rest of the church, she must be recognized as growing in her journey of salvation and to be learning how, simultaneously, to be a member of the community, receiving and giving as disciple, spouse, parent and citizen.

Women clergy are often to be found helping all the ordained to re-evaluate the pervasive metaphor of self-sacrifice that dominated expectations of priesthood during much of the twentieth century. They demonstrate the negative effects of self-sacrifice and self-denial. Women are daring to remind the whole Church of the damage inflicted by allowing a culture that encourages anyone to lose touch with their own needs to experience a loss of self-esteem and the absence of a voice in the community. Some have written of their experience of a reservoir of bitterness and anger building up in women when self-sacrifice leads to overfunctioning on behalf of others and underfunctioning on behalf of themselves. Above all, an overemphasis on the self-sacrifice of the clergy, whether male or female, undermines genuine intimacy and mutuality in the local church. At worst it can lead to relationships of exploitation and domination, portraying nothing of the triune God of mutual relations.[53]

How do we develop a Church that does not exclude others on account of their gender? Self-development and self-awareness may be the most important ways of learning, so that we know as far as possible the effect we are having on people and situations – not patronizingly, assuming the right to talk while others listen, or to overrun the boundaries of people with no apology. We should end the myth that church or ministry is already all that it should or could be. A growing-up Church can acknowledge that and, as a consequence, see its place in the world more sharply.

In a church community focused on mission, the presiding priest will have a care for many issues great and small, and will somehow have a feel for the entire enterprise – that is central to her being there and is at the heart of the task. At the same time, the role involves an awareness and concern for the development of the church's outreach, internal developing as well as concern for people. There is a parallel with the trinitarian relatedness that is God. It is not in any one particular, but in the sum of them all, in their variety and mutual interrelatedness, that the heart of presiding rests. The parish priest – and all others in the ministry team – contributes to the navigating task of standing at the crossroads at the heart of the mission and Eucharist of the people of God. The parish priest, with others, needs to ensure that the Eucharist (and other worship) can speak truly to many differing occasions and groups of people. The possible improvisations are endless, but not without boundaries.

Part of the discerning ministry is to have a sufficient awareness of the Christian tradition of theology, spirituality, liturgy and practice to be able to assist the community in bringing it into play with the other factors of context and mission. Only those who have been utterly immersed in the tradition can keep it growing, imaginative, ever fertile with new awakenings. Part of the ideal of former generations was to ensure stability through perpetuating sameness. Every worship occasion employed the repetition of identical words, gestures and mood, with the priest deliberately effacing himself. The manuals and liturgical text books emphasized the importance of the repetition of the familiar.

It seems more appropriate in a postmodern era that worship should be the same and yet different every time. The metaphor of a jazz performance may be helpful, though disturbing to many.[54] Every performance even of the same text will be new and different. To discern the limits of improvisation requires intuitive experience, and presiding at the Eucharist is not a matter for occasional duty. To deal with the heightening of emotion in worship requires all the maturity a priest can muster – and always in relation to other trusted church leaders to avoid self-delusion.

Blessing

Growing the whole Church in mediating God's love

Inherited notions of a parish priest imply a single direction of flow, so that one brings blessings, goodness, holiness and another receives. If the faith we practise is inherently relational, holiness is conferred on all. If the pursuit of holiness, planning of worship, leading of prayer groups, leading of pastoral teams and following Jesus' self-giving way with full commitment has become the field that includes all the baptized, what are clergy to be or do? Although the Church and the clergy may be privileged agencies of God's saving work, God mediates salvation to all through every conceivable avenue.[55] How then can the worship and life of the local church support, critique and resource society as if purveying a 'holy trust'?[56]

To nourish the framework and networks of families, friendships, society and international justice, peace and stability, churches, through the mediation of the *episkope* of clergy and laity together, must expect to be suffused by God's triune life.[57] *Episkope* in a *koinonia* church will mean that the whole community, in its complementary callings, learns to mediate God's intensive holiness among as much of creation as possible.

This is especially focused when, drawn together and led by the priest with others in Eucharist, the whole community offers itself to God without protection.[58] Risking everything, we draw out genuine relationships of intimacy with other worshippers, we allow God to refine our attitudes and behaviour and to heal our brokenness, and we choose to be a community that enacts the holiness of God, together, and seeks to promote God's refining work in the world. The mediating, presiding priest is to be a primary agency for this development of the whole *laos*, including him- or herself.

Encouraging and modelling the fullness of life that comes through blessing God's name and loving the God of unlimited love must be a priority for the entire congregation, facilitated by the ordained with others. As, late in the proceedings, Jesus gave to a wedding feast absurd quantities of good wine, the mediator encourages all to expect to grow through the expectation and blessing of God in all creation. The response God invites requires all our capacities, including our intellect, to create a church that embodies the *communion* wisdom of God. The church is the place where we have conversations to learn to cross a threshold of consciousness or make a leap to a new state of being. In the Eucharist, the heart of the church's life, we enjoy God's intense hospitality. People are gifted because of God's nurturing and reconciling presence.

In the Eucharist, we learn how to live in ways that are interconnected, a drawing out of the being-in-relation that is God's life. African Christians in particular show how living in God's blessing is both a match for every act of violence against humanity and the most authentic witness to the world. When thousands have died of disease, when the rains have not come or when faced with genocide, their subversive acts of joyful celebration point others to their eschatological vision of a God who is present, acts and will act, so that one day all will find their peace in him.

None of this is dependent on the parish priest in the capacity of intermediary. Rather, just as the whole baptized church is concerned to know and be a blessing in the context of God's desire for creation, the parish priest is to be a sign of God's eschatological blessing running through every aspect of the church's life. The Eucharist transforms the baptized community – through word, sacrament and relationships of loving intention – into its truest self by fulfilling what God promises by inviting disciples to be 'in Christ'. The parish priest has a particular role in enabling the liturgical performance of sacramental acts that are in truth and reality blessings. Through the Spirit, and within the body of the church, they make real what they intend: baptism, Eucharist or reconciliation. In the Eucharistic assembly and in worship, preaching, prayer and study, the triune God is blessed.

There are also para-sacramental blessings, such as might be given to children by their parents, and by children to their parents or mutually between friends, spouses or partners; there are many healing and intercession ministries; and there are pastoral, evangelical and serving ministries, which for the Eucharistic community are known as blessings from God. Mutual blessings come between God and his people when there is work undertaken for wholeness in the created order. All blessings now are a promise of that final state of blessedness, when all things come together in Christ to be given, through the Spirit, into the hands of the Father.

Blessing is mutual affirmation, made possible through the *communion* we have within the life of the Trinity. In a frightening and scarred world it is one of the most significant gifts the church can offer. To reassure people of their goodness and potential begins the process of creating the reality of their maturity – it is to set their feet on the path of their eschatological destiny. A blessing touches the original intensive goodness, of which Genesis speaks, and calls forth persons and communities to be true to their vocation. Once we know our blessedness, we can be free to reassure others of theirs.

Parish priest as mentor and coach

The parish priest's ministry of blessing requires the recognition of her primary task, not as being personally on the front line of mission all the time, but more humbly assisting others to recognize their own ministries and potential for growth. In this context she and those in the ministry team will be a resource: both as challenge and support. How can such a church come into being? There has to be a recognition of priorities with which people can align themselves so that the church can mediate God's holiness to the widest range of people and situations in society. All God's people need to be enabled to learn to practise the wisdom of Christ.

Forms of education therefore overtake traditional diocesan courses for the banking of more knowledge by the few. Instead, precious resources must be used to give skill and vision for the growth in learning of the many in the situations where they live and work. The priestly mediator will give careful attention to the distribution of tasks, not delegated as though from his own work but by discovering the tasks that are appropriate and sustainable locally and matching persons and gifts through recalling that the church exists as a purposeful and intensive engagement with the meaning of the gospel. The people so ordered need to be cared for, expected to grow in the knowledge and love of God, and have their tasks and allocated times regularly reviewed.

Teaching the congregation to exercise episkope

A church that identifies itself as difference-making *communion* will know about generosity and trust. The priest navigator will stimulate and resource the community in recognizing its own overall responsibility for the shape and quality of its ministry and mission. The navigator rescues the church from the politeness that prevents tough love and rigorous decision-making; he or she will also find ways for the community constantly to be reshaped as opposed to falling into chaos and trackless entropy. So no one, ordained or lay, is seen to be able to carry the whole of the church's meaning or work or responsibility. In an attitude of mutual care and trust, tasks are distributed according to gifts, and the infrastructure of the church redesigned accordingly.

This requires the parish priest to know and understand her office as the one who centrally, though with others authorized in some way by the community and not just personally chosen, knows the people and the strategy and can facilitate the community to 'carry out their work in Christ-mediated and Spirit-animated service of others, neither displacing others nor making decisions independently of a "reception process".'[59] As we explored in detail earlier, the local church and its president exercises its mission within the strategic organization and guidance of the bishop and synod. Their task is to create a safe and challenging ecology of catholicity within which the local church can flourish through navigating its character and purpose in the flux of any particular context.

The practice of faith

To navigate a church of this order requires faith and trust.

1 There is no true building of a reciprocal church on grounds of mere equality. Equally beloved by God, we serve in the church in complementary but diverse ways. Church, to be church, has to be exuberant with its chief resource, which is faith itself.[60] Navigating priests and communities serving the Father's will need only to be in Christ through the Spirit. Eucharist, Scripture, prayer, learning, community life must all aim at filling our minds and hearts with the love of God.

2 The true mediator learns to stop controlling people, and in peace allows room for Christ. This means letting his followers live in the freedom the Spirit brings. The navigating priest will not protect people from mistakes or danger but, having warned them of dangers and given them the horizons for their appointed tasks, with open hands lets them stand and walk. I know how personally challenging I myself find this. The dreadful adage 'It's quicker to do it yourself' is the reminder that 'it' cannot be done by yourself because Christian faith is inherently relational. The response of the church to God's invitation to mission is shot through with the love, energy and freedom that is the triune God. The challenge for the mediator is, 'Am I working in the power of the Spirit or am I fuelling my false self and massaging my ego?' The only one who can perfect the church is God in Christ, so all our strategies, portfolio measurements and good desires for mutual accountability need to respect the work of the Spirit, differently in each person and situation.

Witnessing

The parish priest's personal witness

For all that has been said about the relationship of priesthood to the whole Church, often the priest is expected to represent the faith of the Church that God is with us in all suffering and joy. Some weeks bring the urgent call to the hospice and the funerals, weddings and baptisms that are personally deeply demanding. Or the phone rings and a stranger who has taken your number from the notice board needs an urgent conversation. The presiding priest will be called on to represent the Church with intelligent, wise love and to be constantly treading boundaries. Deliberately we recall that the Church exists for the world's healing and not for itself. As the one who helps the local church navigate its context in faith and mediate Christ's love, alive and present in the world, she is also to be an authoritative representative of the Christ of Christmas and Easter, of Bethlehem and Golgotha.

In *Transforming Priesthood* and *Practising Community*, I defined the witnessing role in these terms: the parish priest is called personally to represent the local church to and from the wider Church, ecumenically.

1 The priest has the time, experience and privilege of relating to the wider Church, ecumenically, the insights and needs of the local church. This also works in reverse. Partly because of his itinerant ministry and partly because he reads and attends conferences and synods, he is able to bring back to the local church catholic insights from the wider Church for reflection and perhaps action. He relates personally, though not separated from lay representation, to diocese, bishop and the worldwide Church. There is a necessary aloneness, not loneliness, in this aspect of the task to embody the link, even though numerous laity will be part of deanery and diocesan and ecumenical networks and task groups.

2 The navigating priest has to be soaked sufficiently in God's love and wisdom to be able to embody and speak for the gospel in countless places. The parish priest is given reflective time to make apt connections between the texts and themes of Scripture, liturgy and tradition, and the lives of individuals and of the world community. This is a key part of the role and task – not just to be fitted in if there is time.

A witnessing community

Looking back now, I would want to affirm this but also double the expectation that the priest will usually make it a priority to assist the whole congregation to know with confidence its own ability and responsibility to be an honest and reliable signpost of that call to grow into a more mature humanity which, in the Spirit, the Father offers to all who look to his Son in faith and hope. There has been a long tradition of parish priests who, serving for many years in one place, have provided a still focus for a community, a person in touch with the Divine, to whom all may turn regardless of their formal relationship to Christian belief.[61] The parson-shaped hole in the neighbourhood may still exist in many places. However, increasingly her task will be to encourage and support others in understanding their vital role of mediating Christ in their own spheres of influence. For some laity this will involve attendance at synods and conferences, there to promote two-way processes of listening and speaking, the reciprocal communication that with the bishop is the exercise of *episkope*. It also involves witnessing to the community beyond the church and those on its fringes, as one of those who have been trained to reflect on God's presence and activity, on the great issues people face, of illness, suffering, dying and bereavement. There will be some for whom, by temperament or in given situations, the personal testimony of their lives and conversation will be a primary element in their vocation. Where the priest's own expertise may often need to come to bear is in representing the catholic to the local church. Firmly probing old assumptions and language, she asks whether the theological witness of the rest of the world Church supports or challenges accepted positions and whether the local church intends to remain independent.

Conclusion

This chapter has considered the role of the local parish priest and ministerial colleagues in terms of an extension of *episkope*. Relating specifically to the notion of presidency with the three interrelated concepts of discernment, blessing and witnessing, I have re-explored how the local church needs parish priests who know they are called to a ministry of navigation so that the whole Church can grow in the capacity to mediate and represent Christ. Anglican ecclesiology thrives on the cut and thrust of dialogue. We shall always require a cluster of metaphors to explore the stimulus required for developing a rich diversity of ministries within a Church that is a sign of the world's fulfilment.[62]

If the Church is itself 'like sparks among the stubble', an agency of God's visitation, parish priests are called to dedicate themselves to discovering how to be true to this vocation in each time and place. The eschatological company of the Church happens through the intensification of love of God, the extensification of knowledge of the world, the affinity of true *communion* to mediate the world's transformation. Such a church learns through a truly reciprocal navigational priesthood how itself to become more truly *episkope* for God's passionate desire.

5

Practising *episkope*

Traveller, there is no path.
Paths are made by walking.[1]

The work of Christian intellectuals is not done in the abstract, it is
effective participation in the world, and in the building up of the
Church. This is why we cannot act here simply in a free way; this is
not an intellectual gymnastic to which we are called; it is, above all,
in prayer and meditation that intellectuals will rediscover the sources
of an intelligent life rooted in the concrete.[2]

The priests the Church needs now   ·

So what does it look like on the ground when parish priests deliberately adopt an *episkope* emphasis in their role? I have explored
how a theology of church might be woven around the broad themes
of richness, range, contact and transformation. Further, I have discussed the urgent need for parish priests to live out an *episkope* in
the local church so that all the baptized may enter into their responsible callings. How far do these radical proposals for a *koinonia*
Church seeking the world's fulfilment have any chance of influenc-
ing practice within the historical, legal and sociological realities
of a contemporary institutional Church? Journalists frequently offer
statistics with dubious interpretations of the ailments and attendance of British Christian churches.[3] When the house church
movement is so clearly flourishing and older 'institutional' Churches
are struggling, there is neither sanity in attempting to maintain
the *status quo*, nor any point in advancing wholly unrealistic
expectations.

I have argued, from my own awareness of the Church's tradition and practice, for *episkope* as a metaphor for the work of the
whole Church, of which the *episkope* of bishop and parish priest
are a sacramental sign and effective stimulus. This is in no way to
diminish the diaconal and presbyteral aspects of church and the
orders that signify them. The driving motive of this study is to re-
store the balance when the mission of the local church needs priests

who ensure that the *episkope* role is active for the fulfilment of the Church's character and purpose.

In practice, what could this look like? In order to develop an eschatological community rooted in *communion*, what will be the content and character of the navigating *episkope* of the parish priest, with the others, ordained or commissioned to different and complementary ministries within the whole? Clearly there are human factors, issues of social context, the number of churches in a group, the level of co-operation between churches and the particular skills, experience and personalities of the clergy and team.

The history and paraphernalia of the Church of England's organization sits uneasily with the movement towards being an eschatological company characterized by the triune *communion*. Despite decades of collaborative rhetoric, the general assumption is still largely that the parish priest will decide policy and delegate some tasks to those with energy and spare time. In Chapter 2, I concluded from the diaries of those interviewed that there are many signs of an *episkope* ministry in which bishops and parish priests are already stimulating a Church rooted in *communion*. These I summarized as:

- beginning to value and learn from the experience of women in their struggle to be recognized and heard and to honour their different approaches to relating and speaking;
- continually being readdressed by Scripture and linking many aspects of its learning and performance to the liminal biblical journey of God's people;
- drawing deeply on God's gift in Eucharist and recognizing the celebration as a unique place of transformation for persons, communities and the world's life;
- recognizing itself and the teams within church community as held by God in times of personal growth, crisis, bereavement;
- promoting learning for its own sake as well as to support the burgeoning discipleship and ministries in congregations;
- letting prayer be the live current that, in connecting the church community with the triune God, releases resurrection energy for hope;
- attempting to be exemplary in accompanying local communities without expecting a return;
- accepting the opportunities of handling disagreement with maturity, so that radically different people and views can connect with respect and creative outcomes.

Evidence from a suburban parish

My own contemporary working context is a medium-sized congregation in a suburban parish. I shall conclude this study with a description and review of the possibilities of a navigator (*episkope*) approach to the work of the parish priest within this setting, in the hope that others will be able to make connections for their own situation. I want to note that the pitfalls of this kind of report are obvious if anything of value or authenticity is to emerge. There are a number of factors that give us gifts, challenges and opportunities.

1 I am well aware of the luxury of there being here a number of clergy, readers and imaginative and committed lay teams of various kinds, and an efficient and welcoming parish office.

2 However, as in every place, church practice is thoroughly embedded in its context. In the North East of England, churches, like voluntary groups, charities, local political groups as well as schools and hospitals, share in a deep resistance to 'ordinary' people finding a voice or taking a lead when there are professionals to hand on whom communities can be both dependent and also place the blame for institutional failure.

3 In comparison, say, to the *de novo*, deliberately egalitarian, practice of a Local Shared Ministry church, the default position of St Mary's, Monkseaton is benignly hierarchical, with a preference for stability. Given its history since the 1920s, shaped by successive robust incumbencies, within central Anglicanism, this is no surprise.

4 There is an expectation that people's views may be expressed and heard. At a recent meeting of some 40 of the lay people who in various ways provide leadership within the congregation, the facilitator enabled everyone to voice their views on how recent changes had been introduced, discussed, communicated and reviewed. In an atmosphere of prayer, laughter and a total absence of adversarial debate, a great honesty was expressed about the anxieties that change evokes. For example, concern was expressed about 'neglecting' the high altar when we worship in the nave, but also a deep sense that 'things will work out the way they should without bad feeling'.

5 There is an atmosphere of hope and expectation. In this congregation I see evidence of a growing recognition that an attitude about 'being church' that amounts to more than some tasks being 'delegated' from the clergy to the laity is essential and

even desirable. There is also the possibility of holding this in tension with being a church that serves the entire community and also supports the working lives and daily responsibilities of parishioners.

The cultural shift in which a growing number of people are openly glad to be involved at St Mary's would be both similar and different in a market town, scattered rural or inner city situation. I hope that in what follows I leave enough imaginative possibilities for presiding clergy with readers and lay team members working collaboratively to make connections with their own situation and work.

Owning my own agenda

As I have proposed repeatedly, I believe that the future of churches depends not on attempting to renew previous attitudes, structures and practices; rather it will emerge out of the patient learning, by a critical mass of a congregation, of a transformed attitude about 'church', through knowing and responding to the triune God in diverse and yet fundamentally connected circumstances. Vitally, every local church is both encouraged and constrained by a catholic attachment to the bishop and diocese. I was completely open about my perception of the future needs of the Church in the role of parish priest in discussions both with the bishop and the wardens while negotiating my appointment as parish priest.

Learning about the social context takes its appropriate energy and time, but part of the *episkope* role is to remind every local church of the wider context of the world and of the need for dialogue with the catholic and apostolic Church. I had returned to the task of parish priest after two decades of diocesan and provincial education and training roles and having published several studies on mission and ministry. Naturally my apprehension was high, and I had to watch out for the intrusion of too much of my ego in the agenda. I have been fortunate in having had many opportunities to experience and reflect on parallel developments within the Anglican, Episcopal and Lutheran Churches, internationally. Every situation is unique but always connected to the lively unfolding of the Christian tradition, reaching towards Christ's perfecting of the world, through the Spirit.

But inevitably, I questioned whether my memory of developing priesthood in a collaborative community over 20 years before was a delusion. Were my expectations of lay involvement in the church's mission totally unrealistic? Or would people follow my leadership and begin to embrace a new understanding and practice? Would 'it' work, whatever 'it' was? What kind of crisis would there be for the congregation if it didn't? How would I cope personally if this approach failed? These were inevitable questions and challenges to my personal spiritual maturity, and have needed attention through study, prayer, conferences and many one-to-one conversations with others pursuing a similar route elsewhere. Encountering dread of our own daring and a lack of expectancy in others leads so easily to creating dependencies and becoming anxiously overactive to adverse comment. Not always trusting that others will have the courage or desire to explore and develop the church, in their way, with no less commitment than my own, is a trap that can limit possibilities for the entire enterprise.[4]

For the parish priest to lead and be part of the church in the particular way I am advocating, invites an increasing proportion of the congregation to be glad to recognize themselves as belonging to the church in unfamiliar and often demanding ways. A key challenge to the parish priest (and team) must be to discern the balance of motivations: between following God leading us in this direction, rejuvenating a dying church system, and the ego or anxiety of dominant leaders. How do we demonstrate that this is not an ambitious project disconnected from the work of the Spirit or from the mutual love between the Son and the Father that Jesus advocates and illustrates? How might God be able to work for good, even within our own need and brokenness? Another challenge is to question by what authority you lead in this direction. What contribution does the bishop have in encouraging, watching out for and critiquing such confident developments, rather than focusing primary attention on churches struggling to survive?

Mission action planning: making Christ known through building his Church

The connection between my own *episkope* and that of the diocesan bishop had a high profile, in that at the time of my induction as Vicar, all parishes were asked to devise and implement a 'Mission Action Plan' and to share this with the bishop. A small group of volunteers within the parochial church council (PCC) worked together with me in my *episkope* role. We chose to describe our mission statement under the elastic heading, 'Making Christ known through building his Church'. Well aware that most of those associated with St Mary's had a view of themselves primarily as worshippers on a sliding scale of regularity, we knew that finding comfort and having a regular space for personal devotion were strong factors in their attachment to church.

We were aware too of the danger that an unintentional message given off by this strap-line could be an apparent polarized opposition between a closed 'hothouse' church practice and one fully open to the neighbourhood. The theory of church in Chapter 3 and recurrent arguments question the inevitability of such a dualistic interpretation of expecting an intensification of the faith and discipleship of worshippers. The passionate commitment I communicated was that we could work towards discovering, in this particular place now, a practical style of church that is a deliberate attempt to interweave an intensification with God's triune life with a concern to extend constantly the Church's *koinonia* involvement with human concerns and disciplines for the eschatological transformation of the neighbourhood and global community. That is not the language with which I chose to communicate it in the parish magazine. I have written as well as preached recurrently on this theme. In an evolving congregation, the recommunication and refining of the message is a permanent task.

Initially I took time to find out about the place, the people, the immediate history, and who was offering for leadership roles. Several readers and retired clergy and I maintained and began redeveloping the worship, preaching and teaching, while the wardens, PCC and I explored priorities for the church's next step. I was sharply aware of the need to make a confident place for new work to be developed, but also of the danger, personally, of being pressed too quickly into giving a 'big picture' of the way ahead and being desolated if there were no warm response. The final remark of one of the wardens after our initial conversation was still in my mind: on his door step as I was leaving he had said, 'Remember, although we are looking for a priest who will love us, we are looking for a priest whom we can love.'

Some gladly heard my enthusiasm for a collaborative church as an 'open door' to the shared ministry for which they had expressed a strong desire when I was invited to become their parish priest. Others who appreciated the comfort of traditional worship and coffee mornings were disappointed not to have a 'proper vicar' who did everything and visited them at home as a major priority.[5] Yet others struggled, and still do, as they claimed to prefer 'traditional' ways or assumed that in a collaborative church no one is 'in charge', least of all the parish priest. This is a challenge that has been laid at my own door, as though I were advocating a single 'flat' ministry just with different facets, rather than a *koinonia* of different ministries that face and build up each other.

In order to stretch the congregation's notion of church and to underline the urgency of a major cultural shift, I know I have not always been patient with those who so far have not recognized their 'God' or 'proper church' in the picture I have stimulated and that we are now developing. This is not the same, I believe, as not loving parishioners. A tough love cannot always deliver what people think they need. And North Easterners well know how to tease their clergy into noticing our mistakes and shortcomings.

Mission co-ordinators of the PCC

Recurrently in this chapter I shall refer to 'the staff team'. The membership has varied but essentially it means this: a recently retired priest acts as close associate for much of the week; the reader and one in training, both recently retired from paid employment as managers in their fields, are now able to offer a considerable amount of time and insight to the parish church's work; the parish also has in training as a curate a priest, formerly a senior police officer, whose present full-time occupation is in a local coffee shop with his wife.

Six months after my arrival, 'mission co-ordinators' emerged, as volunteers but with the obvious goodwill of the PCC, from the initial probing of how to develop leaders and a way forward that would allow for imaginative strategic thinking, gather energy and distribute responsibilities. They were all members of the PCC and their positions were ratified and commissioned publicly in the Sunday liturgy, even though we had little clarity about what they would do. Initially four, their purpose was identified as:

- to help shape and develop the Mission Action Plan within the urgent needs of the parish;
- to encourage others to begin to engage in ministries to develop the plans in practice.

The co-ordinators shared enthusiastically in the *episkope* of which, as parish priest, I was the sacramental focus. Together we set about uniting, encouraging and drawing out in others, ministries for worship and spirituality, learning, young people, building community, resources and developing the church's buildings. As one parishioner commented, it seemed appropriate at the time for the co-ordinators to be appointed to enable work to be done, but the learning since then is that in the future we should make sure that co-ordinators (in the selection procedure) should have an authority given not only by the PCC but by the whole congregation. The idea and practice of having co-ordinators had served well initially, and had generated and organized collaborative work for which the PCC held responsibility, but now another step was required.

Initially some staff team members (clergy and readers) were keen to act as co-ordinators. It seemed more likely that we would develop the energy of the congregation if the staff team acted as encouragers and facilitators, helping to frame and develop ideas linked with the question: 'Where is God in our context and how can we collaborate?' As parish priest, I carry the particular role of head of the community and as such have occasionally to intervene when a co-ordinator has felt threatened by the work or attitude of another. A number of comments, such as, 'I don't know what a mission co-ordinator is', illustrate how those who are now involved, but who were not two years ago, can only guess at the initial conversations about the role of the co-ordinators. This highlights the need for continual communication, and at a recent meeting of leaders the lack of success in regular communication was highlighted. The PCC, while appreciating the enormous contribution made over the past two years by the work of co-ordinators, believed that now was the time to find a less managerial style of holding together and developing people and projects.

Five principles to identify the church

The richness, range, contact and transformation broad-brush themes challenge me to ask: 'What are the attitudes, qualities and tasks that are required in a parish priest and all those who share in the extended *episkope* to maintain and extend the church in its character?' Even those most closely involved in the church resist the pressure to regard themselves as being competent intellectually, spiritually or ethically to regard themselves as 'a missionary community'. When it was first proposed that we stand around a nave altar to share Holy Communion, some were initially diffident, declaring their own deep sense of unworthiness to do so.

Looking back over two and half years, I see that the four theological elements of church have been expressed implicitly in a working practice we have come to regard as five very basic principles of operating. I have no doubt that many churches aspire to them, at least some of the time:[6]

1 We believe passionately that we are all God's beloved, sisters and brothers of Christ, filled with the Spirit. Recognizing our own woundedness and imperfection, we also aspire to resurrection hope.

2 Just as our church doesn't have to 'do it all', so in the congregation no-one should be involved in more than a couple of areas of ministry. No one is called to the ministry God has in mind for someone else; no one is so strong or so weak that they are always or never called to minister to others.

3 Authentic ministry is not a solo performance. Those holding ministry leadership roles work in teams, where sharing work is an essential element of the character of church.

4 Anyone bearing a significant role for the community needs a written job description, with specific expectations regarding accountability, especially concerning the amount of time involved week by week and the period of service the PCC seeks of any office holder. Annual reviews and regular support meetings offer a way of avoiding frustration and lack of effectiveness.

5 The call to ministry by a church community has to be matched by the capability and faith of the person concerned in the particular circumstances of life in which they find themselves. Praying is a vital work in which all can be involved without the pressure of meetings and leadership responsibility.

I had the opportunity to receive comments on these practical principles through a review that paved the way for the writing of this chapter.

Reviewing the work

The theology explored in this study certainly needs a reality check. The main purpose for me in writing has always been to reflect on parish practice in the light of developments in ecumenical study and reflection on my own experience. When this, in part at least, connects with others, I have a deeper confidence in my navigational art and point of reference for the future. I invited 50 regular worshippers at St Mary's to respond to a series of questions to provide evidence for the final chapter of this study. They related to the particular contribution of the parish priest and staff team and co-ordinators in the identification of the task of the PCC and congregation, and how they are supported in carrying it out.

The accompanying letter from me said this:

> As you may know, I'm completing the writing of a book about the future priorities for the particular work and life of the parish priest. The book focuses on the steadily decreasing proportion of clergy who are paid full time as 'parish priests', with the teams that collaborate with them. Increasingly clergy are being trained and ordained to 'part-time' posts that combine with their continuing secular employment or some form of self-support, for example retirement.
>
> One of the key themes of the book is that the Church is centred in all of us and not just the clergy. In coming decades, with parishes grouped in clusters, stipendiary (paid) clergy will probably be required to act in such a way as to draw out ministries in others and find ways of supporting people in them. It assumes baptism, rather than ordination, as the gateway to ministry. In such a community of Christians, the parish priest takes a very particular, rather than a generalized role. One way of saying this is, 'What the bishop does for the diocese, the parish priest will do for the parish(es).'
>
> You'll perhaps have noticed that this is the experimental approach that I am advocating and attempting to model during my time as your priest at St Mary's. This is a huge culture shift for the Church of England, in which laity, though often given delegated tasks, still assume a largely passive role. It is vital that the theories described in the book are matched by a truthful account of our experiments together. This is why I am recruiting your involvement please.
>
> I intend that the final chapter will contain practical clues for those reading the book – about the attitudes and actions that draw out a mutual, mission-shaped Church. Our experience at St Mary's could become an important encouragement to others and more so if we can be truthful about our 'failures' as well as 'successes'.
>
> I wonder if you'd be kind enough to make a response to the questions below. Your responses will be known only to me personally, though they will feed into the wider picture painted by the others involved. If you decide you don't feel able to take part just let me know. Thank you.
>
> Your parish priest
> Robin

I am especially grateful for the time and insight of those parishioners who, through answering these questions (set out below), have given thought to what, in our situation now, seems to contribute to the effective exercise of the ministry of *episkope*, and what holds us back.[7]

> '1 Please comment on the five principles and the role of clergy, readers, mission co-ordinators and wardens within them.'

The five principles

These practical principles were generally accepted to be valuable and worthy of wider communication. I was especially interested to note, in verbs such as 'articulate', 'formulate', 'help', and 'check regularly', how much of the parish priest as *episkope* was implicit in the replies. Also I was watching out for how the co-ordinators shared, by extension, in this *episkope*. A key PCC member writes, 'Not so sure about being "God's friend" – otherwise I am very comfortable with the principles.' It was widely agreed that a key role for the parish priest lies in articulating the principles by which we operate and checking they are being followed, for example by quality assessment monitoring with those in leadership roles. One writer says of the parish priest, 'Your role has been to help formulate, communicate and to put into practice the principles, and I think that the co-ordinators have also had some input here.' Another believed it was primarily the co-ordinators' task, with the parish priest, to 'check regularly' that the principles are being followed in practice.

Most respondents were clearly unaware of these principles or how they were developed, despite their being presented in varying forms, in sermons and magazine articles by the staff team. But another writes, 'Our parish priest has allowed the people asked by the PCC, and to an extent the wider congregation, to start as the core team to develop an understanding for themselves of what the five principles involve for them individually. Obviously the basic premise has been something Robin has thought about throughout his ministry. He has not sought to impose them upon us. This gives a greater feeling of buying in to them and allows enthusiasm to develop and make them work.'

Almost all identified with them as 'clear', 'ideal', 'sound', 'realistic', 'full of hope' or 'setting the tone', recognizing that they help us work out 'what we want to do' and 'are good management practice apart from anything else'. Co-ordinators, team leaders and members have experienced the value of principle 5 through regular support meetings with the parish priest and other staff, and with one another.

There is a view that there has been less overt leadership in relation to principles 2, 3 and 4. It wasn't at all obvious at the start what the workload of the co-ordinator roles would be, and to a large extent they have created their own job descriptions as they have discovered what the work involved. Nor is it at all easy to identify a successor or get people to commit to more meetings as part of a formal group. One expressed anxiety that this approach to being church is far more demanding on everyone's energy than they might have anticipated when they started. For some this would be an argument for maintaining the tradition of thinking of the congregation as passive, occasional visitors to uplifting, high-quality worship provided by the staff team. A recent meeting of the coordinators recognized that at any one time only a few people would be willing and available to fulfil the task and that this will be a decisive factor in moving gradually to a more organic process of *episkope*.

A sharp distinction was clear between those who look for high standards in management, review and continuity, especially in how people treat each other in a voluntary organization, and those who believe this to be too ambitious or demanding. Developing 'business practice', in terms of training, learning and development in managing the work of the church, has brought clarity about the purpose and outcomes of time given to planning. It now needs to be tempered by the more overt relating of our future plans to God's will.

One person was concerned that principles 3 and 4 were 'offputting' for a church, which is not a business and cannot expect this level of commitment from volunteers with busy lives and careers. Some warned against attempting to enforce them in an organization where everyone is free 'to vote with their feet'. In similar vein, another writes of anxiety that talk of 'mission' sounds very business-orientated. That person's desire is to worship God and learn more about Christ. Another emphasized that the church is a small business and that management must be as effective as leadership. Another parishioner identified with the principles, believing that 'the parish priest should act as the managing director to ensure that they are followed – the priest's role is as the executive leader who not only innovates but also ensures good governance along with the wardens and the PCC.'

A respondent wrote that the principles add to the sense of 'ownership and responsibility, giving those who wish to do so opportunities to carry out important ministries that have had a real impact'. Evidence for the value of this approach could be seen in the far wider cross section of people now taking an active role in the mission of the church for the first time. The move from being a disparate group of worshippers to a community where people engage with one another is evidenced in the increase in knowing each other's names in a large congregation. One celebrates the 'strong management team approach' that creates long-term direction in which 'each has a role and a way to be within that'. This person also noted that they were relieved not to be made guilty because of being able only to make a small contribution from time to time – 'There is stuff to enjoy as well as stuff to do'.

The mission co-ordinators' role

The flow of mutual support between the co-ordinators, even when there was disagreement, had found appreciation. However, a consistent view is that the role of the co-ordinators is unclear to most people. Some expected the wardens and the PCC to have a greater strategic role than is evident. Wardens vary in their time commitment and past experience. In this parish there are four wardens at any time, serving for three years. So 'pastoral wardens' shadow those legally elected for either one or two years. At the start, each of the four wardens was paired with a co-ordinator. After a short trial, this apparently sound idea was deemed impracticable and was discontinued. The next step is only gradually emerging. It will seek to combine watching out for people and tasks, but in a more networked way. It will probably work through the congregation inviting (in Local Ministry style) some with recognized roles, experience and spiritual maturity to work as a team that ensures the church is guided by key values, such as friendship, inspiring worship, passionate spirituality, a real sense of belonging, gift-based collaborative ministry, raising up leaders, effective structures and evangelism that is responsive to need.

The role of the parish priest and team

How have people perceived the *episkope* role without naming it as such? A strong view was expressed that the parish priest and team have been instrumental in making everyone aware of the principles through repeating the theme in sermons, magazine letters, meetings and courses. There is also a view that 'much more development work needs to be done among the sizeable number of people who want things to stay as they are'. Consistency of aim was emphasized by several people. Given the PCC's agreement on a way forward, the parish priest must challenge individuals and groups to work towards that and relate valuable energy to the central theme, which will always be about 'growing closer to God'.

Respondents wrote that the priest and team must also struggle to include contrary opinions and attitudes within the whole, without letting any particular one become too great a distraction. This in turn draws out contributions of high quality from others: 'we should revel in our differences' and encourage the ingredients that otherwise would be absent. To speak of the church as 'community', to one has resonances more of Marx than Paul, and denies the individual path of each Christian. Clergy were asked to note that many people engage with or are employed by several communities or organizations that demand their concentrated attention. A 'servant' leader would not concentrate so much on the church as organization but on the encouragement of individual people.

One wrote that in relationship to these principles, the parish priest 'needs to be available to listen, discuss, pray, respond and encourage'. This was echoed by others who notice how worshippers will quietly stop attending church if they are uncomfortable or dissatisfied. Several parishioners believed that what is most needed from the priest is a constantly available support, the sharing of ideas from the wider church and a deep concern for the unity of the congregation. Another looked to a flowing movement of priesthood in which sometimes the priest is leading, for example in spiritual matters, while in other areas she might be 'an interested and encouraging spectator'. An ideal of the priest is offered as 'a sensitive appraising role, leading us to question and test our motives in undertaking activities. We need to be gently helped to use our talents and be aware of our limitations' and be rooted in prayer, self-knowledge and 'a growing relationship with God'.

A number of those who responded emphasized that the personality, experience, training and skill of an individual parish priest cannot be ignored as an important factor. This has both positive and negative implications, in that a successor priest may choose and be given the freedom to lead in a completely different way, with unquantifiable outcomes.

One respondent identified the parish priest and team, as a whole, as 'called into a central supportive role rather than an active lead position'. One commented that 'the role of the staff team is also not clear within the overall governance process.' Another noted that wardens who are willing and able to give the commitment in time and responsibility and can act as managers as well as provide all that canon law requires, are not easily discovered. Without the proper tension that includes the wardens, there could be a danger that the co-ordinators and clergy and readers could usurp the role of the PCC in strategic leadership.

There are some important resonances here with the priest in *episkope* role, with consequences for the ministry of others. But there was also evidence of anxiety and nostalgia for the priest to be omnicompetent and allowing of a passive congregation. The communication and acceptance of the principle requires continued attention.

> '2 A local church, by definition, exists through the permanent task of rediscovering its character and priorities for serving God's mission in constantly changing circumstances. How far do you accept this? In this connection, what is the unique role of the parish priest and team? To what extent are we being effective?'

Some wrote of their expectation of the parish priest – and team – as a catalyst to help the whole congregation accept the need for change, especially in regard to a renewed understanding of the role of clergy and readers. It was judged that 'This is best done through example, persuasion, and occasionally, judiciously, and not forcing the issue.'

Others recognized that the parish priest needs the gift of being an innovator or instigator, with a persuasive rather than adversarial approach. 'To enable the church to have a clear mission and direction' is emphasized by one. It seemed clear that the majority of the congregation have not 'grasped the concept of what being a Christian is about, let alone understood what "*Making Christ known through building his Church*" is really pointing up'. This person looks for 'clear direction and leadership and a skill in getting people to think about what is being proposed and being willing to go with it – even when they are either not sure where "it" is or whether they have the skills and abilities to help with the task'.

'Priests', says another, 'must be willing to risk inviting people to consider a ministerial role in the church, not afraid of the inevitable occasions when they are rebuffed'. One emphasizes how vital is the role of the priest as the public representative of the 'God' of this local church. When many are 'sceptical about Scripture and riddled with doubts about belief', the ability of the local priest to make apt connections between this 'God' and people outweighs structures or plans.

Another respondent looks for the role of guide and facilitator in the parish priest to enable the congregation 'to enjoy the freedom of being part of the church's mission'. However, the same person notes with enthusiasm that evidence has shown how a web of wardens, readers, co-ordinators, Mothers' Union, men's group and those with long experience in the church contribute already to the encouragement of task groups and identifying individual strengths. One writes, 'Even after all these years of serving on various PCCs, I struggle to see how the tensions between priorities are held together.' Some look for clarity of purpose to be explained and maintained by the parish priest, while others sense that this is not a priority for many in the congregation who simply want to worship on Sundays.

Anther respondent suggests that the parish priest and staff team make a strong contribution by helping the congregation to make connections between apparently conflicting issues and to show how differing groups can resource each other, rather than being mutually suspicious. One who had played a key role in the PCC wrote that:

> With a few years experience behind us we can and should get into a strategic planning cycle, in which we ask ourselves every so many years (not less than three, not more than five) the classic strategic review questions: How are we doing? Where do we want to be? How do we get there? What shall we do in the light of actual resources and abilities? This ought to provide a more strategic approach to priorities, although of course there are likely to be more agendas than can be coped with, given finite resources, and the final choice will always be affected by the familiar factor of personal preference.

A priest also needs to be 'a Christian educator', according to one respondent, 'enabling us to learn how to do it'. That a parish priest needs to be a committed educator is the conclusion of one response, recalling a series of meetings early in my time as parish priest here, entitled 'Who is our God – who do we worship?' This gave opportunities for 80 members of the congregation to reflect on priorities and to exchange experiences and insights with each other.

Mission action planning happened through arranging initial PCC discussions about mission priorities and shape, followed by a congregational meeting. The same respondent writes of the vitality of a priestly attitude that expects lay people to be capable and willing to engage in various aspects of mission, and to have the experience and discernment to understand who might have talents for a particular role. One responded that 'The church is moving forward and changing despite a strong resistance to change from elements of the congregation.' Another, that it is 'bigger and happier'.[8] For this development, priests must 'hold' the process and act as 'sounding board, reflecting back what they hear and pulling themes together'.

One spoke of priests 'moving us on when we get stuck, demonstrating that they have heard objections but appealing for objective discussion based on facts and including all points of view'.

The co-ordinators were also valued for giving positive and encouraging support to others, such as the Baptism Support Group, in the face of some negative initial comments. It was also noted how individuals have been supported by clergy, readers and co-ordinators to develop ideas, organize, create artwork and help others express their faith. The same group of leaders was commended for the 'reason, tact and dignity' engendered in debating contentious issues about experimenting with the layout of furniture for the Sunday Eucharist, to promote a greater sense of community. In similar vein, one praised the renegotiation with the congregation after it transpired that initial plans to reorder the church were 'unrealistic and un-affordable' in the contemporary climate.

There was a comment that the PCC as a body should play a key role in setting the agenda: 'As someone who is no longer on the PCC, I'm not clear how much they have led this work of identification and how much they have just gone along with it either because they are individually on board with the proposals or because they are content to agree with whatever is proposed!'

On the issue, 'Does it matter who is the parish priest?' one replied unequivocally that in an increasingly complex community, what works is a priest who shares his dream with anyone who will listen, engages with everyone who wants to take part, expects small microcosms of activity to take place that are self-resolving and above all trusts that this will be so and lives with the consequences (without blame) if it is not so. A priest in this community needs to admonish and yet encourage, welcome and yet reject, and above all stick to the main aim. This priest needs to be basically creative, a good communicator, a sensitive listener and 'a believer in chaos theory'. Clear objectives for all in their different roles need to be identified, communicated and supported.

Another wrote:

> Having been very involved in the PCC away day when you first brought forward your vision for St Mary's, and although the

co-ordinators helped identify the issues, I'm not convinced the PCC came up with anything different from the things we had already discussed in the small planning group. This piece of work is yours – and you should be proud of it! . . . A lot of the important work has come from your suggestion – the importance of baptism and the Baptism Group that has grown out of that has had a clear lead from you.

The same person questioned perceptively how much communal prayer had really undergirded this discernment process.

Diocesan advisers, facilitators, visiting preachers, leaders of quiet days and chance visitors on holiday were mentioned by one as adding to the mix of influences. Above all, everyone who wishes has contributed to the mutual support of people and groups in their work, rather than always to the parish priest. 'So new people choose to get involved and new things happen', writes one respondent.

Every reader will come to this chapter with their own experience and views on how flat or not should be the church's governance patterns. This is one of the key elements in the debate to which I want to contribute in this book. Rather than coming to the conversation with preconceived or historically freighted opinions, I believe that, in the light of a trinitarian ecclesiology, we need to be testing out what is *episkope* and reflecting on how it functions in many different situations and through differing personalities. What emerges here is a growing appreciation of the *episkope* role, held by the parish priest but also shared and dispersed. Questions linger about how truly dependent the PCC and congregation remain on the parish priest for direction, confidence and energy. I also see the need to be realistic at this stage concerning the contribution of the navigator priest's experience of the wider Church together with his educational and persuasive skills. There is also plenty of evidence of the ability of the congregation to challenge the priest and to demand more in the way of communication and discussion. In turn, this puts on the line the internal emotional robustness of the priest and her capacity for self-awareness and reflection. The value of regular work consultancy needs to be logged here too.

> '3 We are committed to developing and celebrating worship in differing styles on various occasions to enable a wide variety of people and age groups to follow their journey with and to God. What is the contribution of the parish priest and colleagues, ordained and lay?'

'This should be one of the more significant areas of leadership for a parish priest, after all he has had the training', writes one, adding:

'They should, however, set the broad parameters and be prepared to allow significant lay involvement not only in leading the worship but in seeking original ways (within the set limits) to promote the concepts being followed.' This has worked well during the period in which the lay worship co-ordinator held her post, though few people probably understood her remit, which developed and then changed radically when more clergy joined the team.

Another says:

> I have a picture in my head of a religious order which is non-hierarchical and where everyone shares in the work and people's particular talents, including those for leadership, are equally recognized and used. So clergy and staff team should certainly play a strong role in leading and creating worship but recognize that we all learn and deepen our faith through being actively involved.

One believed that much of the work around worship planning should be given to the clergy who 'have the knowledge', 'have travelled the path before us'. Those on the edge of the church will have this expectation. 'I think this is the one area where the parish priest should be seen to be taking a lead – not doing it all but certainly seen to be taking the lead in worship.'

Another spoke up for more lay leadership in this area, 'guided' by the staff team. One says that the clergy should always have 'a handle' on worship but there should be provision for all kinds of liturgical leadership. The worship co-ordinator does not need to be ordained, even though 'a lay person' needs guaranteed support at short notice when disputes arise. There was, indeed, praise for the first occupant of the co-ordinator role. Whether lay or ordained, this co-ordinator needed the capacity to draw on the resources of the wider church and to balance pastoral care with innovation.

A reply suggested that spirituality is often a hard concept for people to grasp. If you ask the question: 'How would you describe your spirituality?' many would be hard pressed to give a coherent answer. In a congregation where so many have previously worshipped in different denominations and traditions, there is a wide variety of assumptions about how conversational or formal, prescribed or spontaneous, plain or aesthetically complex, worship might be. 'In this area I don't think the parish priest necessarily needs to lead the exploration (for that is what it is) but needs to support whoever is taking it forward. It should go hand in hand with learning.'

Understandably, there was a great deal of concern that the parish priest should help the church navigate its way around worship issues. There is evidence of a genuine tension between nervousness and lack of confidence among the laity about these developments, but a strong sense that it is too important just to be left in the hands of the clergy as providers of worship.

> '4 We have determined that adult Christian learning is vital for personal and community growth. What is the contribution of the parish priest and colleagues, ordained and lay?'

There was a general opinion that the needs in this area should ideally be discerned by the congregation as a whole taking part in a learning exercise. This would give a stronger feeling of ownership and therefore participation in projects. Guidance from the parish priest on delivery and content should be sought but must not appear prescriptive. One person comments: 'I feel there has been a good deal of publicity around this area but, as yet, not a great deal of originality of approach.'

It was suggested that the parish priest and team have a key role in promoting learning through spiritual guidance, preaching, encouraging prayer, reading and action but, writes one:

> We learn best if we are active rather than passive and when we learn from one another, not just from clergy. So learning through creating and leading courses, prayer or worship, needs to be a priority . . . What was the remit of the learning co-ordinator? I think to foster the journeying of all members of the congregation. This was well publicized at the beginning but may need reiterating in the same way that we continually refer to 'Making Christ known through building his Church'.

Various comments present a picture of growing strength in this key area. Another says the focus of what is to be learnt could be clearer, and is supported by one who insists that the 'responsibility for monitoring the programme must be a concern of the priest or a carefully chosen and trained deputy'. A variety of task groups, working with the co-ordinator, were able to create and deliver occasional courses. They used the skills of people in the church to pull together a course that added to people's understanding of their faith and the gospel story.

The point was made that communicating what is planned and recruiting volunteers is a task best addressed within a team approach. There was a strong voice that all that is represented in the congregation's combined fund of knowledge should be released.

This seems to give strong support to the navigating *episkope* role of the parish priest, welcoming lay participation in planning and delivering learning as a key element in learning itself.

'5 Developing the faith, imagination and belonging of young people is a vital task of the whole congregation. What is the contribution of the parish priest and colleagues, ordained and lay?'

That the parish priest should be involved in establishing what we are trying to achieve for young people, and then allowing others to take it forward, was a frequent comment. The young people's co-ordinator describes the remit as 'to keep young people's ministry on the agenda for St Mary's, to identify gaps in provision and seek to fill them. I have a job description. I drew it up myself and it was agreed by the other co-ordinators and the parish priest at the first co-ordinators meeting I attended.' The initial priorities were largely set from a meeting of parents before the co-ordinator role had been created. The major aspect of supporting parents bringing children for baptism was handed over from the building community co-ordinator. The co-ordinator had received support from parents and the parish priest in the major tasks of leading a Children and Holy Communion course for the first time, organizing a crib service and finding someone to lead and establish a baptism support group.

Some spoke of learning how to facilitate from the parish priest's own experience, not least in terms of finding a greater understanding of where a particular contribution fits into the wider picture of God's mission and deepening the faith of individuals through all of this.

One writes of the value of being believed in and encouraged by clergy and the staff team to trust in their capabilities in doing a job.

Communication between different parts of the young people's work had improved with time, but 'the lines of communication are still blurred', showing that the team needs much more development. Contemplative prayer together as the basis of regular meetings of the Young People's Core Group has proved very creative, even though it has to be balanced within people's pressured lives at work, in the family and other communities, as well as church.

The progress of this work has been publicized through informal conversations, presentation to Mothers' Union, sermon discussion slots, magazine articles. There was a general sense that dedicated lay leadership, of 'those who relish the task', is required – with clergy support – in this area. The annual report to the congregation high-lighted for one respondent the experienced and committed leader-ship among the small teenage group, and the godly play approach to children's worship and learning. The role of the young people's co-ordinator was invented after it became clear that learning for all ages was too great a task for one co-ordinator.

Many commented on the effectiveness of this work, which may in some part be because of the clear sense of *episkope* implied in the original job description and the impossibility of one person being seen as able to deliver on all fronts. The creativity of the many pockets of activity was linked with resourcing both in the parish and through the diocese. In early discussions with the other co-ordinators the task was identified as to discern the need and sup-port the PCC in meeting that need. The co-ordinator was appointed to stimulate a network of communication between the organizers of disparate activities.

The potential benefits were seen to be keeping young people's work/spirituality/outreach/place within the church's activities high on the agenda, improving communication between leaders of young people's activities, having an obvious point of contact for people interested in participating in this area of work, and having some-one with an overview of all the young people's activities, able to identify any needs now and in the future and work towards fill-ing them. Pitfalls were identified as being seen as the person to *do* everything in relation to young people. The person appointed had to be able to delegate and network, liaise with other co-ordinators, churchwardens, clergy and young people's workers. Other consider-ations were: the need to have good networks within the church, to be aware of current legislation in relation to young people, to have a good understanding of issues relating to young people's interests and lifestyles, and especially how this relates to their spirituality.

It is clear that few people have a grasp on what the co-ordinator attempts. One person writes: 'This is probably my fault for not tak-ing the trouble to ask, though I have nothing to offer in that area'.

One is anxious that a concentration on one age group can lead to the neglect of another: 'It's like motherhood and apple pie – no one can object, but given the congregation we have, made up of many newly retired people, middle-aged and other groups, others are just as worthy of support in the overt way we approach the young.'

The *episkope* priestly role works effectively when it is clearly understood and accepted and lay people can bring a combination of passion for young people to become disciples combined with the professionalism they have accumulated in their working disciplines.

The navigating priest has to know when to support and challenge and when to trust others and stay in the background.

'6 Building community. What is the contribution of the parish priest and colleagues, ordained and lay?'

The key to this area of mission is to 'Make Christ Known' through connections with the wider community. An attractive parish newsletter, budgeted for and carefully prepared and delivered to every house in the parish, is an illustration of the attempt of this group to create a wide net of communication of attractive and useful information about what St Mary's offers the neighbourhood.

In a relatively prosperous, leafy suburb by the sea, this parish church has for several years lived with the dilemma of wanting to serve people locally at their deepest point of need and yet been unable to discover a substantial project to get engaged with. Involvement practically and financially with building and community projects in more vulnerable churches, an asylum-seeker centre and unemployed young people has long been a feature of this parish's life. The availability of the church hall (with the overheads involved) to many young people and leaders and other community groups can easily be overlooked as a vital service to the neighbourhood.

The co-ordinator who had filled this role for 18 months writes:

> Good ideas like Posada (an adapted Mexican Christmas pilgrimage), the Passion play and several others were proposed in an atmosphere of collaborative work in which we all knew that unless we were proposing something completely off the wall, there was no question of being slapped down by the Vicar. Your attitude has been more to help us think about our ideas in a godly context, and to consider how one idea might link or support another.

Others are adamant that this should be a clergy role – part of being known in the wider community, as the public representative of the parish church. One of the clergy team, who works full-time in his own coffee shop, already acts as a very broad bridge between St Mary's congregation and the neighbourhood, ecumenically. People of all kinds of faith and none take the chance through him to link their lives with that of God.

This building-community work, says one person, is probably the hardest but most important area to define: 'Just looking at the things the retiring co-ordinator has been involved in shows that.' Another writes:

> I see now that everyone in the church should be involved in this in some way, and perhaps we should think about house groups/home groups/cells (call them what you will) to model this first before going out there and building more. I used to think that building community meant building the church as community first and then looking beyond that.

One respondent wrote:

> The best bit of community building that has happened in St Mary's recently is the rehearsal and performance of the Passion from Tony Harrison's *The Mysteries*. People have been changed as a result of three months' involvement in this dramatic production, and we shall build on that by holding a meeting of all involved to ask ourselves what we have learnt.

The 'expertise of the co-ordinator, with an extensive network of contacts and knowledge' was seen by many to be the key to the success of this role. Some of those involved in the Passion have continued to meet, asking how, for themselves and the church and community, there can be further outcomes. Connected with this work is the long-running question of the redevelopment of the church buildings, apart from necessary renovation. The remit of the buildings redevelopment co-ordinator is to lead a group on the process of making our buildings more fit for worship and outreach in the twenty-first century. There is a growing realization of how large a piece of work this is in the current economic climate. The process has been publicized through congregational meetings, discussions, articles and an occasional flare up of anxiety about changing the ordering of the furniture. Someone long seasoned in this process writes:

> I think clergy need to keep the vision of what we are doing this for and keep reminding us, but it is entirely appropriate to have someone with business and negotiation experience leading it and someone the congregation see as one of us rather than a priest who is only here for a few years.

The parish priest, says another,

> should be the lead voice but not the only one in establishing what any redevelopment is meant to achieve, but not in a dictatorial way. It has to be the decision of everyone. Otherwise no feeling of ownership and support will be forthcoming. The parish priest must be seen

to be fully supportive of whatever is finally taken forward. There has to be extensive consultation at every stage and the congregation has to be taken along. In this area we have I think been most careful in the consultation process.

Another co-ordinator keeps an eye on everything regarding resources finance, administration and the parish office. His remit is to 'make sure we have resources in place to play our part in God's mission'.

That co-ordinator writes:

The parish priest's main task under this heading is to identify members of the congregation who can deliver whatever has to be resourced. This requires skills that can only be developed over time. The basics of people management can and should be taught in the training schools. Not every parish priest is a natural manager, but is expected to be so from day one. Some sort of skills register of the congregation will help, and advice from these experts should be sought.

The view was widespread that clergy should know what is going on but not be doing it in this area: 'It's much better to have someone who is focusing on these skills.' Ownership of this work has been achieved 'through publicity, congregational meetings about the use of our buildings and more recently in stewardship discussions, and notices'.

Again in broad terms the *episkope* role of the parish priest has been grasped with some enthusiasm, releasing the energy and gifts of many. This in no way diminishes the possibility of the parish priest witnessing personally through opportunities for involvement in the educational or strategic life of the wider community.

'7 "Ordering" the range and complexity of different tasks and people and holding in unity the many groups and strategic tasks is essential. What is the contribution of the parish priest and colleagues, ordained and lay?'

One writes:

There is so much more going on in a more co-ordinated way than ever before and I don't want my parish priest dropping from complete exhaustion every night of the week because he has had to do every sick visit, baptism visit, lead every teaching activity and take the youth group bowling.

The parish priest shares with the bishop the overall task of *episkope*, and this extends throughout the team of clergy, readers, mission co-ordinators, wardens and PCC. One respondent with business experience considered that a parish probably needs to find a basic management structure that is not merely pyramidical or hierarchical. A clear critique is that: 'At the beginning this was not being done. We tried to do too many things too quickly.' We are now recognizing that we need to prioritize and commit resources, energy and people to the most important tasks at any particular point in time. Regular review and assessment is needed as well as keeping all the community informed.

One-off initiatives tend to run smoothly. It is when we undertake medium- and long-term projects that difficulties arise. Churches on the whole resist the experience that people bring from their working lives of the 'management of information', keeping track of initiatives, coaching people to 'deliver' and making the difficult decisions when something does not work out. As one respondent writes: 'We to a degree self-assess how effective we are.' This routine church culture is also challenged by one who wrote:

> I agree that tasks need to be properly 'ordered' – this is an absolute given. In a business (or school or hospital or government department) this role belongs to the executive team – my problem is that I cannot work out who the executive team at St Mary's is! Is it the PCC, the Wardens, the staff or the co-ordinators or any combination of the above? It should be the PCC, it might be the staff team – I really don't know. This may just be my ignorance – the PCC may well be functioning in this executive role and I'm just not aware of it – if they are we need to publicize what they do more clearly (the PCC minutes stuck on the notice board in the porch just doesn't do it).

'Holding the reins, however lightly' was identified as a key task of the parish priest in this movement: 'The parish priest needs to be a leader with particular skill in making clear our individual roles in shaping the vision, so that many laity can become involved.' There was an eagerness expressed for 'becoming church' rather being 'just attenders'. The priest has the task of instilling a belief that these things can happen.

The mission co-ordinators, together and individually, must meet regularly with the parish priest. Existing channels of communication, such as the magazine, news-sheet and sermons, should be informed and inspire the congregation 'about what's going on but also how this fits in with our knowledge and understanding of God'. Diocesan and other resources are seen as a key agent in:

- inviting people to use their talents, e.g. journalist as newsletter editor, semi-professional theatre director for community drama, a doctor and nurse on the healing team;
- creating opportunities for people to use embryonic talents, e.g. playing guitar in very small intimate service;
- challenging people, with adequate support, to go beyond their comfort zone, e.g. in creating and leading a Preparation for Holy Communion course with children;
- creating a simple directory, frequently revised, of those of the congregation who wish to be in it makes it easier to contact people.

Frequent comments were made on the need to improve communication. In a growing and increasingly complex congregation, keeping track of who's doing what is often difficult. 'Perhaps we should have created some ground rules earlier around logging what people are organizing in the office diary, accountability for use of equipment and where things are stored, what things need to go to the PCC for approval.' An induction session for new PCC members would enable them to become effective much sooner. One wrote that it is not always clear in advance what a role involves when it is new and evolving. 'Clearer statements of the need and goals of any function should be made.'

The results of our present way of working were assessed by some: 'More things happening – a variety of worship and learning opportunities, and the regular distribution of the newsletter are examples.' 'New people are getting actively involved.' 'There were more nominees for the PCC than vacancies.' 'We hear positive feedback from those on the fringes.' This is made possible by a lot of hard work inspired by a vision of 'what it means to be church'. When individuals with roles and tasks 'aren't getting things in place or people are getting stressed', clergy or readers have dealt with it by picking up the organization of tasks themselves, finding others temporarily or increasing the support for the individual concerned. Support is offered for individuals through discussions in relation to role and spiritual guidance. We get people together in meetings and social situations to build relationships, hearing each other's stories and finding ways to move forward with our part in God's mission. 'It's happening because in our congregation we have a high proportion of people who can deliver – I would suggest that we have a higher than average IQ as a demographic group and a lot of us have management experience – so we can identify what needs doing and get on with delivery.' 'I think it has happened because of the work of the Holy Spirit.'

'8 Guidance and watching out for people. What is the contribution of the parish priest and colleagues, ordained and lay?'

Under this heading, which is specifically about an *episkope* approach to the work of a parish priest, there was a gathering up of recurrent earlier comments. 'If the question is, "Who should be available to offer guidance and support?" then the bottom-line answer is, "The parish priest", not as a last resort but in the end the priest should have the sign on their desk that says: "The buck stops here".'

> Guidance has been given in a sense collegially following discussions, and in a way that has not been overt or too managerial. However, eventually something will go 'wrong' and need to be resolved and there will need to be refocusing. This may well be the role of the parish priest who, confident of the support of others, would be seen as the 'safe' person to do this.

The priest must keep reminding us of our vision and offer support for individuals in relation to role and through enabling spiritual guidance.

There is a need to draw people together in meetings and social situations, 'so we are building relationships, hearing one another's stories and finding ways of moving forward with our mission'.

The presiding priest and team are to watch out for when people might be getting overstretched, that work is well distributed and that the five principles are used as a regular tool for corporate and individual reflection.

'9 Ensuring provision for the ones at risk – the sick, housebound, those in hospital. What is the contribution of the parish priest and colleagues, ordained and lay?'

This is about the relationship between the diaconal and episcopal aspects and orders in the community. It was frequently remarked that the detailed care for those at risk should not be seen as the sole responsibility of the parish priest, or any other single person or even a small group. There was a sense that all should be aware of our part in this aspect of church life and take action without being asked or cajoled. Some central recording system would be useful: 'This I think is how we currently operate and it seems to be working reasonably well.'

'This seems to work really well on a word-of-mouth basis', writes one. The parish priest needs to make sure it happens, but preferably by others who feel this is their mission – 'Our church is naturally good at this so a light oversight is all the parish priest needs'. Another person comments that people can have unrealistic expectations of the parish priest visiting in hospital: 'We need to work on these assumptions'. Taking this further, another writes:

> I think we need to do some education here – if we are *all* the *ecclesia*, then we *all* have the responsibility. There are certain things only a priest can do – extreme unction for one – but we need to get people to understand that the pastoral visiting team has the authority from the church and represents the church's concern for those who are sick. Small groups that *everyone* belongs to (even if they don't often turn up) with a leader who is responsible for making sure 'their' people don't fall through the cracks, may well be the way forward.

A respondent writes: 'I think we've got it right – using the pastoral visiting team, although the answer to this question is that it is every member of the church's role to ensure that the housebound and sick are provided for.' Some church members clearly don't feel they have been visited by 'the church' unless someone wearing a dog collar turns up – 'The joke being that you tend to turn up when people are *really* sick – so a visit from you is bad news!'

One notes that she is glad the annual meeting placed growth in prayer as a very high priority for the year ahead. 'My concern (which I know is shared by others) is that we don't pray enough corporately for this work. Daily Evening Prayer has a steady but low attendance and is still beyond people's traditional expectation. Prayer is the powerhouse that should drive everything we do.'

Relevant to this is the comment that, 'We have made a start with the contemplative prayer sessions, concentrating on finding direction with our work among young people, and I know there are prayer cells that meet regularly.' Another writes, 'I've long wanted us to do some teaching on prayer that will stimulate more corporate prayer to support the work God has called us to do.'

On the specific issues of this book, one writes:

> I've answered most of the questions based on our experience here, but I assume that you are trying to articulate a model for the Church at large. I think several things are clear:
>
> 1 What we are doing here is very radical – and to encourage others to consider working with these core ideas requires an almost complete mindset change by both clergy and laity. How far do we need to work together to understand the presiding priest as

managing director? Is this language likely to be rejected by many without understanding its implications?

2 This (or something very like it) has to be the way forward – if we don't change, the Church of England will expire on its feet because we can't afford to pay the clergy and because people on the fringe of the church will be repelled by the hierarchical model that has served well in the past.

Another member of the congregation ventures:

The early Church (and by that I mean the Church as portrayed in Acts) worked because they were risking becoming an open community. Much as I am attracted (occasionally) to community living, I'm not saying that there is a one size fits all approach. We do need to keep finding twenty-first-century models of community where every member, much of the time, is responsible for something – it may be that they are representing Christ in daily work and life, are welcomers or chalice administrators or deliver parish magazines in their street – but we need to grasp the fact that the body of Christ can only be fully functioning if we all pull together.   (1 Cor. 12.9–19)

My response

In reflecting on the interweaving and sometimes conflicting views that parishioners have warmly offered here, I feel a sense that the central ideas of this study is being accepted, even if in fragile and uneven ways. At the time of writing, the co-ordinators in post are just three, which makes an opportunity for the PCC to discuss whether the model is effective and how it should be adapted in a new phase. I sense a figure emerging of a church that can be both urgently orientated to God's purposes for the world and also patient with those who need more time and understanding in order to let go of long-inherited patterns of church.

Those present at the Annual Meeting (2008) spent a while in groups discerning the PCC's agenda for the coming year. Three priorities emerged:

1 inviting the congregation to give realistically to save finance constantly dominating conversation;
2 encouraging many ways of growing intimacy with God;
3 further strengthening provision for the faith development of the young ones as a process involving all ages.

The wardens, myself and the co-ordinators came to the view that a year-of-spiritual-growth group should be a priority. To lead this,

12 people, across the age profile of the congregation, should be chosen by the PCC to take part in a weekend at a retreat house, including myself, with the stimulus of the Local Ministry Adviser. Nominations sent in by the PCC, collated by myself and the vice-chair, were corroborated by the PCC once those nominated had accepted. At the time of writing, the agenda is open, except that it is hoped that we shall find new ways of combining our track record in being well organized with the unpredictability of expecting our communal and personal relationship with God to become more open and vibrant.

The *episkope* of the parish priest

Reflecting on my experience in this parish and my sense of the anticipation of what is yet to come leads me to believe even more strongly in the central argument of this book. Parish priests are required now who can serve the church as stimuli and teach others to act similarly. Of course there will be many occasions when planning to attend the strategic meeting suddenly pales into insignificance through urgent pastoral need. However, the long-term work is the careful and often humorous building-up of confidence in Christ's presence in the church for many to know their vocations and to follow them. And for many this will be in their everyday professions, tasks and caring responsibilities and in attending to such Kingdom issues as ecology or neighbourhood building.

To begin to make a list of the elements of this parish priestly work, often against the prevailing culture and not necessarily popular until its fruits are seen, I would include the following:

- Believing wholeheartedly that all Christians, ordained and non-ordained together, are the *laos* (people), in the tradition of both the Hebrew and Christian Scriptures;
- Working on the basis that the role of the parish priest and that of other ministers and the whole congregation cannot be defined separately;
- Deliberately working in the belief that it is baptism that makes this faithful people, each one equally with the *laos* of God;
- Creating patterns of governance in the church that assume the responsibility (*episkope*) of the whole people in maintaining the church in its character faithfully and in making decisions contextually about its structure, purpose and effective working;

- Holding consciously in mind the organic link between the *episkope* of the bishop, the diocese, the parish and the parish priest;
- Preaching, designing liturgies and encouraging learning and discussion on the role of all Christian disciples in the world of work, family, neighbourhood and global issues as well as in active ministries within the parish;
- Taking care that the whole *laos* has access to opportunities for growth in discipleship, learning and spiritual development and that they are leaders in this process;
- Recognizing and encouraging connection with the expertise of lay people at work and in church;
- Choosing people for leadership roles in the parish on the basis that the people and priest share discernment together;
- Ensuring that parish priests in their professional formation include not only theological and scriptural learning but skills in group process, learning styles, management and leadership;
- Promoting the preparation for baptism, Eucharist and confirmation as opportunities for the whole church to be involved in communicating the gospel, welcoming newcomers and growing in their own personal faith;
- Expecting lay people to grow in forms of prayer that are appropriate to their situation rather than an adoption of monastic or clerical patterns;
- Taking with great seriousness, as part of their vocation, opportunities for work consultancy, review and life-long learning.

Those who select and nurture ordinands and support their initial ministerial education have a great responsibility in this respect. But the responsibility or *episkope* must not be scapegoated on to a few. Every disciple and minister in all their diversity is called to look out for the Church and to choose to make themselves as fit as possible for the hard but rewarding life of a Christian community of reciprocal engagement. Those of us already parish priests have a vertiginous task in teaching and modelling the Church that can emerge if we truly believe that baptism is the key to freeing God's poor ones to be advance signs of that future that is God's passionate desire for all creation.

Openness to God's future will mean that we shall never crudely expect tight, linear progress when looking for the experience of salvation for all, partly through the agency of the graced work of church communities composed of frail human beings. Those who share *episkope* for the Church's demanding journey now are facing immense cultural and institutional change. There can be no forcing or control but rather a watchful 'going with the flow' and constantly reflecting:

> Just go with it. You cannot be fixed in how you're going about it any more than you would be fixed if you were setting about to paint a great work of art. Be alert, be self-aware, so that when opportunity presents itself, you can actually rise to it.[9]

I am wary of any notion of separating practical things from so-called spiritual matters (to free the clergy for their proper business) because it forgets the incarnational principle that, like Christ, all are to be involved in every aspect of life. Equally, I cannot merely subscribe to the parishioner's suggestion that the presiding priest is managing director or CEO. For the one who holds the vision, who holds the people together, who articulates theology and ensures an institutional framework so that we can work together, also belongs to a people, not a corporation. The earlier emphasis on church as *koinonia*, communion, a participation in the Trinity, emphasizes that the Church is always a web of interwoven relations, dynamic interplay, the intimate connection of Jesus with the Father and the sending of the Spirit, the fellowship between Jesus and his first companions. The parish priest, united with the bishop especially when presiding at the Eucharist, is one who, like Jesus, accompanies God's people as they follow the way of the cross.[10]

We're not starting from nowhere. In some ways the Church has always enacted these marks of its character, but in every generation it has to perceive how to re-find itself. Bishop and diocese and parish are a network stitched into the fabric of the life of the entire neighbourhood and location. Not everything is entrusted to a local isolated congregation. The extended *episkope* of bishop and diocesan officers and structures are there to provide a safe and challenging-enough environment for each local church to flourish and fulfil its own particular calling. The invitation to us all as church today is to let our imaginations run freely to picture what church might be like and how we can be an enzyme for making it happen. Trevor Beeson says of diocesan bishops that they need to become 'pioneers, strategic thinkers, and therefore men and women of considerable ability'.[11] I have argued that the same principle applies to the parish priest as navigator.

God's inexhaustible resourcing of our innovative efforts at church empowers us to expect that the promises to Mary in the Magnificat will be realized, but in ways that are unpredictable and personally demanding. The ordered life of church community with God, as a distinct identity, is riskily active in the world, as 'yielding buoyancy for a different life in the world'.[12] Tradition is never settled, it constantly heaves, recapitulates, risks, dreams, engages and relates precisely to people and situations:

> The story of the early Church is not the settlement. It is rather the slow, troubled, long-term meditation on the tradition, always prob- ing and moving, and finding itself led to newness where it ought not to go, led there by its Lord who is the pioneer as well as the per- fecter. The story in the book of Acts is about openness of the com- munity to those beyond the old categories of holiness, welcoming precisely those who are habitually excluded and disregarded. In such a daring maneuver, over which Paul presides, the Church continues that trajectory already strongly at work in antecedent Judaism.[13]

A potent musical analogy is offered by Jeremy Begbie:

> Over and over in tonal music we have closures which are positioned in the metric matrix in such a way that they 'stretch forward' for further resolution. This lends the piece an incomplete character, an 'opening out'. We are given a tension that is not fully resolved, or which is only dissipated in the silence which follows the piece. Promise 'breaks out' of sound.[14]

With a delicate lightness of touch, those who exercise *episkope* in local churches, on whatever scale, are to be navigators, helping the community discern a sense of direction. This means keeping an eye out in parish, neighbourhood and congregation for every sign of God at work, and on what seems to be the way ahead and for all the people. The navigator acts with vigilance and firmness, con- soling, encouraging the weary and uncertain, and sometimes con- fronting and teasing the desperate desire in some for a church of mere privacy and comfort. The parish priest is never simply man- aging director, but makes sure that the church is not deprived of some of those key MD functions.

It will be in our common *episkope* that profound change can happen to match the speech of a Church that defines itself in terms of richness, reach, contact and transfiguration for the sake of the Kingdom. If bishops and all concerned with the initial education of those who are to become parish priests will engage with the tenets of this book, there will be implications for others to draw out and improvise. Archdeacons and Area Deans have an opportunity, in searching for future ministerial patterns for local mission, to give parish priests the emotional support to risk challenging ways of re-perceiving themselves and their task. Along with a confidence in knowing Scripture, liturgy, pastoral care and administration, parish priests need to be practised in the art of group process and, through contemplative prayer of many kinds, need to rely on the Holy Trinity to find a true and reliable way. To be comfortable with the *episkope* role, priests need to have the courage to let go of the impossible burden of making 'it' happen. The Holy Spirit will guide us all in uncovering the kenotic forms of God's Church needed now for the sake of the Kingdom. Refracting the irregular rhythms of the Trinity, a learning Church will have the humility to let go of all the structures and behaviours that are too bulky to pass through the eye of a needle.

To practise *episkope*, parish priests must have the courage and determination to concentrate only on what is important for our role. That is to be a stimulus, along with Scripture, Eucharist, learning, deacons and bishops, to help the Church to re-find itself in ever new situations. For the world and the Kingdom the character of this Church will be one of participation, sharing (*koinonia*), proclamation and service. To achieve this we shall need the loving encouragement of the laity, and then together we shall with Jesus Christ pursue the mission of the Father, so that the Spirit will run through the world like sparks among the stubble.

Appendix

Projected numbers of employed clergy
in the Church of England, 2008–17

Distribution of FTE Stipendiary Diocesan Clergy
(Actual and according to the clergy deployment formula)

Diocese	31 December 2007 Actual	Share	Number over under (−) share	Per cent over under (−) share
1 Bath and Wells	222	200	22	10.8
2 Birmingham	179	177	2	1.1
3 Blackburn	201	202	−1	−0.7
4 Bradford	103	104	−1	−1.4
5 Bristol	134	133	1	0.4
6 Canterbury	143	155	−12	−8.0
7 Carlisle	144	134	10	7.6
8 Chelmsford	396	391	5	1.2
9 Chester	251	248	3	1.3
10 Chichester	305	276	29	10.4
11 Coventry	119	126	−7	−5.9
12 Derby	156	163	−7	−4.3
13 Durham	196.5	202	−5.5	−2.7
14 Ely	148	138	10	6.9
15 Exeter	231	233	−2	−1.0
16 Gloucester	142	140	2	1.6
17 Guildford	177	155	22	14.1
18 Hereford	95	112	−17	−15.0
19 Leicester	137.5	149	−11.5	−7.7
20 Lichfield	306	316	−10	−3.1
21 Lincoln	188	222	−34	−15.4
22 Liverpool	209	208	1	0.3
23 London	522	497	25	5.1
24 Manchester	251.5	263	−11.5	−4.4
25 Newcastle	139.5	140	−0.5	−0.4
26 Norwich	201	195	6	2.9
27 Oxford	374.5	385	−10.5	−2.7
28 Peterborough	155	155	0	−0.1
29 Portsmouth	108	110	−2	−1.6
30 Ripon and Leeds	128	139	−11	−7.9
31 Rochester	226	187	39	20.9
32 St. Albans	262	263	−1	−0.4
33 St. Edms and Ipswich	143	152	−9	−5.8
34 Salisbury	209	214	−5	−2.3
35 Sheffield	164	163	1	0.5
36 Sodor and Man	17.5	18	−0.5	−2.8
37 Southwark	355	325	30	9.3
38 Southwell	152.5	163	−10.5	−6.4
39 Truro	110	116	−6	−5.0
40 Wakefield	152.5	156	−3.5	−2.2
41 Winchester	208	221	−13	−5.7
42 Worcester	145	136	9	6.6
43 York	243	265	−22	−8.4
Province of Canterbury	6,095	6,042	53	0.9
Province of York	2,352	2,405	−53	−2.2
CHURCH OF ENGLAND	8,447	8,447	0	0.0

Note: The 'Actual' is the number of full-time stipendiary clergy plus the whole-time equivalent of the part-time clergy. Shares are allocated as whole posts. Some actual halves are shown to remove rounding errors.

Source: Church Statistics, Archbishops' Council

Spring Projections of Diocesan Shares 2008 to 2012, and 2017 As at December each year

Diocese	2008 Spring 2008 projection	2009 Spring 2008 projection	2010 Spring 2008 projection	2011 Spring 2008 projection	2012 Spring 2008 projection	2017 Spring 2008 projection
1 Bath and Wells	199	198	194	191	187	172
2 Birmingham	175	173	170	166	163	149
3 Blackburn	203	202	198	194	190	174
4 Bradford	104	103	101	100	98	90
5 Bristol	132	131	129	127	124	114
6 Canterbury	156	155	152	149	147	134
7 Carlisle	133	132	129	126	124	114
8 Chelmsford	389	386	378	371	364	333
9 Chester	246	244	239	234	229	210
10 Chichester	276	273	268	263	258	236
11 Coventry	125	124	121	119	117	107
12 Derby	163	161	158	155	152	139
13 Durham	199	197	192	188	184	169
14 Ely	138	137	135	132	130	119
15 Exeter	233	231	227	223	218	200
16 Gloucester	139	137	135	132	129	119
17 Guildford	155	153	150	147	144	132
18 Hereford	112	110	108	106	104	95
19 Leicester	148	146	144	141	138	127
20 Lichfield	313	310	303	297	291	266
21 Lincoln	223	222	217	213	209	192
22 Liverpool	206	203	199	194	190	174
23 London	498	494	485	477	469	431
24 Manchester	261	259	254	249	244	223
25 Newcastle	138	136	134	131	128	117
26 Norwich	195	194	190	187	183	168
27 Oxford	382	378	371	363	356	327
28 Peterborough	154	153	150	148	145	133
29 Portsmouth	110	109	107	105	103	94
30 Ripon and Leeds	138	136	134	131	129	118
31 Rochester	185	184	180	176	173	159
32 St. Albans	262	260	255	250	246	225
33 St. Edms and Ipswich	151	150	147	145	142	130
34 Salisbury	214	212	208	204	200	183
35 Sheffield	161	159	156	153	149	137
36 Sodor and Man	18	18	17	17	17	15
37 Southwark	322	319	313	307	301	276
38 Southwell	162	160	157	154	151	139
39 Truro	116	115	113	111	109	100
40 Wakefield	155	153	150	147	145	133
41 Winchester	220	218	214	210	206	188
42 Worcester	134	133	130	127	125	114
43 York	263	261	255	250	246	225
Province of Canterbury	6,019	5,966	5,852	5,742	5,633	5,162
Province of York	2,387	2,363	2,315	2,268	2,224	2,038
CHURCH OF ENGLAND	8,406	8,329	8,167	8,010	7,857	7,200

Notes: Spring 2008 projection based on 337 ordinands in 2008 (206 male and 131 female), an estimated 339 ordinands (218 men and 121 women) for 2009, and thereafter a five-year moving average.
Share projections use diocesan population projections based on ONS 2004-based population projections for Local Authority Districts.
Source: Church Statistics, Archbishops' Council

Projections of Diocesan Shares 2008 to 2012, and 2017

As at December each year

Diocese	2008 Standard projection	2009 Standard projection	2010 Lower projection	2010 Standard projection	2010 Higher projection	2011 Lower projection	2011 Standard projection	2011 Higher projection	2012 Lower projection	2012 Standard projection	2012 Higher projection	2017 Lower projection	2017 Standard projection	2017 Higher projection
1 Bath and Wells	199	198	189	194	196	185	191	193	181	187	191	161	172	181
2 Birmingham	175	173	166	170	171	161	166	169	157	163	166	140	149	158
3 Blackburn	203	202	193	198	199	188	194	197	183	190	194	163	174	184
4 Bradford	104	103	99	101	102	97	100	101	94	98	100	84	90	95
5 Bristol	132	131	126	129	130	123	127	128	120	124	127	106	114	120
6 Canterbury	156	155	148	152	153	145	149	151	141	147	150	125	134	141
7 Carlisle	133	132	126	129	130	123	126	128	120	124	126	106	114	120
8 Chelmsford	389	386	369	378	381	360	371	376	351	364	371	311	333	351
9 Chester	246	244	233	239	240	227	234	237	221	229	233	196	210	221
10 Chichester	276	273	261	268	270	255	263	267	249	258	263	221	236	249
11 Coventry	125	124	118	121	122	115	119	121	113	117	119	100	107	113
12 Derby	163	161	154	158	159	150	155	157	147	152	155	130	139	147
13 Durham	199	197	188	192	194	182	188	191	177	184	188	158	169	178
14 Ely	138	137	131	135	136	128	132	134	125	130	133	111	119	125
15 Exeter	233	231	221	227	228	216	223	226	211	218	223	187	200	211
16 Gloucester	139	137	131	135	136	128	132	134	125	129	132	111	119	125
17 Guildford	155	153	146	150	151	143	147	149	139	144	147	124	132	139
18 Hereford	112	110	106	108	109	103	106	108	100	104	106	89	95	101
19 Leicester	148	146	140	144	145	137	141	143	133	138	141	118	127	133
20 Lichfield	313	310	296	303	305	288	297	301	280	291	296	249	266	281
21 Lincoln	223	222	212	217	219	207	213	216	202	209	214	179	192	202
22 Liverpool	206	203	194	199	200	189	194	197	183	190	194	163	174	184
23 London	498	494	473	485	489	463	477	483	452	469	477	403	431	453
24 Manchester	261	259	247	254	256	241	249	252	235	244	248	209	223	236
25 Newcastle	138	136	130	134	135	127	131	133	123	128	130	110	117	124

Diocese	2008 Standard projection	2009 Standard projection	2010 Lower projection	2010 Standard projection	2010 Higher projection	2011 Lower projection	2011 Standard projection	2011 Higher projection	2012 Lower projection	2012 Standard projection	2012 Higher projection	2017 Lower projection	2017 Standard projection	2017 Higher projection
26 Norwich	195	194	185	190	192	181	187	189	177	183	187	157	168	177
27 Oxford	382	378	361	371	374	353	363	369	344	356	363	305	327	344
28 Peterborough	154	153	147	150	152	143	148	150	140	145	148	124	133	140
29 Portsmouth	110	109	104	107	108	102	105	106	99	103	105	88	94	99
30 Ripon and Leeds	138	136	130	134	135	127	131	133	124	129	131	110	118	124
31 Rochester	185	184	175	180	181	171	176	179	167	173	176	148	159	167
32 St. Albans	262	260	249	255	257	243	250	254	237	246	251	210	225	237
33 St. Edms and Ipswich	151	150	144	147	148	140	145	147	137	142	145	122	130	137
34 Salisbury	214	212	203	208	209	198	204	207	193	200	204	171	183	193
35 Sheffield	161	159	152	156	157	148	153	155	144	149	152	128	137	145
36 Sodor and Man	18	18	17	17	18	17	17	17	16	17	17	14	15	16
37 Southwark	322	319	305	313	316	298	307	312	290	301	307	258	276	291
38 Southwell	162	160	153	157	158	150	154	156	146	151	154	130	139	146
39 Truro	116	115	110	113	114	108	111	113	105	109	112	94	100	105
40 Wakefield	155	153	147	150	151	143	147	150	139	145	147	124	133	140
41 Winchester	220	218	208	214	215	203	210	213	198	206	210	176	188	199
42 Worcester	134	133	127	130	131	123	127	129	120	125	127	107	114	121
43 York	263	261	249	255	257	243	250	254	237	246	250	210	225	237
Province of Canterbury	6,019	5,966	5,705	5,852	5,897	5,570	5,742	5,824	5,433	5,633	5,746	4,825	5,162	5,440
Province of York	2,387	2,363	2,258	2,315	2,332	2,202	2,268	2,301	2,142	2,224	2,264	1,905	2,038	2,150
CHURCH OF ENGLAND	8,406	8,329	7,963	8,167	8,229	7,772	8,010	8,125	7,575	7,857	8,010	6,730	7,200	7,590

Notes: The 2008 figures are based on 337 ordinands (206 men and 131 women) and the 2009 figures on an estimated 339 ordinands (218 men and 121 women). From 2010 onwards, a moving average has been used to calculate the standard projections. Higher projections assume that the highest recent estimate of ordinations into stipendiary ministry is achieved and maintained. Lower projections assume that an average of the three most recent years of ordinations is maintained.
They also allow some changes in the age profile of ordinands following the pattern of recent years.
Source: Church Statistics, Archbishops' Council

Notes

Introduction

1 Schori, 2006, p. 169.

2 At one level this is straightforwardly expressed in ordination rites and Anglican theological agreed statements, e.g. 'The calling of a priest or presbyter is to represent Christ and his Church, particularly as pastor to the people; to share with the bishops in the overseeing of the Church; to proclaim the gospel; to administer the sacraments; and to bless and declare pardon in the name of God.' Anglican Consultative Council (ACC), 1997 (*Virginia Report*), 3.18.

3 The term *tó presbytérion* occurs in the New Testament for 'the Sanhedrin' and 'the council of elders' in the church (cf. Luke 22.66; 1 Tim. 4.14). Common in Ignatius, the term signifies for him the council of presbyters, which parallels that of the apostles (*Philadelphians* 5.1) and functions as the bishop's council (8.1).

4 ACC, 1997, 4.10.

5 ACC, 1997, 4.22 and 4.25–27.

6 'What we are seeing, then, is the stepping back of theology into the public domain and a consideration of its relation to the whole of human thought and action . . . it occupies the domain of what Balthasar called "the suspended middle" between grace-imbued faith and natural understanding. This domain for him and for Henri de Lubac was that of the paradoxical "natural desire for the supernatural".' Milbank, in Smith, 2004, p. 12. See Morisy, 2004.

7 I am grateful to Jim Dawson, New Zealand historian, for this insight.

8 See Philips, 1956.

9 Yves Congar notably explored the origins and developing function of the biblical term *laos*, in Congar, 1965. For a résumé of Congar's contribution to an ecclesiology rooted in *koinonia* and the call of all Christians to holiness, see Lakeland, 2003, pp. 52ff.

10 'In the last three decades or so, *koinonia* or communion has become an increasingly popular model of the church. The church is constituted as communion by its grace-enabled participation in the communion among the divine persons, and is thereby drawn into the life of the Triune God.' Healey, 2007, p. 122.

11 'It is because we are united to Christ who is bone of our bone and flesh of our flesh, and participate in the risen Humanity of Christ so that we are bone of His bone and flesh of His flesh (Eph. 5.30), that eschatology is so essential to our faith and life from day to day. Union with

Christ means union with the Christ who rose again from the dead, who ascended to the right hand of God the Father, and who will come again; and therefore union with Him here and now carries in its heart the outreach of faith toward the resurrection of the dead and the renewal of heaven and earth at the Second Advent of Christ.' Torrance, 1999, p. 43.

12 '. . . crises are brought about by the divine dynamic itself. Even more we hope that this world will continue to go through constant crises in its imperial power structures, in its authoritarian dogmatisms and cultural pretensions, in its profit-seeking economies that forget the poor. Because it is in these crises, and in the need to restate our own conception of what it is to be human time and again, that we discover the ongoing saving dialogue God holds with us.' Miguez, 2007, p. 68.

13 Elizabeth Schüssler Fiorenza writes, 'Women are church and have always been church.' Cited in Watson, 2002, p. 1.

14 'Postcolonial analyses of colonial and neo-colonial discourse offer the possibility to intricately and carefully map the shifts in the production of power/knowledge and to formulate an equally intricate response to those shifts.' Grau, 2004, p. 33.

1 Church for the world's true life

1 Hauerwas, 2004, p. 14.

2 Hopkins, G. M., in Nicholson and Lee (eds), 1917; Pennington, 2000, p. 46.

3 'The internal organization of the church has symbolic power: it sends a message to society and supports corresponding cultural trends. What the church thinks about democracy is not so much communicated through its prophetic official teaching as through its own institutional life.' Baum, in Wilfred and Susin, 2007, p. 59.

4 See Anglican Consultative Council (ACC), 1997, 3.1–3.4.

5 See Alan Billings and others in the *Church Times*, 1 February 2008.

6 'The practice of "otherness" is not about close rules of contamination. It is about the simple, obvious, daily practices of respect and enhancement that mark the neighbour into well-being.' Brueggemann, 2006, p. 191. See ACC, 1997, 5.1.

7 'Every act of God is an act of the undivided Holy Trinity. The very being of the Church is thus dependent upon the outpouring of God's gracious love, the love of Father, Son and Holy Spirit.' ACC, 1997, 2.12.

8 George, 2003, p. 4.

9 Pattison, 2000, ch. 8.

10 'By turning difference into division through the rejection of the other, we die. Hell, eternal death, is nothing but isolation from the other, as the desert Fathers put it. We cannot solve this problem through ethics.

We need a new birth. This leads us to ecclesiology.' Zizioulas, 2006, p. 3.

11 ARCIC, 1999, 23.

12 Watts, Nye and Savage, 2002, p. 129.

13 See Watts, Nye and Savage, pp. 250ff.

14 Kegan and Lahey, 2001.

15 Nationally and locally, the Church of England is in a process of preparing for Clergy Terms of Service. Rather than being merely rooted in competency, the desire is to establish a learning culture. In this radical change of culture the core text is the Ministry Division's *Review of Clergy Terms of Service*, 2004.

16 See Rooms and Steen, 2008.

17 ACC, 1997, 4.5.

18 See Torrance's discussion of ordained ministry within the Body of Christ, taking note of John Robinson's groundbreaking study, *The Body*. Torrance, 1999, pp. 23ff.

19 'Perhaps you are like me, so enmeshed in this reality that another way is nearly unthinkable . . . We are seldom aware that a minority report may be found in the Bible, the vision of some fanatics who believe that the royal portrayal of history is not accurate because it does not do justice (*sic*) either to this God or to these brothers and sisters . . . God, unlike his royal regents, is one whose person is presented as passion and pathos, the power to care, the capacity to weep, the energy to grieve and then to rejoice.' Brueggemann, 2001a, pp. 36f.

20 'The royal consciousness leads people to despair about the power to move toward new life. It is the task of prophetic imagination and ministry to bring people to engage the promise of newness that is at work in our history with God.' Brueggemann, 2001a, pp. 59f.

21 Keller, 2005.

22 Watts, Nye and Savage, 2002, pp. 121ff.

23 See Brueggemann, 2000, p. 76.

24 See the fundamentally reordered ecclesiology in the work of Cardinal Suenens in preparation for Vatican II. Suenens, 1968.

25 Leech, 1977 and Peterson, 1989.

26 Ecclesiology is the study of the nature, story and character of the Church as a community related to the coming of Jesus Christ. It is a multidisciplinary topic that is currently an important focus for theological study. For a sense of the growing literature and sub-disciplines, see Mannion and Mudge, 2007.

27 As Torrance summarizes, 'the corporeal nature of the Church as shaped by the Word of the Gospel, and informed by the Spirit in the power of the resurrection, means the breaking up and the relativiz-ing of the historical forms of the Church throughout its mission.' Torrance, 1999, p. 71.

28 Hull, 1991.
29 Boyett and Boyett, 1998.
30 Tiller, 1983.
31 Zizioulas, 1985, pp. 123ff.
32 Hunt, 2005, p. 4.
33 For a discussion of this theme in the Vatican II Constitution on the Church, *Lumen Gentium*, see Hunt, 2005, pp. 121f.
34 '[A]t Pentecost the Word of the Gospel is effectually realized in the creation out of the matrix of Israel of a new *soma*, the Body of Christ, the Church. But here in this Body there takes place a parallel movement from particularity to universality, for filled with the Spirit of Christ who has ascended to fill all things, the Church is caught up in the movement of *pleroma*. As such it is the first-fruits of the new creation (Ja. 1.18; Rev. 14.4; cf. Rom. 8.23; I Cor. 15.20), the new humanity in concentrated form, as it were, pressing out immediately in expansion to the utmost limits.' Torrance, 1999, p. 26.
35 Zizioulas, 1985, p. 18.
36 The Greek, *perichoresis*, meaning 'mutual indwelling', refers to the concept of the coinherence of the three divine Persons in the one God. Gregory of Nazianzen first uses the Greek for 'around a place' to speak analogously of the Persons of the Trinity mutually containing and interpenetrating one another while maintaining their incommunicable differences. See Torrance, 1994, pp. 32f.
37 Johnson, 2008, p. 265.
38 Johnson, 2008, p. 270.
39 Moltmann, 1989, p. 190.
40 Johnson consider trinitarian language as a 'naming towards the divine' so that analogy acts like an arc or vector. Johnson, 2008, pp. 113–17.
41 Johnson, 2008, p. 198.
42 Johnson, 2008, p. 221.
43 Moltmann, 1997.
44 Zizioulas, 1985, pp. 43 and 53ff.
45 Schwöbel, 1995.
46 'The true humanity of Christ is constituted by its assumption by the Son. Conversely, it is only in being the hypostasis of the humanity of Christ that the divine Son is the incarnate Son. The identity of Jesus Christ is then described as terms of the union of the person of the Son, who is constituted as the Son in his relation to the Father in the Spirit, with the humanity of Jesus, which is constituted in its relational structure, precisely through its hypostatic participation in the person of the Son in its relations to the Father and the Spirit. The hypostatic being of the Son is the eschatological promise for the whole of creation, realized in the person of the incarnate Son. It is the ground of its possibility, and the promise of its realization.' Hunt, 2005, p. 67.

47 See Jamieson, 1997, p. 35.
48 'Either the *entire* Christian narrative tells us how things truly are, or it does not. If it does, we have no other access to how things truly *are*, nor any additional means of determining the question.' Milbank, in Smith, 2004, p. 51.
49 'but if St Paul is right, then *ecclesia* as founded by Christ names the only polity, or at least possibility of a polity, which collectively lives, beyond death, as an exception even to the law of exception, because it replaces the political animal with the pneumatic body of grace-given mutual trust.' Milbank, 2008, pp. 21f.
50 Mannion, in Mannion and Mudge, 2007, p. 127.
51 Ammicht-Quinn, 2003, p. 42.
52 Catherine Keller writes attractively of the 'fallacy of the binary alternative'. Drawing on postcolonial theory, she describes hybrid identities created through the braiding of ambiguity and celebrating the grey shadows between binary poles. Keller, 2005, pp. 102ff. Field theory, Gestalt theory and the approach to geo-justice advocated notably by Freeman Dyson, demonstrate the inadequacy of binary or adversarial approaches to solving complex problems. Dyson's combination of ethics, scientific theory, technological adventure, psychology and flair, suggest the attractiveness of reimagining the universe in terms of diverse and holistic field forces. See Greenwood, 2002, pp. 56ff. Decision-making processes used by the People of the First Nations in Canada and other aboriginal cultures avoid adversarial methods, based on the 'white man's *win/lose* model'. Native peoples meet and conduct trials in a circle, which affords an opportunity for the *win/win* model to prevail. (Originally they also camped in a circle, lived in a circle (the tepee) and ate in a circle, a holistic practice deemed to be empowering.) As a native writer has pointed out 'The circle is a decision-making process that includes prayer as a key element. The traditional circle emphasizes equality; everyone is at the same level. This process is less intimidating, garners more information, and empowers the community. It makes it less easy for ego to prevail.' See Fraser, in Bird, Land and Macadam (eds) 2002, p. 114.
53 Greenwood, 1988, p. 216.
54 Secular practices of democracy from ancient Greece to eighteenth-century France and even now have oppressed slaves, foreigners and women. As Sobrino writes, 'This is exactly the opposite of what lies at the root of the biblical tradition: at its centre is an oppressed people, lacking power, lacking life, which is hoping for liberation.' Sobrino, 2007, p. 73.
55 Petrella, 2008, p. 132.
56 Althaus-Reid, 2001, p. 5.
57 Sobrino, 2007, p. 77.

58 Patzia, 2001 and Longenecker, 2002.

58 Gooder, 2007, pp. 23f.

60 See Morisy, 2004, pp. 38ff.

61 Petrella, 2008, p. 136.

62 'Justice, however, does not merely mean the equal distribution of goods by those in power, but rather, a community in which all are welcome, in which everybody is celebrated as part of the body of Christ, a gathering of those who are church together with others. A feminist community is not based on "helping" others, but on being with each other in the image of the Triune God.' Watson, 2002, p. 47.

63 Watson, 2002, p. 17.

64 See Grau, 2004, p. 6 note 13. The 1940s Mission de France led by Godin and Suhard was an earlier attempt to reform the Church to evangelize the 'real milieux'. Lakeland, 2008, p. 25.

65 Carter, 2007, Avalos, Melcher and Schipper, 2007 and Ross, 1994, p. 119.

66 Grau, 2004, p. 40.

67 McFague, 2001, pp. 146, 151.

68 Milbank, 2008.

69 Jinkins, 1999.

70 God is known where God is most self-revealed, in Jesus' paschal mystery, especially in his death on the cross. von Balthasar, 1968, p. 71.

71 Doyle, 2000, pp. 178f.

72 ACC, 1997, 2.15.

73 Advocating a hermeneutic of resurrection in the midst of life's contingencies, Ford writes, 'The eschatological thrust, with its cries of passionate longing, warning, fear, and anticipatory joy, meets the confusion of cries thrown up by the sufferings and joys of ongoing history; and wisdom at the cutting edge of life now is continually challenged, stretched and opened up in contradiction, paradox, offence, agony and exultation.' Ford, 2007, p. 41.

74 To save any possible misunderstanding, from all that has been already said, it should be clear that I am not here advocating a church that takes the moral high ground or sees itself as on an apocalyptic power trip. See Keller, 2003.

75 Torrance, 1999, p. 42.

76 'The dynamic of Christian unity lies deep in the heart of God, in the *koinonia* between the three Persons of the Holy Trinity. God desires that nothing less than the intimate communion between the Father, the Son and the Holy Spirit should be reflected in the life of the Church.' WCC, 1999, 2.1. See Grundy, 2007, p. 11.

77 As with all ordained ministry, this *episcope* should have three dimensions: the personal, collegial and communal. The Meisson Declaration affirms that 'a ministry of pastoral oversight (*episcope*) exercised in

personal, collegial and communal ways, is necessary to witness to the unity and apostolicity of the Church.' *On the Way to Visible Unity: A Common Statement*, para. 15 (ix), in WCC, 1999, 5.4.2.

78 General Synod, Anglican Church of Australia, 2004, section 1.

79 ACC, 1997, 5.6–8.

80 'The exercise of the *sensus fidelium* by each member of the Church contributes to the formation of the *sensus fidelium* through the Church as whole. By the *sensus fidelium*, the whole body contributes to, receives from and treasures the ministry of those within the community who exercise *episkope*, watching over the living memory of the Church.' ARCIC, 1999, 29.

81 ARCIC, 1999, 36.

82 ACC, 1997, 5.10.

83 ARCIC, 1999, 28.

84 WCC, 1999, 5.4.2.

85 Lakeland, 2008.

86 Collins, 2002.

87 So the bishop acts 'in the person of the community' and represents the local to the wider Church at councils or synods, which requires a maturity in the faith. See Evans, 2007, p. 38.

88 Zizioulas, 1985, pp. 252, 247 and 257.

89 WCC, 1999, 5.4.2.

90 Bonhoeffer, 1955.

91 'The movement is down, down, down, until it finds the sickest, the most afflicted, the most helpless, the most alienated, the most cut off. The truest symbols that we have of Jesus are the lamb – the lamb led to the slaughter, a sheep before its shearers being dumb. Total poverty . . . the weeping of Christ riding into Jerusalem on a donkey.' Alexander, 2007, p. 51.

92 'Ignatius believed in the importance of engaging in prayer not only feelings, but also the intellect, memory, will and imagination to help retreatants discover God's will and purpose for them.' Ternier-Gommers, 2007, p. 53.

93 See notably Rohr, 2006 and Alexander, 2007.

94 'When we perceive more and more clearly our true self in God, we are all but dazzled by the wonder of this image of God. But at the same time we are profoundly humbled. For we know that we are made in the image and likeness of God . . . And we know that, but for the grace of God, it could be wholly lost.' Pennington, 2000, p. 49.

95 'Through this False Self the infant builds up a set of relationships, by means of introjection even attains a show of being real, so that the child may grow up to be just like the mother, nurse, aunt, brother, or whoever dominated the scene. The False Self has one positive and very important function: to hide the True Self, which it does by compliance

with environmental demands.' Winnicott, D. W., *The Maturational Processes and the Facilitating Environment* (Hogarth, London, 1965), cited in M. Davis and D. Wallbridge, *Boundary and Space: An Introduction to the Work of D. W. Winnicott* (Brunner-Routledge, New York, 1981), p. 48, in Alexander, 2007, p. 17.

96 'The false self is formed, then, by fulfilling all the internalized rules and requirements to gain acceptance and approval from those we value – including God. Often we are not even aware that we have transferred these beliefs on to God, yet we spend our time living according to certain internalized patterns of behaviour that we think will gain God's approval . . . Most of us do this all the time, but some people escape this.' Alexander, 2007, p. 17. See Rulla, 1986 and Greenwood and Burgess, 2005, ch. 3.

97 Greenwood and Burgess, 2005, p. 24.

98 See Robertson, 2007.

2 What's in your diary?

1 Maybee, 2001, p. 15.

2 'A clutch of models needs to be replaced by a single overarching theory, a description with reasonable pretensions to being taken with the ontological seriousness that would correspond to its providing a verisimilitudinous account of what is actually going on, at least at a level of detailed structure.' Polkinghorne, 2007, p. 75.

3 E. Monro, *Pastoral Work*, 1850, pp. 53–5, quoted in Russell, 1980, p. 129.

4 Despite the groundbreaking work of John Collins, within UK Anglicanism the majority of those serving as deacons expect to be ordained priest within a year.

5 I appreciate the time given by some who were prepared to be interviewed by members of the group who have supported the writing of this book. The five bishops were male; of the 40 priests, 19 were female. The identities of individuals have been deliberately disguised and profiles overlapped so that issues cannot be linked just to one person.

6 See Grundy, 2007, ch. 8.

7 There is a parallel perhaps in the teachings of yoga, where although the teachings of past masters carry significance, accumulated practice is the principal medium of learning. Theories of leadership need to be suffused with Jesus' invitation to become as little children. See Irigaray, 2000, p. 54.

8 See the accounts from Brazil and Latin America in Bingemer, 2002. I am grateful for discussion with Manon Parry of her doctoral research on the relevance, from a feminist pastoral theology, of the self in understanding and critiquing the practice of giving and receiving pastoral

care and ministry, with particular reference to the Anglican Church in North Wales.

9 '[T]he building of a public space and exercise of citizenship in a new way, on the basis of "difference" restated as a valuable and important element in the whole process, including a redefinition of the very concepts of "public" and "private"'. Bingemer, 2002, p. 105.

10 Sedgwick, 2006, p. 150.

11 Kung, 2001.

12 See Farley, in Gunton and Hardy, 1989, p. 73.

13 See Hardy, 'Afterword: Evaluating Local Ministry for the Future of the Church', in Greenwood and Pascoe, 2006, pp. 131ff.

14 Robert W. Jenson asserts that the traditional understanding of the Father begetting the Son and spirating the Spirit is inadequate because incomplete. Every act of God is a trinitarian act. He suggests that the Spirit liberates the Father for the Son and reconciles the Son to the Father. Defending this position, Jenson explores the events of Gethsemane and the baptism of Jesus. In the Garden, the will of the Son is 'reconciled' to the will of the Father. Although it is not explicitly stated, it is reasonable to assume the Spirit's involvement. The Son says, 'Not my will but yours.' The utterance itself is, of course, pre-cisely the act of his will to be one with his Father, but nevertheless this very act is itself a reconciliation of two wills. Were Gethsemane a scene in anyone else's life, we would not hesitate to say that what we see here is a man being reconciled to his destiny or to one who determines his destiny. The evangelists do not explicitly name the Spirit as the agent of this reconciliation. But the classical trinitarian tradition names the Spirit as the *vinculum amoris* between the Father and the Son, and if the love of the Father and the Son includes a reconciliation between them, then the Spirit is the agent thereof. Jesus' baptism, though, is more explicit. There the Spirit mediates between the Son and the Father, and this mediation is essential to the Son being the Son. The prophetic and creative Spirit, known throughout the Old Testament, appears *between* them, as the power of the proclaimed relation. In Gunton, 2003, pp. 158ff.

15 'The dynamics of this intra-trinitarian community could be imagined as a dance, a perichoretic celebration of God's love for God. In this intra-trinitarian perichoresis, suppression of difference into a central-ized sameness never takes place, because it is precisely in sharing-difference that the rhythm and dynamics of this one perpetual flow beyond unity dances . . . The exchange of the gift in the trinitarian com-munity is both excess and reciprocity, and it does not occur outside of, or prior to, its being given received, and shared.' Mendez, 2005, p. 17.

16 I am persuaded by John Polkinghorne of the many parallels between the work of scientists and theologians in the various ways of searching

for a 'description with reasonable pretensions, to being taken with the ontological seriousness that would correspond to its providing a verisimilitudinous account of what is actually going on, at least at a certain level of detailed structure'. Polkinghorne, 2007, p. 75.

17 Lakeland, 2003.

18 In dialogue with several contemporary theologians: Walter Brueggemann, David F. Ford, Daniel W. Hardy, Nicholas M. Healey, Graham Hughes, Catherine Keller, Miroslav Volf, Samuel Wells and John D. Zizioulas.

19 Dulles, 1978, p. 178.

20 Dulles, 1978, pp. 194–8.

21 I am glad to acknowledge a debt of gratitude to the work of Daniel Hardy. See Hardy, 2001.

22 'Today as in every age, a constant temptation for preachers or ministers of the Gospel, and indeed for believers of all kinds, is to water down this "wine" of the Gospel with bland ways of thinking and speaking, and to join those among our contemporaries who are leaning, as it were, on the sad "bar-counter" of average addiction, or average distraction.' Murray, 2006, p. 1.

23 '[P]urposeful action and prayer . . . both informed by the wider resources of ecclesial wisdom, tradition and experience that contribute to constructive theological understanding and, crucially, shape Chris-tian identity. Otherwise urban mission can easily become a matter of personal taste, untutored theological sloganizing or a potentially dangerous religious enclave . . . its grammar of faith will appear thin and meagre.' Milbank, 2007.

24 '. . . the reciprocal knowing of Father and Son. *The uniting of joy, responsibility, and the intimate knowing of love centred on full recognition of the other, is simultaneously the source of the cry of rejoicing and the content of divine wisdom.*' Ford, 2007, p. 25 (italics in original).

25 See Wainwright, in Jeanrond and Theobald, 2001, pp. 96ff.

3 Church: communal practice of Good News

1 Brueggemann, 2007b, p. 165.

2 Hardy, 1996, pp. 222ff.

3 Hirst, 2006.

4 'There is a core insight into the nature of wisdom that has been discovered in the Old Testament, New Testament and the Christian Tradition. This: *God is to be loved for God's sake*'. Ford, 2007, p. 225.

5 Johnson, 2008, p. 45.

6 Describing God's holiness, Hardy writes, 'More fundamental, however, is its capacity to maintain its fullness according to its own kind, without reference to, or collapse into, other kinds. Suffice it to say

that *"propriety"* and *"purity"* or *"self-capacity"* and *"capacity for self-maintenance"* are primary ways of designating what is "holy".' Hardy, 2001, p. 9 (italics in original).

7 John Wesley, in Keller, 2003, p. 23.

8 '[P]erichoresis: a sociality of rhythmic interrelations in which inside and out would no longer bifurcate'. Keller, 2003, p. 18. Sere Jones finds the trinitarian reality of Barth's God, 'radically multiple, radically relational, and infinitely active'. Keller, 2003, p. 87; Volf, in Torrance and Banner, 2006, p. 110. See also Elizabeth Johnson, 2008.

9 Ford and Hardy, 2005, p. 13.

10 Wells, 2006, pp. 36ff.

11 Hardy, 1996, p. 186.

12 Hardy, 2001, p. 16.

13 'Here what is emphasized is not difference as such, but being-in-relation and co-participation. And, because of their (self and other) participating in God's excess, their desire for one another and for God perpetually increases as it moves forward into the culmination of history: the promise of perfect communion as a state of eternal ecstasy.' Mendez, 2005, p. 19.

14 Keller, 2003, ch. 4, pp. 65ff.

15 '[T]hat infinitely deep interconnectedness . . . the matrix in which everything is interrelated in the relativity of the universe . . . the inescapably reciprocal character of the continuum of relations'. Keller, 2005, p. 146.

16 Keller, 2003, ch. 9, pp. 157ff.

17 'The Eucharist is the ecclesial performance and celebration of the gift of God's most intimate presence. But, more, as communion, the Eucharist is transformative, and so calls us to be people of God through communion with God on the one hand, and also with the world, and most urgently toward those who hunger for bread, justice and love.' Mendez, 2005, p. 19.

18 'Christianity is characterized by the simplicity and complexity of facing: being faced by God, embodied in the face of Christ; turning to face Jesus Christ in faith; being members of a community of the face; seeing the face of God in creation and especially in the human face, with all the faces in our heart related to the presence of the face of Christ.' Ford, 1999, pp. 24f.

18 Brueggemann, 2006, p. 157.

20 'It is through the very movement of God's holiness towards mankind in the life, death and resurrection of Jesus Christ that mankind is purified and redeemed.' Hardy, 1996, p. 169.

21 Wells, 2006, p. 205.

22 Mendez, 2005, p. 15.

23 '[I]n the Eucharistic feast, God's excessive love feeds all our longing for God in a manner that satiation fills us with desire to taste more of God-self, to have in our mouth what is still yet-to-come. And this erotic movement forward enkindles – and never diminishes – our desire for God, making us feasting pilgrims within history moving towards the *eschaton*: the final and total partaking of God's super-abundant banquet.' Mendez, 2005, p. 15.

24 '[I]t is in the movement of worship (focused in praise), together with the movement of reorientation which accompanies it, that the dynamics of divine order in human life are found in most concentrated form.' Hardy, 1996, p. 15. See The *Virginia Report*, ACC, 1997, 2.20.

25 '[Apophatic theology] is speech about God which is the failure of speech; it is failure in the sense of speech slowing to a halt in awed wonder before the presence of what is always more than one can say'. Denys Turner, in O'Murchu, 2007, p. 147. 'The message of apophatic theology was precisely that the closed Greek ontology had to be broken and transcended, since we are unable to use the concepts of the human mind or of creation, for signifying God – the truth. The absolute otherness of God's being which is found at the heart of biblical theology is affirmed in such a manner that the biblical approach to God contrasts acutely with that of the Greeks.' Zizioulas, 1985, p. 90.

26 Hardy, 1996, p. 168.

27 'Christ is present in his word and speaks through Scripture with the people of God who are assembled around him. The role of the homily is to help to integrate that divine speaking into the lives of the faithful, so that they increasingly be formed in the breath or Spirit of God and so live lives that are opened out with thanksgiving into the compassionate creativity of God.' Davies, 2004, p. 129.

28 Brueggemann, 2006, p. 12.

29 Brueggemann, 2006, pp. 8f.

30 Brueggemann, 2006, p. 75ff.

31 Hardy, 2001, p. 19; 1996, p. 166.

32 'The praise has power to transform the pain but conversely the present pain also keeps the act of praise honest. Praise about old transformations by themselves may permit the old troubles to seem remote from the present moment. But the present reality of pain within which praise is done reminds Israel that this longstanding formulation of praise was articulated and utilized precisely in a context of pain, namely the pain of slavery. Just as this pain was sung in the midst of trouble and oppression, so now it is peculiarly germane in the present pain. As praise recontextualizes pain, so pain refocuses praise.' Brueggemann, 1988, p. 139.

33 See Brueggemann, 2007b, ch. 1.

34 Soelle, 1984, p. 90.

35 O'Collins, 2007, pp. 181ff.

36 Brueggemann, 2006, pp. 158 and 160.

37 Brueggemann, 2006, p. 180.

38 See Greenwood, 1996, ch. 3, pp. 44ff.

39 Volf, in Torrance and Banner, 2006, p. 110.

40 'God communicates himself to us, we enter into communion with him, the participants of the sacrament enter into communion with one another, and creation as a whole enters through man into communion with God. All this takes place in Christ and the Spirit, who brings the last days into history and offers to the world a foretaste of the kingdom.' Zizioulas, 2006, p. 7.

41 'Such are the things that *in principle* and by *an act of faith* – not by way of failure to apply the true faith – lead to a kind of communion that disturbs Trinitarian, Christological, Pneumatological and ecclesiological faith.' Zizioulas, 2006, p. 7.

42 *Cyprus Agreed Statement*, ACC, 2006, 12.

43 The failures of the Church do not hold back the work of the Kingdom because in humility the Church can see signs of the Kingdom in many places elsewhere. Wells, 2006, p. 34.

44 Volf, in Torrance and Banner, 2006, p. 110. J. Ratzinger's ecclesiology assumes that the universal Church precedes the local and that the highest ministry has the task of keeping in order the local. See Zizioulas, 2006, p. 145.

45 Zizioulas, 1985, p. 141.

46 'A healthy complexity is needed, in which local churches exemplify a sensitivity to the special needs of people, while knitting them into a dynamic society both local and world-wide.' Hardy, 2001, pp. 88f.

47 '[T]he persons [of the Trinity] do not simply enter into relations with one another, but are constituted by one another in the relations.' Gunton, 1993, p. 214 and Volf, in Torrance and Banner, 2006, p. 111.

48 *Cyprus Agreed Statement*, ACC, 2006, 4.

49 'The person exists not in possession of its own nature, in opposition to others, but in giving itself wholly into the life of others'. *Cyprus Agreed Statement*, ACC, 2006, 4.

50 Zizioulas, 2006, p. 5.

51 Zizioulas, 1985.

52 'The critical mandate of the community of the Torah, as this tradition voices it, is to be a community matched in its life and practice to the very character of YHWH. The tone of that obedience is command; the substance is holiness, utterly, singularly, peculiarly devoted to and matched with the very character of YHWH.' Brueggemann, 2006, p. 178.

53 'Sociality' refers to a full rather than flattened quality of *communion* life lived through Eucharist, in interaction with God's holiness and in the search for justice, stable relations and mutual trust. See Hardy, 2001, p. 22.

54 See Forsyth, P. T., in Hardy, 1996, p. 200.

55 Hardy, 2001, p. 23.

56 Hardy, 2001, p. 249.

57 Keller, 2003, p. 111.

58 'It is not that the church's theological absolutes are no longer trusted, but that the *old modes* in which those absolutes have been articulated are increasingly suspect and dysfunctional. That is because our old modes are increasingly regarded as patriarchal, hierarchic, authoritarian, and monologic.' Brueggemann, 2007b, p. 21.

59 Torrance, in Torrance and Banner, 2006, p. 185.

60 'In the post-Christendom situation, when Christians are liberated *from* the obligation of upholding and legitimating all the "values" of their host cultures, they are simultaneously liberated *for* a greater and more sensitive awareness of the world at large, particularly those whose destiny is adversely affected by the exclusionary side of global politics.' Brueggemann, 2001b, p. 19.

61 Tomlinson, 2008.

62 Wells, 2006, pp. 52f.

63 'It is by the power of Christ in us, that the Lord is able "to accomplish abundantly far more than all we can ask or imagine". What we need to learn, more and more, is how to open up our lives – our living – to that cross-defined loving of the baptismal vocation.' Watkins, 2006, p. 69.

64 Ford, 1999, pp. 164f.

65 'And that faith is the confidence to act in the face of an open-ended future, thus to act in great humility and in great love.' Keller, 2005, p. 151.

66 Miroslav Volf explains this clearly: 'The self is shaped by making space for the other and by giving space to the other, by being enriched when it inhabits the other and by sharing of its plenitude when it is inhabited by the other, by re-examining itself when the other closes his or her doors and challenging the other by knocking at his doors.' Volf, in Torrance and Banner, 2006, p. 112.

67 'The *Logos* performs an act of dispossession not as making self-sacrifice an end in itself but – from the context of the resurrection and of the Eucharist – as a practice of nourishment, hope and trust for a return in God's superabundant love and fidelity.' Mendez, 2005, p. 18.

68 Volf, in Torrance and Banner, 2006, p. 115.

69 Wells, 2006, p. 49.

70 '[W]e always fall back into the subject/object dichotomy, and in more
   general terms, into the logic of binary oppositions: hot/cold, active/
   passive, masculine/feminine, with sensibility no longer a feeling between present subjects, but a kind of experience in which a subject
   is reduced to an "object" which arouses or experiences sensation.'
   Irigaray, 2000, p. 51.

71 Moltmann, 1985, p. 16.

72 Adams, in Brueggemann, 2001b, p. 27.

73 'My definition implies that the quality of one's ministry is enhanced
   when we discover the presence of God. The process of theological
   reflection helps us to consider what difference God's presence makes
   in our lives and assists in the "moment toward insight" about "God's
   ongoing revelation in the world" (Lamoureux, 'An Integrated
   Approach to Theological Education', *Theological Education*, 36.1,
   p. 145)'. Paver, 2006, p. 43.

74 'The imposition of a life-giving order that makes the world a safe, joy-
   ous, peaceable place is due cause for celebration. Israel celebrates the
   wonder and goodness and beauty and reliability of creation even as it
   celebrates the wonder of its own life in the world as a gift of YHWH
   (see Gen. 1.1—2.4a; Psalm 104).' Brueggemann, 2006, pp. 66f.

75 'In theological reflection there are at least three points of interpretation at which God is involved: human experience, religious tradition
   and culture. It is my belief that God is known only partially in each
   of these points of interpretation or conversational partners. I believe
   we do an injustice to the purpose of theological reflection when we
   neglect some points of interpretation and highlight others.' Paver,
   2006, p. 43. See Hardy, 1996, p. 71.

76 'If my God is the God of the Bible, the living God, the "I am, I was,
   I am coming", then God is inseparable from the world and from
   human beings . . . My action, then, consists in handing myself over to
   God, who allows me to be the link for his divine activity regarding
   the world and other people. My relationship to God is not that of a
   cultic act, which rises up from me to Him, but rather that of a faith
   by which I hand myself over to the action of the living God, communicating himself according to his plan, to the world, and to other
   human beings. I can only place myself faithfully before God, and offer
   the fullness of my being and my resources, so that I can be there where
   God awaits me, the link between this action of God and the world.'
   Congar, Yves, 'Action et Contemplation: D'une letter du Père Congar
   au Père Régamey' (1959), *La Vie Spirituelle*, 152, 727 (1998), p. 204,
   in Murray, 2006, pp. 22f.

77 Hardy, 2001, pp. 168ff.: 'Methods of theological reflection have
   evolved to assist in the discovery of God's presence, clues to or signs

of God's Spirit in human experience.' Practical theologian Mary Ellen Sheehan writes: 'Theological reflection assumes the involvement of God in human history, which mediates his prophetic and healing presence in word and sacrament.' She goes on to say: 'But the experience and recognition of God in history requires interpretation which includes explanation and understanding as well as commitment to responsible action toward releasing the liberative love of God that constitutes revelation.' Mary Ellen Sheehan, 1984, 'Theological reflection on theory–praxis integration', *Pastoral Sciences*, 3.31, in Paver, 2006, p. 43.

78 'The caution sounded by feminist thinkers from Virginia Woolf to Mary Daly is as relevant to the hierarchical model of trinitarian theology as it is to the human cavalcades: beware the processions of educated men.' Johnson, 2008, p. 197.

79 'Christianity emerged from a monotheistic milieu. The claims associated with Jesus because of his special relationship with God, calling him "abba", his identification with the eschatological "Son of Man", his appellation, "Son of God", and above all, his Resurrection and Ascension, which led to the application of Psalm 110 to his person, as the "one sitting on the right hand" of the Father and receiving the adoration and worship due, for a Hebrew monotheist to none but the one God, exercised the first pressure on biblical monotheism.' Zizioulas, 2006, pp. 149f.

80 See Torrance, 1999, pp. 92f.

81 Jamieson, 1997, p. 132.

82 Zizioulas, 2006, pp. 116ff.

83 Zizioulas, 2006, p. 143. The Anglican–Orthodox *Cyprus Agreed Statement* expresses this succinctly: 'If divine existence and life spring from and are caused by a Person, the Father, rather than an impersonal general *ousia* [substance], and if this Person is inconceivable apart from his relationship with the other Persons, nothing general can be imposed on the particular. In ecclesiological terms this means that all forms of primacy in the Church are relational in character, as all *arche* (*principle*) *and aitia* (cause), in being personal, cannot but be relational. By assigning causality in God's being to the Person of the Father, we indicate the way the Church, too, should conceive and practise *arche* and authority.' *Cyprus Agreed Statement*, ACC, 2006, 26.

84 I am grateful to Dr Charles Sherlock for his insight, in a personal communication to me, on the Cappadocian distinction of the persons: 'the Word of God is God insofar as God can assume our human nature (made in the *imago Dei*) and still be God; the Spirit is God insofar as God is able to work in and through all created realities and still be God . . . and the Father is God insofar as God *cannot* assume our

human nature, nor work in and through created realities, and still be God.'

85 Williams, 2000, p. 4.

86 Brueggemann, 2001b, p. 7.

87 Keller, 2005, p. 52.

88 In *Power*, which I wrote with Hugh Burgess, one of the primary evangelical tasks of the Church was identified as critiquing and modelling for the world, dynamics of power in community and between people, directed by the identity of the triune God.

89 Sobrino, 2007, p. 72.

90 Johnson, 2008, p. 269.

91 Brueggemann, 2006, p. 37.

92 Hardy, 2001, pp. 136f.

93 Ford, 2007, p. 78 and Greenwood, 1994, p. 5.

94 Ford, 2007, p. 179.

95 Murray records the daring notion of Meister Eckhart that God enjoys himself and God enjoys all creatures. His intuition is that at the heart of the Trinity there lies laughter; 'the Father laughs at the Son and the Son at the Father, and the laughing brings forth pleasure, and the pleasure brings forth joy, and the joy brings forth love.' Murray, 2006, p. 63.

96 Zizioulas, 2006, p. 89.

97 Hardy, 2001, p. 21.

98 'The only exclusion that is permissible – even imperative – is of exclusiveness itself.' Zizioulas, 2006, p. 92.

99 '[O]ffering to God with gratitude the gift of created existence as the body of him who freely assumed this existence in his own *hypostasis* in order to "save" it, that is, to assure and confirm the survival of creation'. Zizioulas, 2006, p. 93.

100 Zizioulas, 2006, p. 95.

101 Zizioulas, 2006, p. 96.

102 '[T]he "forming of human freedom" in ethical responsibility *within* the refining Cross of Christ as restoring the intrinsic relationality and movement of God's holiness. It is this in which the efficacy of the Eucharist consists.' Hardy, 2001, p. 22.

103 Zizioulas, 2006, p. 97.

104 Zizioulas, 2006, p. 98.

105 'It means extending God's invitation to all, ordering the life of the many in relation to God's revelation in Christ, bringing all to repentance, and joining creation's praise.' Wells, 2006, pp. 215ff.

106 'In the proportioning of this world, it is possible for us to realize the kind of fullness which is the inmost character of God. The wisdom of this world *is* best known and lived within the race of God.' Hardy, 2001, p. 61.

107 'The wish to be an alternative society can easily become an end in itself, allowing the church to be a self-constituted "player" in the world's affairs, with the power attendant on it.' Hardy, 2001, p. 39.

108 Hardy, 2001, p. 88.

109 Isiorho, 2008, pp. 98f.

110 Jones, Hester, in Milbank, 2007, pp. 69–87.

111 Milbank, in Milbank, 2007, p. 102.

112 Loades, Ann, in Milbank, 2007, pp. 105ff.

113 Leech, K., in Milbank, 2007, p. 130.

114 Darragh, 2007 pp. 118ff. Feminist reportrayals of Mary, such as by Elizabeth Johnson, redirect imagery of 'nurturing, warmth, protection; compassionate love that empowers, heals and liberates' and of 'mothering' back to God as intimately present, abundantly loving and life-giving. Johnson, 2003, pp. 86–7.

115 I am gladly indebted throughout this section to Ford, 2007, ch. 7 on Loving the God of Wisdom, pp. 225ff.

116 Gunton, in Gunton and Hardy, 1989, p. 75.

117 'The self gives something of itself, of its own space, so to speak, in a movement in which it contracts itself in order to be expanded by the other and in which it at the same time enters the contracted other in order to increase the other's plenitude. This giving of the self which coalesces with receiving the other is nothing but the circular movement of the eternal divine love – a form of exchange of gifts in which the other does not emerge as a debtor because she has already given by having joyfully received and because even before the gift has reached her she was already engaged in a movement of advanced reciprocation. (1 John 4.8 – God conceived as a communion of perfect lovers).' Volf, in Torrance and Banner, 2006, pp. 113f.

118 Volf, in Torrance and Banner, p. 116.

119 Ford, 2007, p. 259.

120 Ford, 2007, p. 260.

121 'What happens at each moment bears the imprint of the will of God and of his adorable name. How holy is that name! How just, then, to bless it, to treat it as a sacrament which hallows by its own power souls which place no obstacle to its action! Can we see what bears this august name without esteeming it infinitely? It is a divine manna which falls from heaven in order to give us a constant increase in grace.' de Caussade, Jean Pierre, *Self-abandonment to Divine Providence*, trans. Alger Thorold (Collins, London, 1977), in Andrew Ryder, 'The Sacrament of Now', *The Way*, 46/2 (April 2007), 7–18.

122 Ford and Hardy, 2005, p. 108.

123 'It is only in Christ and through the power of the Spirit that the created order is enabled to become what it is purposed to be.' Rae, in Torrance and Banner, 2006, p. 206.

124 Ford, 2007, p. 261.

125 'The resurrection of Christ, *the firstborn* of a new creation, is the beginning and condition of the transformation towards fulfilment of the whole of God's creation. And Christ's ascension, to sit at the right hand of the Father in glory, confirms once and for all, this Logos and not our own as the Word by which the world will be upheld.' Rae, 2006, p. 208.

126 'In the midst of numerous counter signs, Christian commitment with others to peace among faiths, higher education and those with disabilities is a sign of ecclesial catholicity.' Ford, 2007, p. 263.

127 Volf, 1998, p. 122.

128 Ford and Hardy, 2005, p. 20.

129 Zizioulas, 1985, p. 144f.

130 'Catholicity, therefore, in this context, does not mean anything else but the wholeness and fullness and totality of the body of Christ 'exactly as' (*hosper*) it is portrayed in the eucharistic community.' Zizioulas, 1985, p. 149.

131 '[T]he Church is revealed to be in time what she is eschatologically, namely a catholic Church which stands in history as a transcendence of all divisions into the unity of all in Christ through the Holy Spirit to the glory of God the Father.' Zizioulas, 1985, p. 169.

132 Strong, 2007, pp. 110f.

133 Hardy, 1996, p. 218.

134 Hardy, 1996, p. 219.

135 Hardy, 1996, pp. 218f.

136 See the discussion of Kathryn Tanner's work on culture and theology in McDougall, 2008, pp. 104ff.

137 Forder, 1964.

138 George, 2003, p. 11.

139 See Chauvet, 1995.

140 Power, David N., 'The Ritual of Life-Passages: Whether or Not', in Lefebvre and Ross, 2007, p. 21.

141 Hardy, 2001, p. 140.

142 'When the church embodies God's ways it is not in vaguely spiritual ways; it is in particular ways that correspond to the ways in which God is active in the ordering of particular parts of the social fabric.' Hardy, 2001, p. 91.

143 'What is seen in Acts 10–11 and 15 is a community working out how to handle traditional identity markers (circumcision, food laws) after being multiply overwhelmed by the life and death of Jesus, his resurrection and the outpouring of the Holy Spirit.' Ford, 2007, p. 174.

144 'Paul sees the community of faith being caught up into the story of God's remaking the world through Christ.' Hays, Richard, in Torrance and Banner, 2006, p. 171.

145 Torrance, in Torrance and Banner, 2006, pp. 169f.

146 Ford, 2007, p. 34.

147 'Israel – and consequently the synagogue, the church, and the mosque – is a "social experiment" in the world, a revolutionary alternative to see whether the daily social relationships, policies, and institutions in the world can be ordered differently.' Brueggemann, 2006, p. 17.

148 'The prophetic tradition is not so much about scolding and threat as it is a massive act of imagination that asserts the world could be different, if the present is informed by a freighted past and an assured future. The mantra of widow, orphan, alien rings in the ears of Jesus as it rang in the ears of Israel.' Brueggemann, 2006, p. 17.

149 Reddie, 2007, pp. 31f.

150 Torrance, in Torrance and Banner, 2006, p. 181, and Volf, in Torrance and Banner, 2006, p. 116.

151 Torrance, in Torrance and Banner, 2006, p. 182.

152 Torrance, in Torrance and Banner, 2006, p. 184.

153 'The task of the church is to ensure that, in all its thinking and its doctrine it is radically true to the all-inclusive nature of God's self-disclosure in the one logos of God to humanity . . . the triune grammar of our covenantal participation in Christ.' Torrance, in Torrance and Banner, 2006, p. 185.

154 Brueggemann, 2001b, Appendix B, pp. 161ff.

155 Brueggemann, 2006, p. 111.

156 Ford, 2007, p. 159.

157 Ford, 2007, p. 186.

158 'Full mediation requires placing the intensity of the gospel in the closest affinity to those lives and societies to which it is addressed.' Hardy, 2001, p. 148.

159 '[Jesus'] *wisdom is shaped through the passionate multiple intensities embodied in all the cries that have pervaded his ministry and which climax now in his passion and death.* It is therefore a wisdom involved in relationships of many sorts; immersed in history, including all its evils and sufferings; and now swallowed up by death.' Ford, 2007, p. 33 (italics in original).

160 'The core practical wisdom of the Christological drama of desire is loving God for God's sake, glorifying God, blessing God, hallowing God's name.' Ford, 2007, p. 191.

161 'The term ["Son"] connotes not just the past earthly Jesus, nor even yet the risen person of "Christ" (if that is individualistically conceived) but rather the transformed divine life to which the whole creation, animate and inanimate, is tending, and into which it is being progressively transformed (Rom. 8.19–25) . . . The "Father" is both source and ultimate object of divine desire; the "Spirit" is that (irreducibly distinct) enabler and incorporator of that desire in creation – that

which makes the creation divine; the "Son" is that divine and per-
fected creation.' Coakley, Sarah, in Ford, 2007, p. 223.

162 Ford, 2007, p. 198.
163 Ford, 2007, p. 210.
164 Davis, in Wright, 1993, p. 190.
165 Patzia, 2001.
166 'For Ignatius, the bishop is not primarily teacher or administrator,
but the one who presides at, and as "*episkopos*" watches over, the
Eucharistic liturgy.' Wright, 1993, p. 19.
167 See Jamieson, 1997, p. 9.

4 The navigator: *episkope* of the local church

1 General Synod of the Church of England, 1990, p. 20.
2 See Letter to the Smyrnaeans, VIII, in Stevenson, 1965, p. 48 and Irenaeus,
III. 38.1; Harvey; III.24.1 A.-N.C.L., in Stevenson, 1965, pp. 116f., and
Danielou and Marrou, 1964, pp. 110f.
3 'Throughout Christian history, there has always been an understand-
able tendency to call the episcopal body to heel and to remind them
that they are not an un-elected senatorial class who know what is best
for the people, but persons appointed through the ministry of the whole
Church, declared worthy and admitted to office for their reliability and
trustworthiness, in representing the Church's faith, doctrine and manner of life.' Halliburton, in Hannaford, 1996, p. 50.
4 'The ecclesiastical loan word "bishop" is too technical and loaded with
late historical baggage for precise signification of usage of *episkopos* and
cognates in our literature especially the New Testament.' Danker, 2003,
p. 379.
5 Stapley, 1996 and Morgan, 1997.
6 Jamieson, 1997, p. 124.
7 Hardy, 2001, pp. 151ff.
8 Service has been highlighted in many recent studies on leadership and
ministry. I am arguing for a confident exercise of *episkope* that resists
domination and communicates that one woman or one man in charge,
except in mutual relations of trust with all others, is an inadequate
model within the Christian tradition. Contemporary disputes about
Scripture and sexuality lose their spiritual credibility in church and
society when protagonist rectors and bishops act in a spirit of trium-
phalist zeal. Whom they truly represent can often become of apparent
secondary importance.
9 Johnson, 2008.
10 Bacon, 2007, p. 221.
11 Bacon, 2007, p. 223.

12 Bacon, 2007, p. 229.

13 '[A]lthough God cannot be divided into ones, there is sufficient difference in order to secure a mutual relationship of love between each centre of personhood ... neither one taking the others for granted but instead as always approaching as if for the first time. Within this context the Trinity can be understood as an economy of desire in which each centre of personhood approaches the others without fear of consummation, secure in their own identities ... boundaries can be crossed without fear of being consumed, with each centre of personhood being embraced by the caress of the others and always invited to become.' Bacon, 2007, pp. 231f.

14 See Greenwood and Burgess, 2005, pp. 132ff.

15 See *Spe Salvi* (*Saved by Hope*), 30 November, 2007 and *Deus Caritas Est* (*On Christian Love – God is Love*), 25 January, 2006.

16 Johnson, 2003, ch. 8.

17 Volf, 1998, pp. 228ff.

18 '[I]n a world where neoplatonism was influential, the urge to think in terms of degrees of reality, of a hierarchically structured world, was compelling in the absence of a drive to think otherwise ... a major achievement of ancient Christological and trinitarian thinking was that it did call in question that very way of thinking about reality.' Gunton, 1991, p. 60.

19 Schillebeeckx shows how this was the wisdom of the Council of Chalcedon (451 CE). Schillebeeckx, 1980, pp. 58ff.

20 Ross, 1988, pp. 116ff.

21 '[A] circle, a Church comprised of people bonded together in common life by their ministry to each other, ordered and made holy in worship. The "pure and vivifying principle" which prevents this from being a dinosaur or a look-alike for other forms of society is its participation in God's life and work. Its future is in participating in that, and thereby becoming a form of society which can show healing to a world faced with the collapse of all lesser forms of society.' Hardy, 1996, p. 225.

22 'In the light of the *koinonia* of the Holy Spirit, ordination relates the ordained man [*sic*] so profoundly and so existentially to the community, that in his new state after ordination he cannot be any longer, as a minister, conceived in himself.' Zizioulas, 1985, p. 226.

23 Gregory Baum offers a succinct account of the continual debate as to the relationship of the common mind of the people and the natural right to rule of an enlightened elite in 'The Church: For and Against Democracy', in Wilfred and Susin, 2007, p. 54.

24 'Elaine Pagels in her study of the Gnostic Gospels suggests the association between monotheism and the power of the bishop originates from the second-century struggle that Irenaeus had with the Gnostics

in establishing the church's doctrinal authority against heresy through the bishop.' Jamieson, 1997, p. 131.

25 'We are fully ourselves as we are loved for our own sake and as we love God and others for their own sakes ... The poor, the despised, the disfigured, the disabled, are specially suited to being at the heart of such a sign. There is little worldly incentive to embrace them in love and friendship, yet their deepest secret is that they are created, chosen and delighted in by God for their own sake.' Ford, 2007, p. 369.

26 The mutuality of ministries within the local church is increasingly articulated and celebrated liturgically when a new incumbent (rector, vicar) arrives and the Local Shared Ministry team or collaborative leaders are addressed, recognized and blessed as part of the next phase of that church's ministry and mission. It still does not avoid, however, defining the chapters in the history of a local church to a large degree in terms of: Who is the parish priest?

27 Ormonde Plater, Archdeacon in the Episcopalian Diocese of Louisiana, proposes that deacons, as mobilizers of the Church in the world, will help to model the interaction of ministries liturgically and so build the Church in mutuality. Plater, 2008.

28 'The Church is nothing other than the work of the economic Trinity applied to us and through us and together with us to the whole cosmos, an image of the Trinity and a foretaste of the *eschata*, when the whole world will become a movement back to the one God, the Father (1 Cor. 15.24) from whom everything, even the persons of the Trinity in their eternal being, comes forth.' Zizioulas, 2006, p. 149.

29 See Sherlock, 1991, Chapter 4.

30 'Carter Heyward has said that one of her understandings of the concept of "call" is that it means to "tell our stories and in telling our stories manifest a new reality".' Isabel Carter Heyward, *A Priest Forever* (Harper & Row, New York, 1976), in Jamieson, 1997, p. 52.

31 Jamieson, 1997, p. 135.

32 Evans and Wurster, 2000, pp. 169ff.

33 Evans and Wurster, 2000, p. 17.

34 Evans and Wurster, 2000, p. 21.

35 Salmond, 2003, p. 35.

36 Moran and Gardner, 2007, p. 19.

37 'I agree with Benjamin Valentin's claim that "our theological discourses must somehow navigate across racial, cultural, gender, and religious lines, to cultivate holistic social arrangements that may harmonize the interests of diverse constituencies and, in this way, facilitate the possibilities for social change".' Petrella, 2008, p. 140.

38 Heenan, in Hilton, 2008, p. 360.

39 Hilton, 2008.

40 Palmer, in Hilton, 2008.

41 Palmer, in Hilton, 2008.

42 Palmer, in Hilton, 2008. The psychologist and author Daniel Goleman uses the concept of navigating in describing the everyday human task of integrating emotional literacy and brain-based learning. Goleman, 1996.

43 'It is also clearly my role as spiritual leader, when the group does not seem to be listening either to the wisdom of the Spirit or to each other or perhaps even to themselves, to recall them to quiet, prayerful, reflection.' Jamieson, 1997, p. 45.

44 'Neither Moses nor the people understood what would unfold when Moses first confronted Pharaoh after seeing the burning bush. We are all called to be open to God's leadership, to respond even when the pathway to the destination is unclear, and to be prepared for God to reveal more of his plans as the journey continues. In the context of developing a vision, congregations need to be as clear as possible in their understanding of God's vision, but they must also be willing to re-examine the vision throughout the change process.' Herrington et al., 2000, p. 61.

45 Speaking of the life of a bishop, 'the words we utter, the ways in which we use them to form and shape our relations, the decisions that we take, and the ways in which those are reached, do have an impact on the spirituality and culture of the church'. Jamieson, 1997, p. 35.

46 'The easy road for change leaders is to assume that their views of reality are "correct". Listening to others and allowing yourself to be influenced by their perceptions of the world is risky.' Herrington et al., 2000, p. 106.

47 Herrington et al., 2000, pp. 96ff.

48 See Bosch, 1996, pp. 420ff.

49 Jamieson offers a number of criteria for group discernment, such as transparency in situations where most people are already known and private intrigue can take the place of public process, safety so that people feel God's presence and human care, making sure that small voices are heard, and that churches refer business to gospel and scriptural reflection. Jamieson, 1997, p. 42.

50 Begbie, 2000.

51 Ford, 1999, p. 144.

52 Thomas, R. S., 'Hill Christmas', in Thomas, 1993.

53 Gilligan, 1988, pp. 310ff.

54 Ford and Hardy, 2005, pp. 26, 179.

55 '[T]hrough the recognition and refinement of the inherent relations of all people in the world in all the dimensions of life in the world,

natural, ecological, historical, societal, political, economic and cultural/ symbolic.' Hardy, 2001, pp. 17f.

56 Hardy, 2001, p. 22.

57 We could call this 'disintermediation' to make the point that the church's richness and reach must never be limited by the energy, skill or imagination of the priest. See Evans and Wurster, 2000.

58 'The church has gifts to give when it acts out of its own peculiarity, out of its "new self", when it comes to "the other" out of its being loved and forgiven.' Brueggemann suggests that the Truth and Reconciliation Commission exercise in South Africa could be a permanent paradigm to pursue. Brueggemann, 2006, p. 195.

59 Dyer and Eames, cited in Hardy, 2001, p. 152.

60 'This could happen if the training of future priests and ministers places formation in prayer and spirituality on an equal footing with academic training. It could also happen if spiritual teaching becomes a regular part of lay ministry.' Keating, 2004, p. 3.

61 Thomas, R. S., 'The priest', in Thomas, 1993.

62 See Lambeth Conference, 1998, p. 130 and ACC, 1997, 2.9.

5 Practising *episkope*

1 Antonio Machado, in Proulx, 1996, p. 11. © 1996 E. Annie Proulx. Reproduced by permission.

2 Ellul, 1967, p. 136.

3 At the time of writing, Ruth Gledhill writes of the Religious Trends Survey demonstrating how an ageing population of churchgoers is about to expire. Experience in local parishes as well as the Government's 2001 census (establishing that seven in ten people in the UK considered themselves to be Christian), often contradicts forecasts of national trends. Graphs plotting inevitable decline at a steady rate ignore the complex reasons for people choosing or not to become attached to a particular church. See Gledhill, 2008.

4 Jaworski, 1998, pp. 118ff.

5 'By now you will appreciate that for me, church attendance and music provide the opportunity to think, remember and reflect.' 'One of the big moans is that you don't "behave like the parish priest" – which translated means *you* don't visit, *you* don't preach more than anyone else, *you* are not always in the parish . . . but leading retreats or staffing Bishops' Advisory Panels. This is the big issue which I guess your book is trying to address – you (and it has to be you, with the rest of us reinforcing the message) have to explain the theory – over and over and over again – in as many different ways as we can come up with. We have an elderly congregation – they hate change (although hatred

of change is not the sole preserve of the elderly!) but we have to get across the messages' (respondents to questionnaire).

6 These principles have been reworked by many churches in the light of the work of Roland Allen. I am especially grateful here for the inspiration of the Diocese of Christchurch in the Anglican Church of Aotearoa, New Zealand and Polynesia, and especially to Jenny Dawson, former Ministry Educator with special responsibility for the development of Local Shared Ministry.

7 I wrote to 50 regular and varied worshippers in the hope of recruiting their active response to the questions that follow in this chapter. I also informally discussed anxieties or made clarifications. Out of the 50 approached, 29 gave a full response, 12 offered a short reply, while nine asked to be excused or did not respond.

8 'The number of people who are involved in doing things in St Mary's has grown out of all recognition – there are groups involved with Baptism, the Healing Service, the Sunday@4 team, the Bereavement team, the Pastoral Visiting team – the list is almost endless. There is a real buzz about the place – more people at the services – including younger families – more involvement in the church by more people, we are even using the task group system to get things done – the group involved in Holy Week is a good example and will be the group who will look at the Parish Weekend.'

9 Bohm, in Jaworski, 1998, p. 88.

10 ARCIC's *The Gift of Authority* places this clearly in the worldwide debate on these issues. Although I find the language and assumptions now starkly limiting, there is an essential truth in the statement that the Bishop's ministry 'is focused in the Eucharist where he (*sic*) presides in the midst of his people and ministers Word and sacrament, and in a different way, in the local synod when the bishop gathers with his priests and people. His authority in all this is in no sense a personal *possession*; nor is it to be exercised according to the world's ideas of power and status. He feeds his sheep as the servant of Christ and servant of the servants of God' (ARCIC, 1999, p. 163).

11 Beeson, 2007, p. 235.

12 Brueggemann, 2006, pp. 18f.

13 Brueggemann, 2006, p. 188.

14 Begbie, 2000, p. 126.

Bibliography

Adair, John and Nelson, John (eds), *Creative Church Leadership* (Canterbury, Norwich, 2004).

Adams, Joanna, 'Atlanta as Church Context', in Walter Brueggemann (ed.), *Hope for the World: Mission in a Global Context* (Westminster John Knox, London, 2001).

Alexander, Irene, *Dancing with God: Transformation through Relationship* (SPCK, London, 2007).

Althaus-Reid, Marcella, *Indecent Theology: Theological Perversion in Sex, Gender and Politics* (Routledge, London, 2001).

Ammicht-Quinn, Regina, 'Whose dignity is inviolable? Human Beings, Machines and the Discourse of Dignity', in Regina Ammicht-Quinn, Maureen Junker-Kenny and Elsa Tamez (eds), *The Discourse of Human Dignity* (*Concilium*, SCM, London 2003/2), pp. 35ff.

Anglican Consultative Council (ACC), *Report of the Inter-Anglican Theological and Doctrinal Commission (The Virginia Report)* (Anglican Consultative Council, London, 1997).

Anglican Consultative Council (ACC), *The Church of the Triune God: The Cyprus Agreed Statement of the International Commission for Anglican–Orthodox Dialogue* (Anglican Communion Office, London, 2006).

Archbishops' Council, *Review of Clergy Terms of Service* (Church House Publishing, London, 2004).

Archbishops' Group on the Episcopate, *Episcopal Ministry* (Church House Publishing, London, 1990).

ARCIC II, *The Gift of Authority: Authority in the Church III* (Catholic Truth Society, London, 1999).

Avalos, Hector, Melcher, Sarah J. and Schipper, Jeremy, *This Abled Body: Rethinking Disabilities in Biblical Studies* (Society of Biblical Literature, Atlanta, 2007).

Bacon, Hannah, 'What's Right with the Trinity? Thinking the Trinity in Relation to Irigaray's Notions of Self-Love and Wonder', *Feminist Theology*, 15/2, 2007, pp. 220ff.

Baginhole, Barbara, 'Prospects for Change? Structural, Cultural and Action Dimensions of the Careers of Pioneer Women Priests in the Church of England', *Gender, Work and Organization*, 10/3, June 2003, pp. 361ff.

Baker, Jonathan (ed.) *Consecrated Women? A Contribution to the Women Bishops Debate* (Canterbury, Norwich, 2004).

Baum, Gregory, 'The Church: For and against Democracy', in Felix Wilfred and Luiz Carlos Susin, *Christianity and Democracy* (*Concilium*, SCM, London, 2007/4), pp. 51ff.

Beeson, Trevor, *The Bishops* (SCM, London, 2007).

Begbie, Jeremy S., *Theology, Music and Time* (CUP, Cambridge, 2000).

Beozzo, José Oscar and Susin, Luiz Carlos (eds), *Brazil: People and Church(es)* (*Concilium*, SCM, London, 2002/3), pp. 102ff.

Bingemer, Maria Clara Luccheti, 'Women in the Brazilian Church', in José Oscar Beozzo and Luiz Carlos Susin (eds), *Brazil: People and Church(es)* (*Concilium*, SCM, London, 2002/3), pp. 102ff.

Bird, John, Land, Lorraine and Macadam, Murray (eds), *Nation to Nation: Aboriginal Sovereignty and the Future of Canada* (Irwin, Toronto, 2002).

Bonhoeffer, Dietrich, *Ethics* (SCM, London, 1955).

Bosch, David J., *Transforming Mission: Paradigm Shifts in Theology of Mission* (Orbis, New York, 1996).

Boureux, Christophe, Soskice, Janet Martin and Susin, Luiz Carlos, *Hunger, Bread and Eucharist* (*Concilium*, SCM, London, 2005/2), pp. 14ff.

Boyett, Joseph and Boyett, Jimmie, *The Guru Guide: The Best Ideas of the Top Management Thinkers* (Wiley, New York, 1998).

Brookfield, Stephen D., *The Skillful Teacher: On Technique, Trust and Responsiveness in the Classroom*, 2nd edn (Jossey-Bass, San Francisco, 2006).

Brown, David, *Releasing Bishops for Relationships* (Foundation for Church Leadership, London, 2006).

Brueggemann, Walter, *Israel's Praise: Doxology Against Idolatry and Ideology* (Fortress, Minneapolis, 1988).

Brueggemann, Walter, *Texts that Linger, Words that Explode: Listening to Prophetic Voices* (Fortress, Minneapolis, 2000).

Brueggemann, Walter, *The Prophetic Imagination*, 2nd edn (Fortress, Minneapolis, 2001a).

Brueggemann, Walter (ed.), *Hope for the World: Mission in a Global Context* (Westminster John Knox, London, 2001b).

Brueggemann, Walter (ed. Edwin Searcy), *Awed to Heaven, Rooted in Earth: Prayers of Walter Brueggemann* (Fortress, Minneapolis, 2003).

Brueggemann, Walter, *The Word that Redescribes the World: The Bible and Discipleship* (Fortress, Minneapolis, 2006).

Brueggemann, Walter, *Praying the Psalms: Engaging Scripture and the Life of the Spirit*, 2nd edn (Paternoster, Eugene, 2007a).

Brueggemann, Walter, *The Word Militant: Preaching a Decentering Word* (Fortress, Minneapolis, 2007b).

Buxton, Graham, *Dancing in the Dark: The Privilege of Participating in the Ministry of Christ* (Paternoster, Carlisle, 2001).

Cameron, Helen, Richter, Philip, Davies, Douglas and Ward, Frances, *Studying Local Churches: A Handbook* (SCM, London, 2005).

Carr, Wesley, *The Pastor as Theologian: The Integration of Pastoral Ministry, Theology and Discipleship* (SPCK, London, 1989).

Carter, Erik W., *Including People with Disabilities in Faith Communities: A Guide for Service Providers, Family and Congregation* (Brookes, London, 2007).

Chauvet, Louis-Marie (ed.), *Liturgy and the Body* (*Concilium*, SCM, London, 1995/3).

Chester, Tim and Timmis, Steve, *Total Church: A Radical Reshaping Around Gospel and Community* (IVP, Nottingham, 2007).

Clark, David (ed.), *The Diaconal Church: Beyond the Mould of Christendom* (Epworth, Peterborough, 2008).

Cocksworth, Christopher and Brown, Rosalind, *Being a Priest Today: Exploring Priestly Identity* (Canterbury, Norwich, 2002).

Collins, John N., *Diakonia: Re-interpreting the Ancient Sources* (OUP, Oxford, 1990).

Collins, John N., *Deacons and the Church: Making Connections between Old and New* (Morehouse, Harrisburg, 2002).

Collins, Raymond E., *The Many Faces of the Church: A Study in New Testament Ecclesiology* (Crossroad, New York, 2003).

Congar, Yves, *Lay People in the Church*, revised edn (Chapman, London, 1965).

Countryman, William L., *Living on the Border of the Holy: Renewing the Priesthood of All* (Morehouse, Harrisburg, 1999).

Croft, Stephen, *Ministry in Three Dimensions: Ordination and Leadership in the Local Church* (DLT, London, 1999).

Danielou, Jean and Marrou, Henri, *The Christian Centuries, Volume I: The First Six Hundred Years*, trans. Vincent Cronin (DLT, London, 1964).

Danker, Frederick William (ed.), *A Greek–English Lexicon of the New Testament and Other Early Christian Literature*, 3rd edn (University of Chicago, London, 2003).

Darragh, Neil, 'Homeplace, Paradise, and Landscape – A New Zealand Perspective', in Marie-Theres Wacker and Elaine M. Wainwright, *Land Conflicts, Land Utopias* (*Concilium*, SCM, London, 2007/2), pp. 118ff.

Davies, Oliver, *The Creativity of God: World, Eucharist, Reason* (CUP, Cambridge, 2004).

Dell, Katharine, *'Get Wisdom, Get Insight': An Introduction to Israel's Wisdom Literature* (DLT, London, 2000).

Doyle, Dennis M., *Communion Ecclesiology* (Orbis, New York, 2000).

Dulles, Avery, *Models of the Church* (Doubleday, New York, 1978).

Ellul, Jacques, *The Presence of the Kingdom* (Seabury, New York, 1967).

Evans, G. R., 'The Church in the Early Christian Centuries: Ecclesiological Consolidation', in Gerard Mannion and Lewis S. Mudge (eds), *The Routledge Companion to the Christian Church* (Routledge, London, 2007), pp. 28ff.

Evans, Philip and Wurster, Thomas S., *Blown to Bits: How the New Economics of Information Transforms Strategy* (Harvard Business School, Boston, 2000).

Fiorenza, Elisabeth Schüssler, *Discipleship of Equals: A Critical Feminist Ekklesia-logy of Liberation* (SCM, London, 1993).

Fiorenza, Elisabeth Schüssler, *Searching the Scriptures: A Feminist Commentary* (SCM, London, 1995).

Ford, David F., *Self and Salvation: Being Transformed* (CUP, Cambridge, 1999).

Ford, David F., *Christian Wisdom: Desiring God and Learning in Love* (CUP, Cambridge, 2007).

Ford, David F. and Hardy, Daniel W., *Living in Praise: Worshipping and Knowing God* (DLT, London, 2005).

Forder, Charles F., *The Parish Priest at Work: An Introduction to Systematic Pastoralia* (SPCK, London, 1964).

Fraser, Irene, 'Honouring Alternatives in the Criminal Justice System', in John Bird, Lorraine Land and Murray Macadam (eds), *Nation to Nation: Aboriginal Sovereignty and the Future of Canada* (Irwin, Toronto, 2002), pp. 114ff.

General Synod of the Church of England, *The Report of the Archbishops' Group on The Episcopate* (Church House, London, 1990).

General Synod of the Church of England, *For Such a Time as This: A Renewed Diaconate in the Church of England*, GS 1407 (Church House, London, 2001).

General Synod, Anglican Church of Australia, *Episcopal Ministry and Women*, 2004.

George, Ian, *The Role of the Bishop Today: Pastoral Address* (Diocese of Adelaide, 20 May 2003).

Gibbons, Robin, *House of God, House of the People of God* (SPCK, London, 2006).

Gilbert, Barbara G., *Who Ministers to the Ministers? A Study of Support Systems for Clergy and Spouses* (Alban Institute, Washington DC, 1987).

Gilligan, C., *In a Different Voice: Psychological Theory and Women's Development* (Harvard, Cambridge, 1988).

Gledhill, Ruth, 'God-shaped hole will lead to loss of national identity', *The Times*, 8 May 2008, pp. 6f.

Goleman, Daniel, *Emotional Intelligence: Why It Can Matter More Than IQ* (Bloomsbury, London, 1996).

Gooder, Paula, 'In Search of the Early Church: The New Testament and the Development of Christian Communities', in Gerard Mannion and Lewis S. Mudge (eds), *The Routledge Companion to the Christian Church* (Routledge, London, 2007), pp. 9ff.

Grau, Marion, *Of Divine Economy: Refinancing Redemption* (T. & T. Clark, London, 2004).

Greenwood, Robin, *Reclaiming the Church* (Collins, London, 1988).

Greenwood, Robin, *Transforming Priesthood: A New Theology of Mission and Ministry* (SPCK, London, 1994).

Greenwood, Robin, *Practising Community: The Task of the Local Church* (SPCK, London, 1996).

Greenwood, Robin, *Transforming Church: Liberating Structures for Ministry* (SPCK, London, 2002).

Greenwood, Robin, *Risking Everything* (SPCK, London, 2006).

Greenwood, Robin and Burgess, Hugh, *Power* (SPCK, London, 2005).

Greenwood, Robin and Pascoe, Caroline, *Local Ministry: Story, Process and Meaning* (SPCK, London, 2006).

Grenz, Stanley J., *Rediscovering the Triune God: The Trinity in Contemporary Theology* (Fortress, Minneapolis, 2004).

Grundy, Malcolm, *What's New in Leadership? Creative Responses to the Changing Pattern of Church Life* (Canterbury, Norwich, 2007).

Gunton, Colin E., *The Promise of Trinitarian Theology* (T. & T. Clark, Edinburgh, 1991).

Gunton, Colin E., *The One, The Three and the Many: Creation and the Culture of Modernity* (CUP, Cambridge, 1993).

Gunton, Colin E. (ed.), *The Theology of Reconciliation* (T. & T. Clark, London, 2003).

Gunton, Colin E. and Hardy, Daniel W. (eds), *On Being the Church: Essays on the Christian Community* (T. & T. Clark, Edinburgh, 1989).

Halliburton, John, 'Order and the Episcopate', in Robert Hannaford (ed.), *The Future of Anglicanism: Essays on Faith and Order* (Gracewing, Leominster, 1996), pp. 39ff.

Hardy, Daniel W., *God's Ways with the World: Thinking and Practising Christian Faith* (T. & T. Clark, Edinburgh, 1996).

Hardy, Daniel W., *Finding the Church* (SCM, London, 2001).

Harmless, J. William and Gelpi, Donald L., 'Priesthood Today and the Jesuit Vocation', *Studies in the Spirituality of Jesus*, 19/3, May 1987.

Hauerwas, Stanley, *Performing the Faith: Bonhoeffer and the Practice of Nonviolence* (SPCK, London, 2004).

Healey, Nicholas M., 'The Church in Modern Theology', in Gerard Mannion and Lewis S. Mudge (eds), *The Routledge Companion to the Christian Church* (Routledge, London, 2007), pp. 106ff.

Herrington, Jim, Bonem, Mike and Furr, James H., *Leading Congregational Change: A Practical Guide for the Transformational Journey* (Jossey-Bass, San Francisco, 2000).

Hilton, Sean, 'Education and the Changing Face of Medical Professionalism: From Priest to Mountain Guide?', *British Journal of General Practice*, Vol. 58, No. 550, May 2008, pp. 353ff.

Hirst, Judy, *Struggling to be Holy* (London, DLT, 2006).

Hull, John, *What Prevents Christian Adults from Learning?* (Trinity Press International, Philadelphia, 1991).

Hunt, Anne, *Trinity* (Orbis, New York, 2005).

Hunter, Alastair, *Wisdom Literature* (SCM, London, 2006).

Irigaray, Luce, *To be Two* (Athlone, London, 2000).

Isiorho, David, 'Faithful Cities and Their Theology of Context: Even our Diversity is Diverse', *Black Theology: An International Journal*, 6/1, 2008, pp. 98–118.

Jamieson, Penny, *Living at the Edge: Sacrament and Solidarity in Leadership* (Mowbray, London, 1997).

Jaworski, Joseph, *Synchronicity: The Inner Path of Leadership* (Berrett-Koehler, San Francisco, 1998).

Jeanrond, Werner G. and Theobald, Christolph (eds), *God: Experience and Mystery* (*Concilium*, SCM, London, 2001/1).

Jenson, Robert W., 'Reconciliation in God', in Colin E. Gunton (ed.), *The Theology of Reconciliation* (London, T. & T. Clark, 2003), pp. 158–66.

Jinkins, Michael, *The Church Faces Death: Ecclesiology in a Post-modern Context* (OUP, Oxford, 1999).

Johnson, Elizabeth A., *She Who Is: The Mystery of God in Feminist Theological Discourse* (Crossroad, New York, 1993).

Johnson, Elizabeth A., *Truly Our Sister: A Theology of Mary in the Communion of Saints* (Continuum, London, 2003).

Johnson, Elizabeth A., *Friends of God and Prophets: A Feminist Theological Reading of the Communion of Saints* (SCM, London, 2008).

Kasper, Walter, *Leadership in the Church: How Traditional Roles can Serve the Christian Community Today* (Herder & Herder, New York, 2003).

Keating, Thomas, *Open Mind, Open Heart: The Contemplative Dimension of the Gospel* (Continuum, London, 2004).

Kegan, Robert and Lahey, Lisa Laskow, *How the Way We Talk Can Change the Way We Work: Seven Languages for Transformation* (Jossey-Bass, San Francisco, 2001).

Keller, Catherine, *Face of the Deep: A Theology of Becoming* (Routledge, London, 2003).

Keller, Catherine, *God and Power: Counter-Apocalyptic Journeys* (Fortress, Minneapolis, 2005).

Kung, Hans, *Women in Christianity* (Continuum, London, 2001).

LaCugna, Catherine Mowry, *God for Us: Living Trinitarian Faith* (Harper-SanFrancisco, San Francisco, 1991).

Lakeland, Paul, *The Liberation of the Laity: In Search of an Accountable Church* (Continuum, London, 2003).

Lakeland, Paul, 'Breaking the Mould of Christendom: David Clark's Challenge to Roman Catholicism', in David Clark (ed.), *The Diaconal Church: Beyond the Mould of Christendom* (Epworth, Peterborough, 2008), pp. 23ff.

Bibliography

Lambeth Conference, 1998, *Official Report of the Lambeth Conference, 1998: Transformation and Renewal* (Morehouse, Harrisburg, 1999).

Leech, Kenneth, *Soul Friend* (Sheldon, London, 1977).

Lefebvre, Solange and Ross, Susan, *Stages of Life and Christian Experience* (*Concilium*, SCM, London, 2007/5).

Lobinger, Fritz, *Like His Brothers and Sisters: Ordaining Community Leaders* (Gracewing, Leominster, 2002).

Longenecker, Richard L. (ed.), *Community Formation in the Early Church and in the Church Today* (Hendrickson, Massachusetts, 2002).

Louden, Stephen H. and Francis, Leslie J., *The Naked Parish Priest: What Priests Really Think They're Doing* (Continuum, London, 2003).

Luscombe, Philip and Shreeve, Esther, *What is a Minister?* (Epworth, Peterborough, 2002).

Mannion, Gerard, 'Postmodern Ecclesiologies', in Gerard Mannion and Lewis S. Mudge (eds), *The Routledge Companion to the Christian Church* (Routledge, London, 2007), pp. 127ff.

Mannion, Gerard and Mudge, Lewis S. (eds), *The Routledge Companion to the Christian Church* (Routledge, London, 2007).

McDougall, Joy Ann, 'Keeping Feminist Faith with Christian Traditions: A Look at Christian Feminist Theology Today', *Modern Theology*, 24, January 2008, pp. 103ff.

McFadyen, Alistair, *The Call to Personhood: A Christian Theory of the Individual in Social Relationships* (CUP, Cambridge, 1990).

McFague, Sallie, *Life Abundant: Rethinking Theology and Economy for a Planet in Peril* (Fortress, Minneapolis, 2001).

Maybee, Maylanne (ed.), *All Who Minister: New Ways of Serving God's People* (ABC, Toronto, 2001).

Meltzer, Lynn (ed.), *Executive Function in Education: From Theory to Practice* (Guilford, New York, 2007).

Mendez, Angel F., OP, 'Divine Alimentation: Gastroeroticism and Eucharistic Desire', in Christophe Boureux, Janet Martin Soskice and Luiz Carlos Susin (eds), *Hunger, Bread and Eucharist* (*Concilium*, SCM, London, 2005/2), pp. 14ff.

Middleton, Arthur, *Towards a Renewed Priesthood* (Gracewing, Leominster, 1995).

Miguez, Nestor O., 'The Crisis of the People of God in Biblical Times', in Felix Wilfred and Luiz Carlos Susin (eds), *Christianity and Democracy* (*Concilium*, SCM, London, 2007/4), pp. 61ff.

Milbank, Alison (ed.) *Beating the Traffic: Josephine Butler and Anglican Social Action on Prostitution Today* (George Mann, Winchester, 2007).

Milbank, John, 'Paul Against Biopolitics'. Society for the Study of Theology conference paper, Durham, 2008.

Moltmann, Jürgen, *The Crucified God: The Cross of Christ as the Foundation and Criticism of Christian Theology*, trans. R. A. Wilson and John Bowden (SCM, London, 1974).

Moltmann, Jürgen, *God in Creation: An Ecological Doctrine of Creation. The Gifford Lectures 1984–85* (SCM, London, 1985).

Moltmann, Jürgen, *The Trinity and the Kingdom of God: The Doctrine of God* (SCM, London, 1989).

Moltmann, Jürgen, *History and the Triune God: Contributions to Trinitarian Theology* (SCM, London, 1991).

Moltmann, Jürgen, *God for a Secular Society: The Public Relevance of Theology* (SCM, London 1997).

Moran, Seana and Gardner, Howard, ' "Hill, Skill and Will": Executive Function from a Multiple-Intelligences Perspective', in Lynn Meltzer (ed.), *Executive Function in Education: From Theory to Practice* (Guilford, New York, 2007).

Morgan, Gareth, *Images of Organization* (Sage, London, 1997).

Morisy, Ann, *Journeying Out* (Continuum, London, 2004).

Murray, Paul, OP, *The New Wine of Dominican Spirituality: A Drink Called Happiness* (Burns & Oates, London, 2006).

Nicholson, D. H. S. and Lee, A. H. E. (eds) *The Oxford Book of English Mystical Verse* (OUP, Oxford, 1917).

O'Collins, Gerald, *Jesus Our Redeemer: A Christian Approach to Salvation* (Oxford, OUP, 2007).

O'Murchu, Diarmuid, *The Transformation of Desire: How Desire Became Corrupted – and How We Can Reclaim It* (DLT, London, 2007).

Ormerod, Neil, 'On the Divine Institution of the Three-fold Ministry', *Ecclesiology*, Vol. 4.1, pp. 38ff., 2007.

Osborne, Kenan B., *Orders and Ministry: Leadership in the World Church* (Orbis, Maryknoll, 2006).

Palmer, Parker J., *The Courage to Teach: Exploring the Inner Landscape of a Teacher's Life* (Jossey-Bass, San Francisco, 1998).

Pattison, Stephen, *Shame: Theory, Therapy, Theology* (CUP, Cambridge, 2000).

Patzia, Arthur G., *The Emergence of the Church: Context, Growth, Leadership and Worship* (Intervarsity, Illinois, 2001).

Paver, John E., *Theological Reflection for Ministry* (Ashgate, Aldershot, 2006).

Pennington, M. B., *True Self/False Self: Unmasking the Spirit Within* (Crossroad, New York, 2000).

Perdue, Leo G., *Wisdom Literature: A Theological History* (Westminster John Knox, London, 2007).

Perri, William D., *A Radical Challenge for Priesthood Today: From Trial to Transformation* (Twenty-Third, Mystic, 1996).

Peterson, Eugene H., *The Contemplative Pastor* (Eerdmans, Grand Rapids, 1989).

Petrella, Ivan, *Beyond Liberation Theology: A Polemic* (SCM, London, 2008).

Philips, Gerard, *The Role of the Laity in the Church* (Fides, Chicago, 1956).

Plater, Ormonde, *Deacons in the Liturgy* (Morehouse, Harrisburg, 2008).

Polkinghorne, John, *Quantum Physics and Theology: An Unexpected Kinship* (SPCK, London, 2007).

Pratt, Andrew, *Net Gains: A Guide for Ministry* (Inspire, Peterborough, 2008).

Proulx, E. Annie, *Accordion Crimes* (Fourth Estate, London, 1996).

Rae, Murray, 'Humanity in God's World', in Alan J. Torrance and Michael Banner (eds), *The Doctrine of God and Theological Ethics* (T. & T. Clark, London, 2006).

Rausch, Thomas P., *Priesthood Today: An Appraisal* (Paulist, New York, 1992).

Reddie, Anthony G., 'HIV/AIDS and Black Communities in Britain – Reflections from a Practical Black Liberation Theologian', in Regina Ammicht-Quinn and Hille Hacker (eds), *AIDS* (*Concilium*, SCM, London, 2007/3), pp. 25ff.

Rigney, James (ed.), *Women and the Episcopate* (*Affirming Catholicism Journal*, London, 2006).

Robertson, David, *Collaborative Ministry: What it is, How it Works and Why* (BRF, Oxford, 2007).

Rohr, Richard, *Adam's Return: The Five Promises of Male Initiation* (Crossroad, New York, 2004).

Rohr, Richard and friends, *Contemplation in Action* (Crossroad, New York, 2006).

Rooms, Nigel and Steen, Jane, *Employed by God? Theological and Practical Implications of the New Church of England Clergy Terms of Service Legislation* (Grove, Cambridge, 2008).

Ross, Maggie, *Pillars of Flame: Power, Priesthood and Spiritual Maturity* (Harper & Row, San Francisco, 1988).

Ross, Maggie, 'The Seven Devils of Women's Ordination', in Sue Walrond-Skinner (ed.), *Crossing the Boundaries: What Will Women Priests Mean?* (Mowbray, London, 1994), pp. 93ff.

Rulla, L. M., *Anthropology of the Christian Vocation*, Vol. 1 (Gregorian University Press, Rome, 1986).

Rulla, L. M., Ridick, Sr J. and Imoda, F., *Anthropology of the Christian Vocation*, Vol. 2 (Gregorian University Press, Rome, 1989).

Russell, Anthony, *The Clerical Profession* (SPCK, London, 1980).

Salmond, Anne, *The Trial of the Cannibal Dog: Captain Cook in the South Seas* (Allen Lane, London, 2003).

Sanford, John A., *Ministry Burnout* (Arthur James, London, 1982).

Schillebeeckx, Edward, 'A Creative Retrospect as Inspiration for the Church of the Future', in Lucas Grollenberg, *Minister? Pastor? Prophet? Grass Roots Leadership in the Churches* (SCM, London, 1980).

Schillebeeckx, Edward, *The Church with a Human Face: A New and Expanded Theology of Ministry* (SCM, London, 1985).

Schori, Katharine Jefferts, *A Wing and a Prayer: A Message of Faith and Hope* (Morehouse, New York, 2006).

Schroer, Silvia, 'The Book of Sophia', in Elisabeth Schüssler Fiorenza (ed.), *Searching the Scriptures: A Feminist Commentary* (SCM, London, 1995), pp. 17ff.

Schwöbel, Christoph, 'Christology and Trinitarian Thought', in Christoph Schwöbel (ed.), *Trinitarian Theology Today: Essays on Divine Being and Act* (T. & T. Clark, Edinburgh, 1995), pp. 113–46.

Sedgwick, Jonathan, in James Rigney (ed.), *Women and the Episcopate* (*Affirming Catholicism Journal*, London, 2006).

Sherlock, Charles, *God on the Inside: Trinitarian Spirituality* (Acorn, East Brunswick, Victoria, Australia, 1991).

Smith, James K. A., *Introducing Radical Orthodoxy: Mapping a Post-secular Theology* (Baker Academic and Paternoster, Michigan, 2004).

Sobrino, Jon, 'A Critique and Unmasking of Current Democracies and Ways of Humanizing Them from the Biblical–Jesuanic Tradition', in Felix Wilfred and Luiz Carlos Susin (eds), *Christianity and Democracy* (*Concilium*, SCM, London, 2007/4), pp. 69ff.

Soelle, Dorothy, *The Strength of the Weak* (Westminster, Philadelphia, 1984).

Stapley, Lionel F., *The Personality of the Organization: A Psycho-Dynamic Explanation of Culture and Change* (Free Association, London, 1996).

Stevenson, J. (ed.), *A New Eusebius: Documents Illustrative of the History of the Church to AD 337* (SPCK, London, 1965).

Strong, Roy, *A Little History of the English Country Church* (Cape, London, 2007).

Stuart, Elizabeth, 'Exploding Mystery: Feminist Theology and the Sacramental', in *Feminist Theology*, 12/2, 2004, pp. 228ff.

Suenens, Léon-Joseph, *Coresponsibility in the Church* (Burns & Oates, London, 1968).

Sugirtharajah, R. S., *Postcolonial Reconfigurations: An Alternative Way of Reading the Bible and Doing Theology* (SCM, London, 2003).

Sweet, Leonard, *AquaChurch 2.0: Piloting Your Church in Today's Fluid Culture* (Cook, Colorado Springs, 2008).

Ternier-Gommers, Marie-Louise, *Catholic Women in Ministry: Changing the Way Things Are* (Novalis, Ottawa, 2007).

Thomas, R. S., *Collected Poems, 1945–1990* (Dent, London, 1993).

Tiller, John, *A Strategy for the Church's Ministry* (CIO, London, 1983).

Tomlinson, Anne, 'Local Collaborative Ministry: liberating the *laos* through learning', in David Clark (ed.), *The Diaconal Church: Beyond the Mould of Christendom* (Epworth, Peterborough, 2008), pp. 119ff.

Torrance, Alan J., *Persons in Communion: Trinitarian Perspectives and Human Participation* (T. & T. Clark, Edinburgh, 1996).

Torrance, Alan J. and Banner, Michael (eds), *The Doctrine of God and Theological Ethics* (T. & T. Clark, London, 2006).

Torrance, Thomas F., *Trinitarian Perspectives: Toward Doctrinal Agreement* (T. & T. Clark, Edinburgh, 1994).

Torrance, Thomas F., *Royal Priesthood: A Theology of Ordained Ministry* (T. & T. Clark, Edinburgh, 1999).

Torry, Malcolm and Heskins, Jeffrey, *Ordained Local Ministry: A New Shape for Ministry in the Church of England* (Canterbury Press, Norwich, 2006).

Volf, Miroslav, *Exclusion and Embrace: A Theological Exploration of Identity, Otherness, and Reconciliation* (Abingdon, Nashville, 1996).

Volf, Miroslav, *After Our Likeness: The Church as the Image of the Trinity* (Eerdmans, Cambridge, 1998).

von Balthasar, Hans Urs, *Love Alone: The Way of Revelation – A Theological Perspective* (Burns & Oates, London, 1968).

Wacker, Marie-Theres and Wainwright, Elaine M., *Land Conflicts, Land Utopias* (*Concilium*, SCM, London, 2007/2).

Walrond-Skinner, Sue (ed.), *Crossing the Boundaries: What Will Women Priests Mean?* (Mowbray, London, 1994).

Watkins, Clare, *Living Baptism: Called out of the Ordinary* (DLT, London, 2006).

Watson, Andrew, *The Fourfold Leadership of Jesus: Come, Follow, Wait, Go* (BRF, Abingdon, 2008).

Watson, Natalie K., *Introducing Feminist Ecclesiology* (Sheffield Academic, London, 2002).

Watts, Fraser, Nye, Rebecca and Savage, Sara, *Psychology for Christian Ministry* (Routledge, London, 2002).

Weller, Paul, *Time for Change: Reconfiguring Religion, State and Society* (T. & T. Clark, London, 2005).

Wells, Samuel, *God's Companions: Reimagining Christian Ethics* (Blackwell, Oxford, 2006).

Wilfred, Felix and Susin, Luiz Carlos (eds), *Christianity and Democracy* (*Concilium*, SCM, London, 2007/4).

Williams, Rowan, *Lost Icons: Reflections on Cultural Bereavement* (T. & T. Clark, Edinburgh, 2000).

Winston, David, *The Wisdom of Solomon: A New Translation with Introduction and Commentary. The Anchor Bible*, Vol. 43 (Doubleday, New York, 1979).

World Council of Churches (WCC), *Baptism, Eucharist and Ministry* (The Lima Text), Faith and Order Paper 111 (WCC, Geneva, 1982).

World Council of Churches, *Episcope and Episcopacy and the Quest for Visible Unity*, Faith and Order Paper 183 (WCC, Geneva, 1999).

Wright, J. Robert, *On Being a Bishop: Papers on Episcopacy from the Moscow Consultation, 1992* (Church Hymnal Corporation, New York, 1993).

Zappone, Katherine, *The Hope for Wholeness: A Spirituality for Feminists* (Twenty-Third, Mystic, 1991).

Zizioulas, John D., *Being as Communion: Studies in Personhood and the Church* (St Vladimir's Seminary, New York, 1985).

Zizioulas, John D., *Eucharist, Bishop, Church: The Unity of the Church in the Divine Eucharist and the Bishop During the First Three Centuries* (Holy Cross Orthodox, Massachusetts, 2001).

Zizioulas, John D., *Communion and Otherness: Further Studies in Personhood and the Church* (T. & T. Clark, London, 2006).

Young, Frances and Ford, David, *Meaning and Truth in 2 Corinthians* (Eerdmans, Grand Rapids, 1987).

Index

administration 23, 37, 40–1, 45, 145
Anglican Church xiv, 5, 21–2, 41, 51, 64, 70, 93, 119, 123–4
Anglican Church in Aotearoa, New Zealand and Polynesia 30
Anglican Consultative Council (ACC) 161–2
Anglican–Roman Catholic International Commission (ARCIC) 21
apostolic 71, 75–6, 79, 88–9, 97, 124
appreciative enquiry 30
Archbishop's Group on the Episcopate 90
Australian Anglican Church, General Synod of 21

baptism 130, 137, 141, 151–2; baptized xv, 13, 34–6, 57–8, 61, 72, 74, 76, 78, 81–2, 86, 97–8, 100–2, 107, 111, 115, 118, 121, 151–2; baptizing community 81
Barth, Karl 10
Beatitudes 17
bishop 2, 4–6, 21–4, 30, 35–51, 75, 80, 88, 91–2, 99, 107, 119, 125, 130, 152, 167, 181, 182
Black Theology 17
blessing xv, 54, 56–7, 70, 73, 87, 101, 111, 114–17, 119, 161
Boff, Leonardo xv, 16, 51
Brueggemann, Walter 6, 67, 162, 172
Butler, Josephine 70

call of God xii–xiii, 30, 37, 50, 55, 57, 69, 78, 96, 99–100, 102, 119, 121, 161
Campbell Seminar 84
Cappadocian theologians 64, 96, 176

catholicity 71, 74–6, 80, 97, 124, 179
cell groups 4
Christendom 49
Christianity 49, 51, 53, 121
Church/church: as Body of Christ xv, 5, 20, 22, 47, 58, 72, 78, 83, 92, 107; character 9, 122, 129, 135; as *communion* 2–3, 10, 12, 19, 104, 122, 161; as community xiii–xv, 1–4, 7, 8, 13–15, 19–21, 23, 26, 31–2, 34, 38, 46, 57–8, 67, 72–83, 85–90, 96, 99–100, 109, 111, 113, 115–17, 122, 129–30, 133–4, 137, 146, 152, 154; identity 1, 8, 9–10, 14, 17, 19, 24, 27, 31–2, 34, 38, 51–2, 55, 57, 60–1, 65, 67, 69, 73, 76–9, 87, 89, 92, 96, 102, 107; participation in 13, 27, 53, 55, 59, 63, 78–80, 82, 84, 94, 141, 153; as People of God xv, 16–17, 21, 50, 84, 89, 92, 122; purpose 120, 122
Church in Wales 30
Church of England 2, 5–6, 9–10, 15, 23, 30, 42, 46, 77, 122, 130; General Synod of 5
Clergy Terms of Service 5, 163
clusters of parishes 3, 38–9, 130
collegiality 21–2
Collins, John 22, 168
communication 2, 89, 102, 107, 128, 131, 135, 137, 140
communications xi, 49, 66, 80, 103, 112, 126, 128, 131, 138, 142
Communion and Women in the Episcopate 88
confirmation 35
conflict 40
Congar, Yves xiv, 161, 175
contact 33–4, 42–3, 52–3, 71, 85, 89, 92–3, 121, 128, 154

201

context xi, 2, 7–8, 25, 31, 52, 60, 75, 90, 92, 109, 113, 122–3, 124, 128, 151; *see also* environment, locality, neighbourhood
Council of Nicaea 71
Croft, Stephen 24

deanery 110
diaconate 22–4, 30, 53, 88, 99–102, 121
difference in relation xvi, 9, 14, 33, 51, 54, 58–9, 62, 72, 74, 78, 80, 89, 116, 122
diocese(s) xi, 4, 6, 10, 42, 82, 88, 103, 109, 116, 118, 123, 138, 146, 152–3
discernment xv, 21, 83, 101–2, 107, 109–10, 113, 119, 125, 138, 152
disciple 4, 62, 87, 96–8, 100, 112, 115, 122, 126, 143, 152
diversity 76, 93, 102, 152
Dulles, Avery 33

ecclesiology xii, 1, 8–10, 15, 18–20, 32, 71, 88, 97, 101, 119, 161, 163; and faith 14; and Holy Spirit 11, 97; and Trinity 10–14, 94, 108; and world 14–15
ecology 20, 55, 74, 82, 85, 184
economics 14, 16, 55–6, 66–7, 82, 103, 184
ecumenism xi, xiv, 2, 4, 13, 21–2, 40, 76, 90–1, 102, 110, 118, 129
elders xi, 90, 161
environment 17, 76
Episcopal Church of Scotland 30
episcopate 21–3, 36, 53, 64–5, 75, 88–90, 124
episkeptomai 90
episkope xii–xiii, 4, 20–5, 29, 50, 52–3, 65, 72–5, 80, 82–3, 87–8, 89–120, 121–55, 167; *see also episkopos*, *episkeptomai*
episkopos 90
equipping 46

eschatology xv, 11, 18–25, 55, 67, 69–71, 76, 88–9, 92, 94, 98, 108, 112, 115, 120, 122, 126; and Christ 164, 166
Eucharist 2, 13, 21, 23, 25, 34, 44, 50, 55, 58, 60, 68–70, 72–7, 79, 81–2, 86–8, 99–111, 113–15, 117, 122, 137, 152–3, 155, 171, 172
Evangelical Lutheran Church in America (ELCA) 30
evangelism 78, 88, 104
'executive function' 105
Exodus 6, 16, 18, 87

facilitation 38, 60, 114, 117, 123, 128, 136
Faithful Cities 70
'False Self' theory 26, 73, 167–8
family 9, 31
feminist theology xvi, 9, 66, 94, 166, 168, 176, 178
For Such a Time as This 23
Ford, David F. xv, 111, 166, 170, 183
formation 27, 108, 152, 185
freedom xvi, 51, 56–7, 59, 64–5, 67, 69–70, 81, 85, 102, 107, 117
friendship 4, 9, 20, 112, 114, 115

Gaudium et Spes 85
Gift of Authority 3, 21
Grau, Marion xvi, 18
group of churches 122
Grundy, Malcolm 166
Gunton, Colin E. xv, 51, 182

Hardy, Daniel xv, 28, 33, 77, 169, 170, 171, 177, 182
healing 15, 36, 39, 45–6, 55, 81–3, 85, 118
hierarchy 5–6, 13, 18, 22, 24, 26, 32, 58, 63–5, 73, 80, 91, 95, 97–8, 101, 103, 123, 139, 146, 150, 182
holiness 53–63, 68–9, 71, 73–4, 78–9, 80, 84, 97, 108, 114, 171

Holy Spirit xv, 11–12, 18, 21, 34, 49, 55, 57–9, 61–2, 64–6, 72, 75–6, 79, 82, 85–7, 89, 95–6, 98, 100, 107–9, 111, 115, 124–5, 148, 155, 169; gifts of 97, 101, 110, 117, 119, 124–5, 129, 155

hope xiii, xvi, 6, 16, 18–19, 34, 49–50, 54, 56, 66, 69, 75, 84–5, 100, 122–3, 131, 174

house church 121

Ignatius 90, 161, 167, 181

immigrants 38, 83

incumbent xii, xv, 4

Irenaeus 89

Israel 8, 18, 55, 57

Jamieson, Penny 93, 102, 106, 184

Jenson, Robert 169

Jesus Christ xv, 6, 8, 11, 15–19, 25, 31, 34, 40, 49, 54–5, 57, 59–65, 67–8, 72, 74–7, 79–85, 87, 89–90, 92, 94–100, 103, 105, 107, 114, 116–17, 119, 125, 132, 150, 153, 161

Jewish faith xv, 12, 15, 54, 69, 95–6, 154

Johnson, Elizabeth A. xvi, 12–13, 51, 94–5

joy 18, 62, 68, 72, 75, 85, 88, 118, 177–8

justice 31, 38–9, 60, 62, 66, 70–2, 114, 166

Keller, Catherine xvi, 54

kenosis 19, 26, 61, 63, 65, 69, 72, 74, 98, 155

Kingdom xiv, 6–7, 13, 17, 19, 40, 51, 58, 62, 71–2, 74–5, 79, 84–5, 94, 107–9, 151, 155

koinonia 2–3, 6–7, 15, 17, 22, 52, 59, 66, 71–4, 78, 81, 83–4, 87, 89, 92, 94, 97, 114, 121, 126–7, 153, 155, 161, 166

lament 2, 55–7

leadership 8–9, 16, 29, 41–2, 46, 60, 70, 88, 90–1, 104–5, 107, 113, 123, 125–9, 131–3, 135, 138–9, 141, 144, 152

learning 4–5, 7–8, 23, 25–7, 35–6, 38, 47, 50, 55, 61, 67–8, 71, 78, 81, 87, 100, 105, 108, 111–12, 114, 116, 122, 124, 128, 132, 139–42, 152, 174

Leech, Kenneth 71

liberation xiii, xv, 13, 16, 18–19, 35, 53, 69, 71, 95, 165

Lima texts 8

liturgy 8–9, 42, 45–6, 59, 69, 81–2, 87, 91, 93, 101, 107, 110, 112, 115, 127, 152; *see also* worship

local church xi–xii, 2, 6, 9, 21, 39, 48, 53, 60, 65, 74, 87–9, 90–120, 121, 124, 153

Local Shared Ministry 3, 5, 32, 60, 97, 108, 122, 133, 183; *see also* mutual ministry

locality 7, 15, 28, 31, 38, 39, 44, 50, 54, 76–8, 82, 92, 99, 108–9, 119, 126, 143

Lubac, Henri de xiv, 161

Lumen Gentium xiv, 22

Lutheran 124

management 10, 50, 131–3, 135, 145–7, 152

Marxist theory 16, 18

Medellin 18

mediation 64, 114, 116–17, 119

Meisson Declaration 166

Milbank, John xv, 15

ministry: collaborative xi, 3, 17, 27–8, 42, 48, 63, 100–1, 105, 122, 124, 126–7, 130; consultancy 4–5, 27, 138, 152; development 5; review 5, 28, 116, 123, 129, 132, 152; team(s) xi–xii, 50, 92, 106, 122, 125, 127–31, 133–4, 139, 145, 148; among young people 38, 128, 141–2, 147

Index

mission of God xii; action planning 125, 136; co-ordinators 127–55
Moltmann, Jürgen 11–12, 51, 62
Moses 6, 66
mutual ministry 2, 6, 12–14, 20, 22, 42, 51, 63, 65, 67, 79, 90, 92, 94, 98–9

navigator xii, xiii, 1, 6, 31, 34, 69, 74, 80, 83–4, 89–120, 122–3, 129, 138, 140–1, 143, 153–4, 183
neighbourhood xi, xv, 5, 126, 143
New Testament 20, 28, 67, 82, 89, 90–2, 161
New Zealand (Aotearoa) xii, xiii
Nicene Creed 58

Old Testament 56
ontology 11, 59, 65, 69, 96, 98–9
Ordained Local Ministry 47
ordinands xi, 8, 15, 27, 108, 152
ordination rites xii, 161

parish priest: as *episkopos* 92–5; as leader of community 128, 139; particular work of 4–6, 20, 30, 101, 108–9, 117, 119, 130–1, 134–40, 142–3, 145, 148–51; as presider 8, 96–7; role models xii, 4, 6, 25, 31, 48, 89, 108; *see also* navigator
parochial church council (PCC) 125–30, 131–8, 142, 146–7, 150–1
pastoral care xii, 18, 23, 24, 29, 35, 37–41, 43, 48–9, 71, 78, 80, 88, 91–3, 106, 116, 149, 155, 161
Paul Report 9
Paul the Apostle 2, 15, 61, 67, 72, 76, 82, 86, 90, 92, 134, 154, 165, 179
Pentecost 62, 67, 74, 111, 164
perichoresis 12, 54, 92, 97–9, 164, 169
person 12–13, 15, 31, 62, 64, 73, 77, 79, 82, 89, 94, 98–101
personhood 13–14, 18, 64–5, 69, 95–6, 182
Polkinghorne, John 168, 170

poor, the 16–18, 20, 62, 66, 75, 80, 85, 99, 152; church of 18–20, 76, 99
postcolonial theology 16
power xvi, 2, 6–8, 12–14, 16–17, 24, 31, 37; God's 18–19, 32, 53, 57, 65–8, 82–3, 85, 93, 97, 103, 107, 109, 112, 162, 166, 172, 177–8
prayer 38, 50, 70, 79, 81, 85, 109, 111, 113, 117, 121–3, 125, 129, 134, 138, 149, 152
preaching xii, 36, 43–4, 49, 51, 88, 101, 110–11, 126, 131, 133, 138, 141, 146, 152, 172
presbyter 22, 53, 121
presiding role xv, 8, 24, 34, 44, 49, 88, 92, 95, 97, 99, 101, 109, 113–14, 119, 124, 148–9, 153, 185
prophet 6, 19, 53–4, 56–7, 66, 70, 87–8, 102, 162, 180

'Radical Orthodoxy' movement 15
range 33–4, 38–42, 52–3, 65, 89, 92–3, 121, 128, 154
reader ministry xi, 8, 22, 99–101, 126, 128, 136–7, 145
reciprocity 12, 14, 18, 31, 55, 62
relationality 7, 9, 11, 13–14, 17, 22, 24, 31, 53–5, 66, 68–9, 71, 73–4, 78, 83, 88, 92, 96, 98, 100, 102, 106–9, 112, 114
representative 45, 48, 96, 135, 161
resurrection life 1, 15, 18–20, 50, 66, 79, 82, 85–6, 89, 122, 129, 163, 166, 179
retreats 4
richness 33, 35–8, 52, 89, 92–3, 103, 121, 128, 154
Roman Catholic Church xiv, 22
Royal Consciousness 6, 163
rural parishes 38
Russell, Anthony 29

sabbaticals 4, 37
sacraments xii, 23–4, 55, 82, 88, 112, 121

salvation xii, 1, 14, 16
Schillebeeckx, Edward xiv, 51
Schwöbel, Christoph 14
Scripture xiv–xv, 2, 6, 8, 16, 35, 50–1, 54–6, 60–2, 64, 73–4, 79, 81–2, 86–7, 89, 94, 111, 117–18, 122, 135, 151–2, 155
sensus fidelium 102, 167
servant leadership 6, 22, 26, 30, 51, 78, 93, 96, 108, 134, 181
shame 3
shepherd 88, 90, 92
Sobrino, Jon 16–17
sociality 70, 74
society xv, 70
Solomon 6
Sophia 12–13
spiritual development xiv; direction 4, 8, 36–7, 108, 140, 148; exercises 26; growth 37, 82, 91, 125, 128, 133, 150, 152
statistics 121, 185
strategy 5
structures 33, 38, 42, 45, 49, 85, 153
suffering 12–13, 40, 48
synod 21–2, 102, 118–19, 186

theological education 7, 8, 108
theological reflection 8, 175–6
Tiller Report 10
Torrance, T. F. 20
tradition 27, 154
transformation, church as agent of xiv–xvi, 1, 2, 18–19, 28, 33–4, 36, 44–50, 52–3, 55–8, 63, 67, 72,

81–3, 85–7, 89, 92–3, 120–2, 124, 126, 128, 154
Trinitarian, triune God xii, 5, 8, 11, 13–14, 19, 31, 58, 61–4, 69, 85, 89, 92, 96, 98–9, 101, 113, 122, 124, 126, 161; *communion* 10, 25, 122; ecclesiology xiv, 25, 31–2, 58, 61, 65, 94, 98–100, 138, 176; language 12–14, 53, 58, 63, 180; unity 23
unity: of Church 21, 58, 71–2, 74, 77, 80, 88, 97, 102, 166; of God 12–13, 59, 78, 82; of world 55, 92
Vatican II xiv, 8, 14, 85
Virginia Report xi, 5, 19, 21
vocation xi, xiv, 9, 35, 42–3, 55, 69, 74, 102, 116, 119–20, 140, 151–2
Volf, Miroslav 51, 96

wardens 126, 133–5, 150
Wells, Samuel 69, 111
wisdom: Christian 93, 107–8, 110; of God 20, 73, 85–7, 114, 116, 118, 184; *see also Sophia*
witnessing xv, 1, 32–3, 36, 42, 49, 59, 71, 77, 79–80, 89, 101, 115, 118–19
women's experience xv, 16, 31, 50, 57, 66, 70–1, 94, 102, 112, 122
World Council of Churches 14, 25
worship xiii, 3, 23, 29, 31, 35, 37–8, 43–7, 50, 53, 55–7, 59, 61, 67–8, 73, 76, 78–81, 84–6, 100, 113, 126, 128, 132, 136, 139, 140

Zizioulas, John xv, 11–12, 14, 23, 51, 96, 173, 183

Transforming Church
Liberating Structures for Ministry

In a world where the Church is faced with declining attendances, financial constraints and a shortage of clergy, is it possible to release a new vitality and energy?

According to Robin Greenwood, if, as a Church, we can let go of the idea that we are marginalized, we can become much more confident, boldly discovering diverse and holistic ways of re-imaging the Church. When faced with diminishing congregations, instead of looking for someone to blame we can ask: 'What is there which is hopeful and fully alive, speaking of the liberating power of God? What can we offer to people and society who are searching for meaning in daily work and relationships?'

In this book, Robin Greenwood argues that in the Local Ministry movement every Christian person has a gift to offer. Everyone in their particular charism, and integrated with everyone else, is set free to do what is necessary for the Church to be Church.

The Local Ministry movement gives a freedom to explore the many connections between faith and life, emphasizing how to have a sense of well-being, celebration, hope and enjoyment. It is in working together in a collaborative ministry that it is possible to halt the decline and renew the Church.

ISBN: 9780281052080

Transforming Priesthood
A New Theology of Mission and Ministry

Transforming Priesthood offers a major theological reappraisal of the present and future role of the parish priest in Britain. Although written primarily with Anglicans in mind, the book is full of insights for partner churches – especially for those in which professional ministers and lay people recognize the need to collaborate effectively in carrying forward the mission and ministry of the whole church.

'At last, here we have a practical, imaginative and intelligent vision of the priesthood for today's Church of England and beyond it. Dr Greenwood is widely experienced in parish ministry as well as at the diocesan level and in academic theology. He is both realistic and theologically perceptive about contemporary England and its churches. His analyses are convincing; he is in touch with the liveliest developments at a local level and in theological thinking; and at the heart of his prescription is a relevant and passionate affirmation of the Trinitarian God. The result is a book that should not only stimulate debate of the right kind at a time of momentous change in all churches, it should also help to nurture Christian vocations, both as laity and parish priests.'

David F. Ford, Regius Professor of Divinity,
University of Cambridge

ISBN: 9780281047611

Risking Everything
Growing Communities of Love

How can Christian living be distinctive without becoming too insular?
How can it be respectful and open to all without losing its character?

In *Risking Everything*, Robin Greenwood seeks to respond to these questions. He focuses on God's call for Christian communities to indulge in the risky business of vulnerable, loving relationships, to be effective signs and agents of mission in the real world. The God who *is* a community of mutual love invites us to form attractive ways of companionship. Fellowship that allows each person an equal but different place in the Church, Canon Greenwood believes, can model the love that God offers, enhancing all human life.

Each chapter offers a variety of resources for group and individual use, including:

- a reflection and a poem
- meditation and prayer exercises
- an exercise in self-awareness and a way to escape the 'false self'
- a way to understand where you are on the journey
- a way to witness to one another.

'Here is a rich resource for the Christian journey from Lent, through Holy Week, Good Friday and Easter, to Pentecost. A book which will help not only individual Christians but parishes to keep their love affair with God well and truly alive.'

Martin Wharton, Bishop of Newcastle

ISBN: 9780281057696

The Ministry Team Handbook
Local Ministry as Partnership

Ministry is for everyone, not just the clergy. The leadership of every church, parish and congregation is the responsibility of the whole of that community. Churches need leadership, but that leadership must empower the whole congregation, fusing them into a dynamic, outward-looking community, bearing witness to the powerful message of the Gospel.

This book provides practical resources for groups of people who want to:

- work with God for the well-being of the world
- become a ministering community
- develop local, collaborative and supportive ministry
- encourage a partnership between clergy and laity
- grow dynamic leadership for mission
- sustain and support local ministry teams
- introduce local ordained ministry into a team.

ISBN: 9780281052790

Local Ministry
Story, Process and Meaning

In the first chapter of this timely and incisive collection of essays on being Church now, Robin Greenwood writes: 'The contemporary world's story is one of violence and exclusion at a time when the Christian Church in the West . . . is experiencing humiliating challenges . . . In the face of most people's bored disengagement with organized religion, we experience both the complacency of preserving outworn routines in the local church and institutional panic that the old order is slipping away.'

How is this situation to be addressed? One answer is through the healthy and creative growth of Local Ministry that focuses on deliberately inter-relational and inclusive practises of gospel community in a mission-shaped Church, for in every age and place the Church has to be refounded. The short reflections in this book give snapshots of imaginative developments in some parts of the Anglican Communion (the British Isles, New Zealand and the United States) and explore ideas about the future identity of the local church.

With a view to encouraging the strengthening and deepening of the Church's response to the Great Commission, Robin Greenwood and Caroline Pascoe have produced a valuable addition to current thought on the Local Ministry movement.

ISBN: 9780281057139